D1083808

OTHER VOLUMES IN THIS SERIES

John Ashbery, editor, *The Best American Poetry 1988*

Donald Hall, editor, *The Best American Poetry 1989*

Jorie Graham, editor, *The Best American Poetry 1990*

Mark Strand, editor, *The Best American Poetry 1991*

Charles Simic, editor, *The Best American Poetry 1992*

Louise Glück, editor, *The Best American Poetry 1993*

A. R. Ammons, editor, *The Best American Poetry 1994*

Richard Howard, editor, *The Best American Poetry 1995*

Adrienne Rich, editor, *The Best American Poetry 1996*

James Tate, editor, *The Best American Poetry 1997*

Harold Bloom, editor, *The Best of the Best American Poetry 1988–1997*

THE
BEST
AMERICAN
POETRY
1998

◇ · ◇ · ◇

John Hollander, Editor

David Lehman, Series Editor

SCRIBNER

SCRIBNER
1230 Avenue of the Americas
New York, NY 10020

Set in Bembo

Manufactured in the United States of America

1   3   5   7   9   10   8   6   4   2

ISBN 0-684-81453-6
ISSN 1040-5763

CONTENTS

Foreword by David Lehman   9

Introduction by John Hollander   15

Jonathan Aaron, "Mr. Moto's Confession"   25

Agha Shahid Ali, "The Floating Post Office"   26

Dick Allen, "The Cove"   28

A. R. Ammons, "Now Then"   30

Daniel Anderson, "A Possum's Tale"   33

James Applewhite, "Botanical Garden: The Coastal Plains"   35

Craig Arnold, "Hot"   36

Sarah Arvio, from *Visits from the Seventh*   41

John Ashbery, "Wakefulness"   55

Frank Bidart, "The Second Hour of the Night"   57

Robert Bly, "A Week of Poems at Bennington"   89

George Bradley, "In an Old Garden"   93

John Bricuth, from *Just Let Me Say This About That (IV)*   94

Anne Carson, "TV Men: Antigone (Scripts 1 and 2)"   107

Turner Cassity, "Symbol of the Faith"   109

Henri Cole, "Self-Portrait as Four Styles of Pompeian Wall
Painting"   111

Billy Collins, "Lines Composed Over Three Thousand Miles
from Tintern Abbey"   114

Alfred Corn, "Jaffa"   117

James Cummins, "Echo"   119

Tom Disch, "What Else Is There"   121

Denise Duhamel, "The Difference Between Pepsi and Pope"   122

Lynn Emanuel, "Like God,"   124

Irving Feldman, "Movietime"   126

Emily Fragos, "Apollo's Kiss" 129

Debora Greger, "Mass in B Minor" 130

Allen Grossman, "Weird River" 132

Thom Gunn, "To Cupid" 134

Marilyn Hacker, "Again, The River" 136

Rachel Hadas, "Pomegranate Variations" 139

Donald Hall, "Letter with No Address" 144

Joseph Harrison, "The Cretonnes of Penelope" 148

Anthony Hecht, "Rara Avis in Terris" 150

Daryl Hine, "The World Is Everything That Is the Case" 152

Edward Hirsch, "The Lectures on Love" 153

Richard Howard, "The Job Interview" 164

Andrew Hudgins, "The Hanging Gardens" 167

Mark Jarman, "The Word 'Answer' " 170

Donald Justice, "Stanzas on a Hidden Theme" 173

Brigit Pegeen Kelly, "The Orchard" 174

Karl Kirchwey, "Roman Hours" 178

Carolyn Kizer, "Second Time Around" 183

Kenneth Koch, "Ballade" 185

John Koethe, "The Secret Amplitude" 189

Rika Lesser, "About Her" 199

Phillis Levin, "Ontological" 203

Philip Levine, "Drum" 205

Rebecca McClanahan, "Making Love" 207

J. D. McClatchy, "Descartes's Dream" 209

Heather McHugh, "Past All Understanding" 211

Sandra McPherson, "Chalk-Circle Compass" 213

W. S. Merwin, "The Chinese Mountain Fox" 215

Robert Mezey, "Joe Simpson [1919–1996]" 219

A. F. Moritz, "Artisan and Clerk" 220

Thylias Moss, "The Right Empowerment of Light" 223

William Mullen, "Enchanted Rock" 225

Eric Ormsby, "Flamingos" 228

Jacqueline Osherow, "Views of La Leggenda della Vera Croce" 231

Robert Pinsky, "Ode to Meaning" 244

Reynolds Price, "The Closing, the Ecstasy"   247

Wyatt Prunty, "March"   250

Stephen Sandy, "Four Corners, Vermont"   251

Alan Shapiro, "The Coat"   253

Robert B. Shaw, "A Geode"   255

Charles Simic, "Ambiguity's Wedding"   256

Mark Strand, "The View"   257

James Tate, "Dream On"   258

Sidney Wade, "A Calm November. Sunday in the Fields."   260

Derek Walcott, "Signs"   261

Rosanna Warren, " 'Departure' "   264

Rachel Wetzsteon, from *Home and Away*   266

Susan Wheeler, "Shanked on the Red Bed"   271

Richard Wilbur, "For C."   273

C. K. Williams, "The Bed"   275

Greg Williamson, "The Dark Days"   277

Charles Wright, "Returned to the Yaak Cabin, I Overhear an Old Greek Song"   282

Contributors' Notes and Comments   283

Magazines Where the Poems Were First Published   327

Acknowledgments   329

David Lehman was born in New York City in 1948. He is the author of three collections of poems: *An Alternative to Speech* (1986) and *Operation Memory* (1990), both from Princeton, and *Valentine Place* (1996), from Scribner. His latest critical book is *The Last Avant-Garde: The Making of the New York School of Poets* (Doubleday, 1998). A revised and enlarged edition of his anthology, *Ecstatic Occasions, Expedient Forms,* was recently published by the University of Michigan Press. He has received a Guggenheim Fellowship in poetry, an Award in Literature from the American Academy of Arts and Letters, and a three-year writers' award from the Lila Wallace–Reader's Digest Fund. He is on the core faculty of the graduate writing programs at Bennington College and the New School for Social Research. He also teaches a "great poems" course in the undergraduate honors program at New York University. He is the general editor of the University of Michigan Press's Poets on Poetry Series. He initiated *The Best American Poetry* in 1988.

FOREWORD

by David Lehman

◊   ◊   ◊

Not very long ago, the coverage of poetry in the national press was dominated by complaint and self-pity: the lament for a lost audience, the noise of interminable debate about the use of poetry in an age of technology, the growl of congressional disapproval. How quickly that has changed. Poets today still face major obstacles as they struggle to gain acceptance or even just to make ends meet. But the prestige of the art has steadily climbed since this decade began, and it has paralleled a growing public appetite for the best poems of our moment. The nation's hot romance with poetry shows no sign of cooling off.

When Ted Hughes's secretly written book about his marriage to Sylvia Plath was published, the *New York Times* carried the story on its front page. Within weeks, Hughes's *Birthday Letters* had displaced Toni Morrison's novel *Paradise* as the number one hardcover bestseller at Colosseum Books in New York City. (Sales nationwide topped the 100,000 mark by the advent of spring.) Robert Hass, America's outgoing Poet Laureate, established the policy of choosing a poem from a new book every week and commenting on it for the *Washington Post Book World*. Robert Pinsky, Hass's successor as Poet Laureate, commenced work immediately on the "Favorite Poem Project," a kind of oral history of contemporary taste. A cross section of Americans from varied backgrounds will be asked to read and record their favorite poems for the Library of Congress. "If a thousand years from now anyone should ask who the Americans were, this archive might help give an answer," Pinsky said.

On the Internet, websites devoted to poetry are proliferating. Poetry Daily, true to its name, highlights a different poem every day; it also "reprints" articles on poetry from major newspapers. (When Poetry Daily learned that I was writing a poem a day as an experiment, they invited me to post my daily poem all through the month of April—a thrilling experience that left me more convinced than ever that poetry is conditioned by the fastest means of transmission available to the poet.) The Academy of American Poets' website offers the browser a brief course in modern poetry. The Poetry Porch provides poems, interviews, and links to university libraries. The Poetry Society of America has an on-line "peer workshop" and is planning to host an interactive cyber-symposium this fall addressing the perennial question, "What is American about American poetry?" For the lively Electronic Poetry Center, the poet Charles Bernstein compiled a list of sixty useful experiments that poets might try. "Any profits accrued as a direct or indirect result of the uses of these formulas shall be redistributed to the language at large," the reader is advised. Visitors to the site are invited to participate in a group collaboration with other plugged-in poets.

Today, when shoe manufacturers plan a new ad campaign, they are liable to consider enlisting the help of poets, the way Ford asked Marianne Moore's help in naming the ill-fated car that management, ignoring Moore's recommendations, called the Edsel forty years ago. Poems are appearing on beer coasters and subway posters. In 1996 the Baltimore Ravens—named after Edgar Allan Poe's "grim, ungainly, ghastly, gaunt, and ominous bird of yore"—replaced the Cleveland Browns ("Nevermore") in the National Football League. Ten pages of Barnes & Noble's 1996 annual report were devoted to poetry. There were quotes from John F. Kennedy and Claude Levi-Strauss, photographs taken at readings, a list of the year's poetry bestsellers (*The Odyssey* and *Canterbury Tales* were right up there with Maya Angelou), a poem by Nobel laureate Wislawa Szymborska, and a letter to shareholders from Leonard Riggio, the firm's CEO, stating his determination to "broaden the marketplace for works of poetry and literature." On Valentine's Day 1997, passengers on Amtrak's Metroliner and guests at Doubletree hotels in Boston, Baltimore, and Atlanta were handed free copies—fifteen thousand in all—of a collection of famous love poems. In 1998 the American Poetry and Literacy Project planned to up the ante by giving away fifty thousand copies of *101 Great American Poems* to celebrate National Poetry Month in April. An aspect of this year's White House sex scandal not usually emphasized but of particular note in this context is that President Clinton gave Monica Lewinsky a copy of *Leaves of Grass*, a book he is said to present routinely to honored visitors and guests.

Whitman's immortal work was recited at the White House—Rita Dove reading from "Song of Myself" and Robert Pinsky from "Crossing Brooklyn Ferry"—when President and Mrs. Clinton hosted a

"Millennium Evening" celebrating American poets and poetry. Hillary Clinton initiated the proceedings by quoting Howard Nemerov's poem "The Makers." The President spoke of having had to memorize 100 lines of *Macbeth* when he was in high school. He credited the experience with teaching him "about the dangers of blind ambitions, the fleeting nature of fame, the ultimate emptiness of power disconnected from higher purpose," with the result that "Mr. Shakespeare made me a better president." The event was beamed to 200 sites in 44 states and was cybercast. A transcript was very quickly made available on the web, and it was no less pleasurable for the accidental transformations that hasty typing produced—as when Wallace Stevens's "the palm at the end of the mind" turned into "the pond at the end of the mine."

The Best American Poetry, now entering its second decade, has from the start committed itself to the idea that the enlargement of poetry's audience can be entirely consistent with uncompromising literary standards. We have wished to perpetuate excellence in any of the forms it may take. At the same time we have done our best to make this book as friendly and hospitable as possible to readers beyond the society of scribes. The poems in *The Best American Poetry 1998* were culled from big-circulation weeklies (*The New Yorker, The New Republic*), university quarterlies (*The Yale Review, Southwest Review*), and independent magazines (*The Threepenny Review, The Paris Review*). More than thirty periodicals are represented in these pages; many more than thirty were consulted (and, in future, we expect to add high-quality Internet magazines, such as *Slate* and *Jacket,* to the list). The seventy-five poems that made the editor's final cut faced stiff competition, and plenty of it. Most of the chosen poets have generously contributed comments on their poems, a section of this anthology that many readers prize—it has the salutary effect of demonstrating that modern poetry is by no means as inaccessible as advertised.

As the series editor of *The Best American Poetry,* I know that the most important decision I have to make every year involves the identity of the year's guest editor—himself or herself a major poet—who is asked to choose the poems and contribute an introduction assessing the state of the art. For the 1998 volume, I could think of no one better qualified for the task than John Hollander. In a poetry culture in which the short, anecdotal or confessional lyric is valued above all else, Hollander has, over the course of his career, given us brilliant examples of formal possibilities that we would be foolish to ignore: shaped verse, satirical epistles, songs, and meditations, as well as long poems and poetic sequences in forms devised by the poet himself. In addition to being a poet of remarkable resource and inventiveness, Hollander is an astute scholar (as readers of *The Figure of Echo* will see) and teacher (whose *Rhyme's Reason* ought to be a required manual for aspiring poets). He is also one of the most experienced anthologists of his generation. I knew that he would make his judgments carefully but confidently and that he would honor the diverse ways in which true poetry differs from what he calls the "canonical bad verse of our time."

To assist the year's guest editor, the series editor is obliged to read as many magazines as he can get his hands on. It is a tall task that is also, fortunately, a pleasure, for the reader of magazines encounters the new when it is truly new. Every year brings its share of discoveries and delights. In *American Poetry Review* I come across "The Winter of Our Discontents & Other Seasons" by Marcia Southwick, a poet previously unknown to me, who wants her poems "to be less Marcia-centric" and to this end decides to write about "*Star Trek*'s Seska the undercover Cardassian spy." The result is charming, as is Dina Ben-Lev's "Response to a Message of Hate on My Machine" in the impressive new magazine *Salt Hill*. In *Chain*, Peter Gizzi has an "Ode: Salute to the New York School 1950–1970 (A Libretto)," which turns out to be a wonderful cento (a poem consisting entirely of lines lifted from other poems) that doubles as an index to a chronological bibliography. The poem of the week in *The New Republic* is "Remembering My Visit to Martha's Vineyard Last Summer" by Ann Claremont Le Zotte. A note indicates that the poem has been "translated, from Sign Language, by the author." The effects of this maneuver are remarkable: "Plum cake tart eat I," the poem begins. Then I pick up *New American Writing* and read Paul Violi's "On an Acura Integra," which proves there is plenty of life left in the rhetorical gambit of the insincere apology. This hilarious poem is in the form of a note left on a wrecked car by the driver who crashed into it and then fled the scene. I mention these five poems, and could easily speak of five times as many, precisely because they did not make the final cut for this year's anthology—a fact that underscores just how bountiful American poetry is today.

One thing that is distinctive about American poetry is the largeness of spirit in which people raise the question, "What is American about American poetry?" The question is asked in earnestness, innocence, and generosity. Compare this to the rigorous and exclusionary procedures of the French Academy, for example. There are other aspects of American poetry that set it apart: a certain lawless energy, a native strain of celebration and self-celebration. American poetry can be said to have issued its literary declaration of independence from Britain when Emerson railed against conformism, Whitman said he could "resist anything better than my own diversity," and Dickinson gave everyone permission to be "Nobody." The history of our poetry seems a history of defiant individuality to the point of eccentricity, and who would want it otherwise? Poetry is freedom, and that includes freedom from social obligations and literary norms. At the same time, the idea of America remains an enthralling possibility for the imagination. "The United States themselves are essentially the greatest poem," Walt Whitman asserted in his prose introduction to the 1855 edition of *Leaves of Grass*. The genius of the United States, he wrote, rests not in its executives and legislatures but in the "unrhymed poetry" of the American people, which awaits "the gigantic and generous treatment worthy of it." The American poet in 1998 continues to find inspiration and sustenance in Whitman's words and in his vision of a country that absorbs its poets as affectionately as they have absorbed it.

John Hollander was born in New York City in 1929. *A Crackling of Thorns,* his first book of poems, was chosen by W. H. Auden for the Yale Younger Poets Series in 1958. The sixteen books that have followed— including *Types of Shape* (1969), *Reflections on Espionage* (1976), and *Powers of the Thirteen* (1983)—demonstrate a rare virtuosity and cunning ingenuity. *Selected Poetry* and *Tesserae,* his two most recent volumes, were issued simultaneously by Knopf in 1993. Mr. Hollander has also written six books of criticism, including *The Work of Poetry* (Columbia University Press, 1997) and a forthcoming volume, *The Poetry of Everyday Life* (University of Michigan Press). He has edited, or been co-editor of, numerous collections (such as *The Laurel Ben Johnson*) and influential anthologies (the definitive two-volume Library of America edition of *American Poetry: The Nineteenth Century*). Together with Anthony Hecht, with whom he shared the Bollingen Prize in Poetry in 1983, he put together *Jiggery-Pokery: A Compendium of Double Dactyls.* In 1990 he was made a Fellow of the MacArthur Foundation. He is currently Sterling Professor of English at Yale University.

INTRODUCTION

by John Hollander

◇   ◇   ◇

The task of attending to so much late—very late—twentieth-century American poetry has been a strange one. The nation's talk about its recent history has been clouded by a modicum of historical self-consciousness about our current fin de siècle. But our decade can nonetheless hardly feel belated with respect to the poets of those original nineties that Yeats referred to as a "tragic generation." Our moment tends to feel temperately shaded rather than darkly threatened by the lengthening shadows of those of our precursors who have come to matter most. In uttering the phrase "fin de siècle" I can't resist telling Richard Howard's story of a student in a course he was teaching on the literature of decadence, in which the 1890s had of course figured prominently. At the end of the semester the student was apparently still puzzled by a phrase his teacher had used throughout the course. "What exactly is 'fantasy-echo,' Mr. Howard?" he inquired.

And yet poetic fancy could see that, after all, the student had somehow got it right: those nineties, suffused with the poetry of Lionel Johnson, Dowson, Davidson, and Symons, were indeed something of a "fantasy-echo" of the compelling call of poetic voices like those of Swinburne, Rossetti, and Meredith (let alone those of Browning and Tennyson). But I have not found the best poetry of our later nineties to be that of the dying fantasy-echo; nor has it been the reciprocally fruitless self-absorption of Narcissus. Our literary fin de siècle shows every sign of having learned from what has gone before without being incapacitated by it.

This occasion has also provided a surprising pleasure for me. Having committed myself to explore an expanding realm of published verse that I had not, in recent years, been able to visit more than occasionally, I was absorbed by what I saw: the kinds of variety (scalar, generic, modal, rhetorical, formal), kinds of accomplishment, and kinds of concern I encountered were quite impressive. What remained invariant was their true poetic character. Particularly notable, for example, were the profound differences between the two very long selections by John Bricuth and Frank Bidart. The first of these, a section of a book-length poem called *Just Let Me Say This About That,* is marked by an intertwining of the high serious and the high comic, quasi—but only figuratively—political in its imaginative venue. In Bidart's poem, the profoundly affecting retelling of an Ovidian tale arises from the most personal of anecdotal accounts, revising Ovid's own kind of intercalation of story within story by way of the modern poetics of memory and narration from Wordsworth through Proust and, in our time, the late James Merrill. The widely varying ways in which these two works form their intense poetic fictions is almost exemplary for the best poetry of our time. There were long mid-range poems, too, such as Brigit Pegeen Kelly's "The Orchard" with its beautiful mode of unfolding, and Edward Hirsch's "The Lectures on Love." The latter exemplifies the structural genre of the poetic suite—Wallace Stevens's preferred form—which differs from the long-stanzaed, ode-like form in English poetry through its highly modern use of dissociation and of the reshaping of sequentiality itself into something beyond narrative, expository, or pre-Romantic lyric order.

I found also that the poems I liked best varied in the mode and degree of figurativeness in their use of the first person. Lyric poetry has always been traditionally associated with a "solitary singer"—as Whitman called his private mockingbird—but that lyric persona has always been some sort of fiction.

True poetry has always striven for, and has come in the last twenty years to perfect, a nobility of expression that is of vital importance for our democratic esthetic, moral, and political culture. A democracy must always see post-feudal nobility of lineage as a horrible travesty of an evolved idea of the outstandingly human. Poetry is a realm in which elegance supplies, rather than vitiates, power of the best kind—power to make and change rather than (in the tunnel vision behind the current official palaver of academic pseudo-literary or "cultural" studies) power over people. Imaginative power is neither coercive nor vindictive and, when effectively employed, results in works of art that, when effectively read, liberate rather than constrain. Canonical bad poetry of the past forty years has included a good deal of naively literal first-person narrative vignette that seemed to derive from the misconstruction of this fundamental trope. It is as if the contemporary equivalent of rhymed jingle were sit-down comic routines for the benefit of friends. The speakers of these hopelessly sincere but rarely authentic poems were always the poets themselves, rather than some fictional personae. The outmoded fashion of "confessional" poetry depended for its somewhat sensational appeal on a kind of prurient interest, particularly among readers who knew little of the devious ways by which poetry manages to get straight to its points. But among the poems collected here are those dealing with an authorial self in plangently figurative ways, such as that of Henri Cole in his "Self-Portrait in Four Styles of Pompeian Wall Painting," where the matter of representation is acknowledged immediately. While distinguished philosophers in the past decade have written learned studies of the history of the notion of self and of autonomy, poets have always been engaged in reconstructing such conceptions.

A travesty of poetry can occur when the immediate interests of any institutionalized moral, political, or sentimental agenda make their unrelenting claims on the poetry's fictiveness. Diverse travesties of the condition of individual *variety* are generated by the culturally and imaginatively disastrous concept of "*diversity*"—a term propounded and brandished by the politico and the apparatchik—which trashes the particular excellences of whatever ethnic culture it can turn into kitsch. The equivalent for poetry of identity politics in the public sphere tends to obliterate the uniqueness of individual poetic voices (a trope that—despite deconstructive attempts to abolish—we continue to find useful). The American poet—inescapably Emersonian as he or she must be—takes our national emblem of *E pluribus unum* in two ways at once: as the motto of federalism and, privately, with the *e pluribus* construed as releasing an independent poetic self. Certainly it is with a marvelous and profound deviousness that Whitman often braids these two meanings into the same assertion, and allows one to stand metaphorically for the other. The poet is a member of a sect of one, consisting only of him- or herself. To be sure, a poet can write almost anything in the way of versified political or religious propaganda; but the more literally it is meant, the further it will be from poetry, which is a matter or trope and not of pattern. Almost anything—a shopping list, an advertisement, a public notice—can be versified, but unless the document has been turned into fiction, it will not be poetry. Thus, for example, the following is true:

> "On this matter I shall be quite terse:
> These lines, not poetry, are merely verse."

The closer poetry gets to the exposition of contemporary specifics, the more deliberately and effectively comic it had better be. The best, most pointed, agile, and telling light verse achieves a mode of poetic status—there are examples of excellent comic verse in this volume—and along with the specificities of fashion and current event that Northrop Frye included in what he called the "low mimetic," political matters of many sorts provide occasions for wit, whether of ridicule or milder amusement. But probably only a mock, or notional, or fantastic, or more-than-satirically parodistic version of a manifesto could be a true poem ("the truest poetry," as we are made to recognize in *As You Like It,* being "the most feigning").

But if it is a gross literalism generally which deafens and blinds potential readers of poems, conversely, it is poetry that undoes the expression of the literal. Past and present, fact and fiction, heights and depths, interiors and exteriors, size and scale—all of these can shift their positions and their relations, can be stood on their hands and made to stand for one another. And yet of course the misconstructions of literalists persist, even among putative poets. (In this connection I am reminded that every year or so dozens of American poets receive at least one letter demanding that as poets they speak out for this or that politically grounded cause. I have always felt that such appeals ought to be made to one as a citizen, and that invoking an unexplained and undefended agenda about poetry and particular socio-political responsibilities condescends to citizenship and poetry at once.)

The vigorous pluralism of American poetry at its best makes itself felt in the varieties of poetic diction on exhibit in this volume. One of the great responsibilities entailed in writing free verse, as T. S. Eliot remarked in an essay in 1917, derives from the fact that the more the rhythms of a poetic line approach those of prose, the heavier the burden will be upon a controlling and characteristic diction. Weak free verse analogous to weak greeting-card jingle often results from a naive belief that *vers libre* comes with the mandate to ignore diction—to ignore, that is, not merely poetic counterparts of Flaubert's individual *mots justes,* but rather the volume of all the particular frequencies that make up a characteristic voice. English, and particularly twentieth-century American English, is a language born of, and nurtured in, a true diversity. And while for poetry there are no real synonyms—I know writers for whom even "grey" and "gray" denote different tones—every corner of our language provides a multitude of alternative means of rhetorically approaching a reader or listener, and these alternatives are far more complex than merely those of what would, in some Renaissance and neoclassic regimens, constitute the decorum of high, middle, and low levels of style. The less one is bound and aided by a canonical style, the weightier is the necessity of being one's stylistic self, and this may start in one's conscious choice of vocabulary. American poetry at the end of this century seems elegantly to recognize the diversities of a native speech that has naturalized so many kinds of linguistic immigrant, as so many of the poets to be read here are acutely aware. Their kinds of vocabulary seem as various as the particular occasions and forms of their poems.

Here I must observe that for some decades now, the question of "form" has been something of a bugbear. The word "formal" keeps coming up with respect to certain poets: I notice that a valuable collection of essays on Anthony Hecht's poetry—containing particularly fine observations by Peter Sacks, Kenneth Gross, John Frederick Nims, J. D. McClatchy, and others—is entitled *The Burdens of Formality.* However the editor construed these "burdens," Hecht shares with James Merrill, Richard Wilbur, and Howard Moss (to name three very different poets) the burden of critical cant that weighs heavily on poetic seriousness. The editor remarked of Hecht's "The Venetian Vespers" that this great meditation "makes the case for formal poetry as much as anything being written today." Though he no doubt meant well, this editor helped perpetuate the false idea that what we call "form" is a property of certain forms of verse and not others. Some of our finest poets have accomplished what they have not because their verse is generally accentual syllabic, and often rhymed. It is because of what they did with that instrument. And just so with major poetry in any mode of free verse. All true poets know this, although occasionally (like W. C. Williams at his crankiest) they may carry on about it in one unhelpful way or another.

For all poetry is "formal," in that its verse is not randomly constructed. In all poetry, frameworks of expectation are put in place that allow various orders of rhythm to inform the language, causing poems to generate their own quasi-musical settings. (Anyone who thinks that poetic rhythm is confined to the alternation of stressed and unstressed syllables—or even to questions of prosodic structure and versification—had better learn a lot more about spoken and written language both.) Any poem can be analyzed formally, and—if it is a really good poem—can be shown to interpret and modify its formal structure. This applies to verse composed in any system—our accentual syllabic, our older purely accentual, our recently adopted pure syllabic, the unmeasured but clearly marked parallelism of the verse of the Hebrew

Bible, Greek quantitative verse and its peculiar Latin adaptation—and in any relation to previous verse. The free-verse modes of Whitman, or Williams, of D. H. Lawrence in his best poems, or of such older contemporaries as W. S. Merwin, John Ashbery, and A. R. Ammons, all have different formal properties.

Many poets have written both free verse and the accentual-syllabic kind that was—at least from Chaucer through Hardy—thought to be normative for English. While Frost and Williams never crossed what they felt to be heavily guarded borders, Stevens, Crane, Moore, Warren, Bishop, Lowell, Roethke, and Swenson all wrote in various ways at various times, and with no harrumphing fuss about it. But for some decades after the late 1950s, third-rate poetry marched under an ideological banner proclaiming that anything other than free verse was "formal," retrograde, and somehow un-American. While Hecht, Merrill, Wilbur, and Moss all continued, as had Frost and Auden, to invent their own ways of using the older mode, they never preached about it like true believers. A poet's use of language is so deeply personal that to institutionalize it is almost—if you know what real poetry is—obscene. Recently, a silly agenda has been laid down by writers calling themselves and others (some splendidly undeserving of the epithet) "new formalists." Like the free-verse ideologues they opposed, such polemicists were unwittingly adopting, in "formalist," what was originally a vicious Stalinist term of anti-intellectual opprobrium. I mention this, because I feel that the term "formal poetry" is itself misleading, and whether used by pro- or op-ponents of it, distracts attention from the true matter of poetry, which is not its verse. Verse of some kind may be a necessary, but is never a sufficient, condition of poetry. It is not meters, said Emerson in a famous passage in "The Poet," but a meter-making argument, that makes a poem. And indeed, one argument (which means "substance," "matter," "stuff of meaning") may make a sonnet-like poem, while another will give rise to varied, unmeasured expository-sounding lines across which run long periodic sentences. The meters will be called up by the stuff of the poem, and will, once framed, summon up more stuff in turn. But the particular meters that the argument makes are a very private business.

If one looks at the history of poetry in English, one can find a wide variety of ways in which poetic form can be variously transparent or opaque. A poet can take one kind or mode of conventionality totally for granted, and write with it as if it had rolled down Parnassus for him or her alone, thus making it seem truly fresh and original. One thinks of

Shakespeare's sonnets, so profoundly radical in their revision of the Petrarchan sequence in England, yet which never try, save in one or two misplaced instances, to vary the three-quatrain-and-couplet form (as opposed to Sidney, in *Astrophel and Stella,* for example, who assertively puts his sonnet pattern through quite a few changes). Or Emily Dickinson's common meter quatrains, a mode infrequently varied, but which nonetheless frame successive poems of such unexpected individuality that one scarcely knows what she will be doing next. Or Stevens's magisterial blank verse, in tercets, couplets, or sometimes longer stanzas.

Conversely, a poet like Hardy will—admittedly within the overall system of rhymed accentual-syllabic verse—be remarkably arbitrary in the wide range of shapes and sizes in his stanza forms. Following him, Auden and James Merrill moved in just that direction, while May Swenson took this way of proceeding along an up-and-down-hill path of her own, varying not merely the form but often the system in which that form was framed. A poet's personal mode of writing verse is a private and almost sacred matter. It involves the peculiar ability of a formal commitment—even if, as so often happens, it is made during the course of a poem's taking shape—to summon up the strongest powers of the poetic imagination to create fictions of—and in, and even about—language. That this is as true of good free verse as it is of good accentual-syllabic verse goes without saying.

Given all the propaganda about form one encounters, it was especially pleasurable to notice the wide variety of shapes in which both younger and older poets frame their poetic language without any regard for fashion or political special pleading. Some of the youngest poets here (Greg Williamson, Daniel Anderson, Rachel Wetzsteon, Joseph Harrison) have felt as much at home in rhymed accentual-syllabic verse as have older masters like Wilbur, Hecht, Thom Gunn, and Daryl Hine; others have worked in different modes of free verse (of which there are so many, albeit unacknowledged in poetry handbooks) with equal assurance and power. Both Richard Howard and Karl Kirchwey (in the first part of his "Roman Hours") deploy pure syllabic verse, but in totally different ways. Likewise, in the strongly turned accentual sapphics of Marilyn Hacker's poem one may apprehend the same kind of assurance in a way of writing and a kind of energy gained from it in return for breathing new life into it.

But best of all, in contemplating some of the best work being done in verse in the United States today, I was gratified by the continued assurances of where, and in what unsuspected ways, a true avant-garde is still leading the way—at this point, into the twenty-first century. Given the evolution even of evolutionary cycles themselves, it was not surprising to find at about the middle of this century that the generation of mere novelty had already become one more convention, and that true originality was not necessarily going to be engaged in a struggle with its routines. But in a period of very late modernity, we have come to see how the older model of what is now called the "cutting edge" has chopped itself up: the authenticity solely of the sensationally problematic—a forceful, fruitful notion in 1922—has dried up into a conventional sort of agenda. A self-conscious avant-garde today is by nature academic.

Genuine originality is born and works in private, and art of any kind is solitary, and often lonely, work. Literary schools and groups and circles have existed at least since the Renaissance, but with different associative paradigms: study groups, social clubs, mini-courts, aesthetico-political underground cells, cabals, and so forth. But they matter little to poets themselves, and are celebrated primarily by journalists and publicists and, eventually perhaps, historians. Within them, the complex dynamics of deep personal friendship, aesthetic affinity and taste, and institutional accident work in mysterious ways. Although some of the older poets represented in this book may have been called members of a group or school, the reader will be unable to determine such an association from their current work. There are no battle lines in the eternal, ever final struggle to become, to remain—and to continue to change the meaning of being—poetically oneself. *La lutte continue!*

Poets propound parables—of the observed world, of the ways in which their lives and times refer to inaccessible inner states, of homely things and beings and of exotic ones, factual or fictional, encountered in the sessions of sweet, silent thought. It is by keeping faith with each poet's commitment to this kind of propounding—whether it sounds like singing, or declaiming, or joking, or proclaiming, or praying, or meditating, or arguing—that poetry continues to move forward and to generate the poetic history that is both smaller and greater than a history of literature.

THE

BEST

AMERICAN

POETRY

1998

◇ ◇ ◇

JONATHAN AARON

Mr. Moto's Confession

◇   ◇   ◇

The famous Tokyo detective looked as if he'd taken a shower
in his linen suit and then slept in it.
He mopped his shiny forehead with a handkerchief.
"Pascal was right," he said, his tenor slightly nasal.
"Men are so necessarily mad, that not to be mad would amount to
another form of madness. What's more," he added, the cat
eying the canary, "contradiction is not a sign of falsity,
nor is the want of contradiction a sign of truth—Pascal again."
He took out his fountain pen. I saw my chance.
Mr. Moto, I asked, should I believe all those stories
I've heard about you? "Please do not," he murmured. "I do not."
He was writing something on a cocktail napkin.
"In fact," he said, his pen continuing to move, "my real name is
Laszlo Löwenstein. I was born in Hungary, I drove myself crazy
as an actor in Zürich and Berlin, and now that I live in Hollywood
I have bad dreams. Last night one of them told me
I'll end up buried alive in a tale by Edgar Allan Poe."
He coughed politely, capped his pen, and getting to his feet
handed me the little piece of paper. "An ancient Japanese
poetic form," he said. Even as I stared at it
the little cairn of characters, each a tiny, exotic bird cage
with its doors open, blurred, melted, and reformed as if rising
to the surface of a well, where these words trembled
but stayed clear enough to read: *As evening nears, how clearly*
a dog's bark carries over the water.

from *The New Republic*

The Floating Post Office

◇   ◇   ◇

(Note: The post boat was like a gondola that called at each houseboat.
It carried clerk, weighing scales, and a bell to announce arrivals.)

Has he been kept from us? Portents
of rain, rumors, ambushed letters . . .
Curtained palanquin, fetch our word,
bring us word: Who has died? Who'll live?
Has the order gone out to close
the waterways . . . the one open road?

And then we saw the boat being rowed
through the fog of death, the sentence
passed on our city. It came close
to reveal smudged black-ink letters
which the postman—he *was* alive—
gave us, like signs, without a word,

and we took them, without a word.
From our deck we'd seen the hill road
bringing a jade rain, near-olive,
down from the temple, some penitent's
cymbaled prayer? He took our letters,
and held them, like a lover, close

to his heart. And the rain drew close.
Was there, we asked, a new password—
blood, blood shaken into letters,

cruel primitive script that would erode
our saffron link to the past? Tense
with autumn, the leaves, drenched olive,

fell on graveyards, crying "O live!"
What future would the rain disclose?
O Rain, abandon all pretense,
now drown the world, give us your word,
ring, sweet assassin of the road,
the temple bell! For if letters

come, I will answer those letters
and my year will be tense, alive
with love! The temple receives the road:
there, the rain has come to a close.
Here the waters rise; our each word
in the fog awaits a sentence:

His hand on the scales, he gives his word:
Our letters will be rowed through olive
canals, the tense waters no one can close.

from *The Kenyon Review*

The Cove

◊   ◊   ◊

Something was out there on the lake, just barely
visible in the dark.
I knelt and stared, trying to make it out,
trying to mark

its position relative to mine,
and the picturesque willow, the moon-silvered diving board
on the opposite shore. I listened hard
but heard

no sound from it, although I cupped one ear
as I knelt in the cove,
wondering how far I should take this, if I should seek
someone to row out there with me. Yet it didn't move

or grow darker or lighter. Most shapes,
you know what they are:
a rock-garden serpent, a house in the mist, a man's head,
an evening star,

but not this one. Whatever was out there kept changing
from large to small.
The mass of a wooden coffin surfaced,
then the head of an owl,

a tree limb, a window, a veil—
I couldn't resolve it. I ran one hand through my hair
as I stood up, shrugging. I had just turned 50
and whatever it was that might be floating there

I didn't want it to be. Too much before
that came unbidden into my life
I'd let take me over. I knelt again and stared again.
Something was out there just beyond the cove.

from *The Hudson Review*

Now Then

◇　◇　◇

You can have your bathroom window open an inch
and if the door is nearly closed, it can slam.

it shut: the wind can: whereas, if the door
is standing open (as perhaps it shouldn't be)

(not if you're doing anything, you know, cool)
a hurricane would do little more than tremble

the door (however much it rattled the window);
may not, contrariwise, the physics be in the

metaphysics: which is to say that major effects
can come of slender spacings, while something

too wide open cannot be bothered by anything:
broadly, therefore, welcome the world, and if

you must have them keep your splinterings and
partitions solidly shut away from transmission:

you are, in other words, everyone, except for
your little exception box to which you may

repair for repair or prayer when the wide
scene loses hold on its outlines: the more to

be said the closer you get to nothing: you
peep out at dawn and say of the whole thing,

look at that, when, later, looking at the
vibration in the microinscriptive, you may

need to call up libraries of language for
poise: it could not be truly said of the

yellowjackets that they are out in the drizzle
today without their jackets, even though it is

true that they are not without their jackets:
if god is in each of us, I wonder if he is

in each of the gorillas, if only in his
gorilla-aspect, a facet the gorillas can see

themselves and be seen by, just as, I suppose,
when we look, we see our own natures, native

and, like ligatures, sewn together: the
yellowjackets that usually streak straight into

the stone socket of the stone wall they nest
in, today buzz broadly about that wet entrance

before diving in: the yellowjacket god is these
motions, and when naked yellowjackets

dip and streak and hunt the clover blooms,
don't think they don't feel at home, right with

their god: for it is true far and wide that
nothing is so true as what breaks into being

this minute from colossal petrifications of
past time and huge issuances into time-to-be:

don't mess with me, or the yellowjackets: we
are in a high place which may or may not explode

but if it explodes nothing will be lost, every
little tiny atom will still be spinning for

the lord: we may go, and scientists may suck
the yellowjackets out of their hole to extract

the sting-venom: have no fear: weep but move
on: if the god is not in residence, he is in

motion, and it is hard to tell which is which:
coco rico, the rooster crows: it is day again

from *Michigan Quarterly Review*

A Possum's Tale

◇   ◇   ◇

He's hauled himself out from a stranger place,
Unnoticed and in turn unnoticing
Of high-beams drifting down the cul-de-sac
Or shafts of street light angling through the limbs.
He makes his way, hunched deep into himself,
A tarnished silver creature bearing down
On corn silk, melon rinds and celery stalks
Dissolving into compost where they fell
One afternoon beside the barbecue.
Three children heading in from kick-the-can,
Their mothers having called them home from play,
Have cornered him beneath a picnic bench.
They pitch small stones and jab him with a stick,
Mistake his grin for a half-sarcastic smirk,
And meddle with his naked, coiled tail.
Enduring simply what he must endure,
He focuses the black beads of his eyes
On tufts of grass and dandelion thorns.
Perhaps he mutters something to himself
When, racing off at last, the boys depart
And he is left to needle into night,
Beneath the neighborhood's display of light,
While windows, like paintings on their easels, bear
Rare glimpses into unfamiliar lives.
Through bronze and copper rooms dark figures pass,
Their liquid shadows trailing after them.
On someone's parlor chandelier glass drops
Cascade like waters from a fountainhead.
Three houses down, high in a gable pane,

A sewing mannequin admires her gown
While he finds loveliness in scabs of moss,
Inspects the gunwales of a garbage can,
And drags behind him in his quiet wake
A strangeness only he can comprehend.

from *Raritan*

Botanical Garden: The Coastal Plains

◇　◇　◇

for Dr. Marianna Breslin

Fever bark, chokeberry, and goat's rue gather.
A persimmon tree and bridge frame muddy water.
Beyond, in a dense tangle, fetterbush twines
wax myrtle the way religion grapples with sin.
Dragonflies complete the pocosin.
Raised above a muck, I let the scene sink in.
I've returned to a miniature of the terrain
where I was born. Sun again boils my brain,
and pine needles sharpen their tips of pain
under snow-mountain clouds, those greedy breasts,
as one bruise-blue underneath now rests
over the pond where a turtle swims—
its below-surface shadow like an omen.
But tags are wired to stems. Plaques on posts
stand to explain, exorcising the ghosts
gathered in yaupon and pine. My father
is missing. Yet this land that entombs
my time has phyla and species, no longer dumb.
The secret dooms, once labeled, take on form.
The absent moccasin, as now I see him,
changes the meaning of his venom.

from *The Southern Review*

Hot

◇   ◇   ◇

I'm cooking Thai—you bring the beer.
The same order, although it's been a year

—friendships based on food are rarely stable.
We should have left ours at the table

where it began, and went to seed,
that appetite we shared, based less in need

than boredom—always the cheapest restaurants,
Thai, Szechuan, taking our chance

with gangs and salmonella—what was hot?
The five-starred curries? The pencilled-out

entrees?—the first to break a sweat
would leave the tip. I raise the knocker, let

it fall, once, twice, and when the door is opened
I can't absorb, at first, what's happened

—face loosened a notch, eyes with the gloss
of a fever left to run its course

too long, letting the unpropped skin collapse
in a wrinkled heap. Only the lips.

I recognize—dry, cracked, chapped
from licking. He looks as though he's slept

a week in the same clothes.—*Come in, kick back,*
    he says, putting my warm six-pack

of Pale & Bitter into the fridge to chill.
    There's no music. I had to sell

the stereo to support my jones, he jokes,
    meaning the glut of good cookbooks

that cover one whole wall, in stacked milk crates
    six high, nine wide, two deep. He grates

    unripe papaya into a bowl,
fires off questions—*When did you finish school?*

    Why not? Still single—Why? That dive
that served the ginger eels, did it survive?

I don't get out much. Shall we go sometime?
    He squeezes the quarters of a lime

into the salad, adds a liberal squirt
    of chili sauce. *I won't be hurt*

if you don't want seconds. It's not as hot
    as I would like to make it, but

you always were a bit of a lightweight.
    Here, it's finished, try a bite.

    He holds a forkful of the crisp
green shreds for me to take. I swallow, gasp,

    choke—pins and needles shoot
through mouth and throat, a heat so absolute

    as to seem freezing. I know better
not to wash it down with ice water

—it seems to cool, but only spreads the fire—
    I can only bite my lip and swear

quietly to myself, so caught
up in our old routine—*What? This is hot?*

You're sweating. Care for another beer?
—it doesn't occur to me that he's sincere

until, my eyes watering, half in rage,
    I open the door and find the fridge

    stacked full with little jars of curry paste,
    arranged by color, labels faced

    carefully outward, some pushed back
to make room for the beer—no milk, no take-

out cartons of gelatinous chow mein,
    no pickles rotting in green brine,

not even a jar of moldy mayonnaise.
    —*I see you're eating well these days,*

    I snap, pressing the beaded glass
of a beer bottle against my neck, face,

    temples, anywhere it will hurt
enough to draw the fire out, and divert

    attention from the fear that follows
close behind. . . . He stares at me, the hollows

under his eyes more prominent than ever.
    —*I don't eat much these days. The flavor*

has gone out of everything, almost.
    For the first time it's not a boast.

    You know those small bird chili pods—the type
you wear surgical gloves to chop,

    then soak your knife and cutting board
in vinegar? A month ago I scored

a fresh bag—they were so ripe
I couldn't cut them warm, I had to keep

them frozen. I forget what I had meant
   to make, that night—I'd just cleaned

   the kitchen, wanted to fool around
with some old recipe I'd lost, and found

   jammed up behind a drawer—I had
maybe too much to drink. "Can't be that bad,"

   I remember thinking. "What's the fuss
about? It's not as if they're poisonous. . . ."

Those peppers, I ate them, raw—a big fistful
   shoved in my mouth, swallowed whole,

   and more, and more. It wasn't hard.
You hear of people getting their eyes charred

to cinders, staring into an eclipse . . .
   He speaks so quickly, one of his lips

   has cracked, leaks a trickle of blood
along his chin. . . . I never understood.

   I try to speak, to offer some
small shocked rejoinder, but my mouth is numb,

tingling, hurts to move—I called in sick
   next morning, said I'd like to take

   time off. She thinks I've hit the bottle.
The high those peppers gave me is more subtle—

   I'm lucid, I remember my full name,
my parents' birthdays, how to win a game

of chess in seven moves, why which and that
   mean different things. But what we eat,

why, what it means, it's all been explained
  —Take this curry, this fine-tuned

balance of humors, coconut liquor thinned
  by broth, sour pulp of tamarind

  cut through by salt, set off by fragrant
galangal, ginger, basil, cilantro, mint,

the warp and woof of texture, aubergines
  that barely hold their shape, snap beans

  heaped on jasmine, basmati rice
—it's a lie, all of it—pretext—artifice

  —ornament—sugar-coating—for . . .
He stops, expressing heat from every pore

of his full face, unable to give vent
  to any more, and sits, silent,

  a whole minute.—*You understand?*
Of course, I tell him. As he takes my hand

I can't help but notice the strength his grip
  has lost, as he lifts it to his lip,

presses it for a second, the torn flesh
  as soft, as tenuous, as ash,

  not in the least harsh or rough,
wreck of a mouth, that couldn't say *enough.*

from *Poetry*

From *Visits from the Seventh*

◇   ◇   ◇

I. FLOATING

I said something nonsensical to them
and they mocked back, "but we're your one design,"
or "you're our one design"—which was it?

The pen slipped and capered on the page,
escorted by ripplings in the atmosphere
like breeze blowing with nothing to blow against.

"We wear no form or figure of our own
—a wisp, a thread, a twig, a shred of smoke—
to tell us from the motions of the air.

We would love to live in even a bubble,
to wrap around its glossy diaphanous,
reaching and rounding, as slinkily real

as a morning stretch or a dance in a field.
But we know only this air, and memory,
once, or several times, removed and turned,

the pang of a once-had, a maybe-again,
that shifting half-light, our home and habitat,
those hours, soft-toned, windless, that favor passage,

the usual relay of twilights. And,
how often a century? The sun eclipsed,
that 'created' half-light, not dusk or dawn:

us glowing through, our light, our element,
in which we show best, glow best, what we are.
Yesterday some snowflakes slipped through us,

refreshing kisses passing through our heat.
Ah, we wanted to say. If we could have,
we'd have laughed right out from sheer surprise."

And what else? "We've got you to stand for us."
And I have you, I said, to float for me.

II. How I Yearn

I had been missing them very badly,
that day and that day and the next—and yet
the solace they offered was imperfect,

airborne and volatile. I invoked them,
yes, often, in lieu of human contact.
Not that they weren't human, just abstracted

from humanness on the physical plane.
But why had they deserted me? I knew
the answer: for spurning them out of hand.

But where, in that case, did they swirl off to?
Did they rise higher, higher, and vanish
into some upper ether or did they

betrayingly visit someone else who
might at that moment seem more receptive?
Calling them back after a desertion

was never simple: I had to turn my mood
soft, bright, calm and dreamily attentive;
then, after a time, they would slip back in,

one by one, refiguring their spirals
in those inevitable rows of seven.
Would they, I once found the courage to ask,

weave together and net the air for me,
linking and looping their remembered limbs,
to break softly my falling if I fell?

"Cradle me, oh cradle me," I whispered.
That was not a service they could do, though.
Life is so complicated for us here,

so troublesome, really, that I wondered
how they found theirs. Did they love it up there
cutting their spirals into cold fronts and

turning somersaults with the storms? Did they
nestle cozy into their troughs of air,
basking in the serene and glossy heights,

the breathtaking vistas of blue-gray seas,
the pink-tinted cloudscapes, the high music—
or did they, as we do, long for blankets

and warm bodies? So I broached that question
when they came soft-shoeing back in this time.
"No memory, no thought," they lipped to me,

"can stand in for the loss of a life of touch."
"Amen," I said, "and that's the life I want."
So I brushed the air to be rid of them.

III. DENMARK

"But how could you tell him? Never ever
have we allowed—have we intimated—
you should share our visits with anyone."
That's I think the gist of what one said.

"All territories have, never forget,
their own imperatives and covenants,
and the tacit ones. Under the so-called
presumption rule—that's Denmark—we presume

that the broader and deeper sovereignty,
crossing all lines, subsuming all bodies,
aquatic or abstract, will override
interior but lesser requisites."

I wanted to argue that telling him
was not so different from telling myself.
"Oh appeal, appeal, if you must," one said.
"We don't mind a hum, a word, a whisper.

now and then, alluding to some other . . .
But outright revelation will only
imperil all that we've done, we and you,
to come to this arrangement—all the hours

at work before dawn in the North country,
the briny, eye-blue Baltic blustering
hard by, the sun rising to never more
than low in the sky, a cold yellow blur

gleaming dull in the iced *fourchettes* of trees."
So, was that all? Was that the sum of it?
Must I then keep mum or suggestive or
throw over all that they had been to me?

"Stay, stay," I happened to hear one murmur.
A song sprang to mind: "Oh, Copenhagen,
wonderful . . . salty old queen of the sea . . ."
(Or some such.) They beamed, for they liked that thought.

IV. DEATH

Well, the night is blooming. Death may not be
(as the atheists would have it) nothing
at all, but rather (think many of us
who've abandoned god for a sense of god)

a moment to move through, on the other
side of which to find, no one knows, but more
than worms and darkness. For some, a power
almost to speak—although "speak" may not be

the term in the absence of lips, tongue, teeth.
"To say." By some means they implant their thoughts
into a person's mind. Mine, for instance.
And thus they go on growing and thriving.

At times they only seem to want to chat
or to make florid gestures, curves and sweeps
and curlicues—*esquisses*! Coy promises
—teases of a vision not to be had;

at others they seem to bud or burst forth
with words pushing to be said, and they nudge
and tickle me to say them for them. They're
working on the matter of openness—

not though, for its own sake, as a value,
but so that I'll be more fertile for them.
Not altogether a noble purpose—
but that depends on the nobility

of the thought they're striving to cultivate.
Doesn't the wish to have one's thought thought of
seem vain, decorative? The lingering
effect of having lived well, maybe, and

not being able to leave it at that.
Always one stroke more to add: another
asterisk, addendum or afterword,
sprig after sprig, petal upon petal.

And if their thoughts are fine ones (most seem so
these nights) I don't mind helping them out by
letting them do their thinking in my thoughts.
Petals of promise; calyces of joy.

I like to fancy them as my teachers;
if they use me well, I may even learn
to use myself. And just now the room fills
with a fragrance of flowers. Or of love—

no, that isn't so. And yet, imagine
a garden, not wild but cultivated,
and richly fragrant. Yes, some spring flowers
turned in a breeze: that fresh, that rapturous.

V. A Flower

"Which ones?" And here they were, with me again,
slipping gently from this topic to that:
"Those for whom earthly senses are almost

not bearable, for whom a rough voice or
vile smell or small abrasion drawing blood
are racking or still worse. Those are the ones

living on the rim of Death, skirting it,
life being too lush, too real, and too rich—
meaning, they're allotted too many nerves."

"And for what? To please themselves, god only knows."
"But you can't have one without the other.
You can't be exquisitely pleasured and

not draw darker data through the senses."
There was the rub. They all laughed. We all laughed.
"And 'we all' know what too much pleasure is.

Or do we? (Paolo and Francesca knew)."
"The truest blessing to the sensitive
is not to live at all. How can a flower

be tolerated, for instance; maybe
it's too grand also, too great a rapture."
"There are many means of passing across,

including the taking of one's own death—
always a mistake viewed from either side."
"The tragedy of course is multifold,

the ones left behind weeping and helpless,
and the departed who must pass forward
through the stations, not having satisfied

a central moment of his destiny—
arduous passage." "For the extra-sensed
are tasked, you know, with negotiating

the difficult domain of the Divide."
I was tired then from too many such truths,
so I said good night, and I retreated.

VI. Moon-Gazing

And here now again: it didn't matter,
or did it, whether life's shifting layers
were "collateral or coterminous";

what was essential was to "look ahead
lightly"—"so very lightly"—and to "fuss
pleasantly over the moment's pleasures"

"without religion and without regret."
For that was all there was. *"Now is ever."*
And with these words, a beam of light streamed in,

a soft moonstripe or a neighboring lamp
through whose shine pranced the palest acrobats,
willful almost wanton and expressing

pure contentment at their own fine fact: *now
is ever.* Wasn't that really the "text
and texture of the higher life?" (This time

not excluding the sex organs.) "High" means
exquisitely sensed or extra-sensed? "Yes."
I've asked them but they haven't told me yet

how they sense without the senses. Oh yes,
the sixth sense, I had forgotten that one.
I feel them humming and clucking gently:

"The sixth sense is sex, silly. The *seventh* is
our sense, the one we sometimes share with you."
(This was a common but crucial error.)

But then how did they gather theirs of us?
I wanted to know so I pressed and pressed.
"Some, dear, have talked of seeing through the backs

of mirrors. And so it is, or almost so.
We live—'reside,' that is—on the far side
of the moon, watching it in negative

against the light of the sun. Do you see?
Dark moon in a sea of light. Oh to us
almost as wonderful and less like cheese."

VII. TEMPTATION

I do know the temptation to beg them
to read me the future or to read me
the present so I can parse the future;

and though they may seem to *clair-voient* my mind,
should I trust them to see someone else's?
If they said, "you are the life of his heart,"

if they hummed, "he is yours, now and ever,"
or, "after this hour, he will come to you,"
what if they visioned there not the true thought

48

but the self-deceit or the subterfuge
and then sang back those thoughts to me? And I
lived my life led by those misreadings?

And what if I said, as I know I did,
where is he now? And they said back "China"?
What China then? A China of the mind,

"mandarin and yes, multifarious,"
where a hex means merely a hexagram,
where a wild goose perching on a bare branch

means barren love. Well, was that our China?
Love that I desire return to me
and the change read, "noblehearted return,"

and return means merely "turning again";
"return from a short distance," read the change.
How far had we gone, how far would we come?

Was that then what our China would be?
"The number of sticks is six, the number
for sex, and thus the number of changing."

"Yes, well, sex *is* a danger to the soul:
it wounds the soul and therefore changes it.
The chaste are always wrong. For sex is change

and change is the essence of everything . . ."
You see? Such mediumistic moments
were fraught with bad turns, missteps and false hopes.

VIII. CANCER

Were they speaking of chemotherapy?
(JM reported that it split the soul.)
Oh? To live one life and not another,

and pass, how? "Shattered in a thousand shards."
I think it must feel like psychosis then.
"The soft wavering balloon of the self

flying in myriad loose flying bits.
Terrifying. Some thoughts this way, some that.
A memory here, a thought over there—

the circle at the center, gone." What would
I do if faced with such a hopeless hope?
I would wish to be moved to pass across

with my soul intact, or to turn to prayer,
or to seek the secret at the crisis
of the splitting of cells. "Would you call it

the demon's foot, the kernel of the fact,
the secret *dolor,* the seed of the seed
sleeping in the garden of memory,

lying in the hothouse of banished thoughts?"
"Would you call it the thorn, the buried pea
that bruised the perfect skin of the princess?"

"The brute instant or the prolonged trauma?"
"And what, after all, will waking it do?"
"Will it kiss away the little one's tears,

will it delete the image, frame by frame,
back to the moment when the day turned wrong?"
"No, probably not, no, certainly not."

"Will it reconceive the deforming cells?"
"Oh, possibly." Was that superstition
or faith? And here the pen slowed audibly:

"Yes, faith in the awful heart of the fact.
Blind believing but in nothing but that.
Irreligious but oh reverential."

This one, for instance, just said (I heard him
through a screen of static or scraping wind—
was it the scratch of the pen on the page?),

"Shun that small soul. Shun that small-natured soul.
Avoid mediocrity at all cost."
This was, yes, "improper interference."

"It's really only the new departures
who want, having just left, to intervene,
driven by the onset of new vision."

And "oh alas, in the time of passage
can they be dissuaded? For they haven't
yet grasped the futility of trying

to spare you your plight, your purpose, your oh
so necessary struggles and strivings.
For without them what would life be? As good . . .

as good as . . ." (here he fumbled and broke off,
mawkishly humming) ". . . oh useless to know . . .
oh love your sweet tears." And into the room

flew the sense of a dark song and a throng
of flutters or rustles—were they whispers
or were they soft wings, oh paler than air,

or merely the sense of the sound of them,
and the sound was as waves lapping, laughing,
the sound was as forests ruffled by wind.

And here now again, urgently pressing:
"Waste your talents on that constricting soul
for the love of a spot of affection?

Do you hope to exalt him? Watch how he
tries to count and control you, watch how he
wants to enclose you." And then this other:

"In time (or out of it) we learn to quell
our frustration, to turn our thoughts elsewhere
(I nearly said 'our minds'—how utterly

we are moved to speak your language to you)
toward the outer worlds. Oh yes, so high-flown
these words I know. But a fact is a fact."

X. MALICE

There are ones out there as false as any
(a 42nd Street of the Heavens),
gypsies and fantasists, con men and creeps:
if you're unbefriended they can steal in

at any hour under any pretext,
wanting you to believe in their goodwill
while secretly witching for your downfall.
They're envious, being those least gifted

or those who mismanaged their gifts in life,
so they can't come around honoring or
answering to honor they couldn't merit.
But do they ask themselves why not, and work

upwards from there? No. After all that time
cavorting idle across the skyscape,
pink, pellucid and cloud-streaked (that alone
should be enough to arouse them to praise),

and grousing about what they didn't do,
they *want* to see you injured or chagrined,
so they can chortle and vent their failure.
An ever-so-alluring deceiver

is the one who tells you your every dream
as though it were the truth of the future;
meanwhile there you stand in a wash of sweat
your hopes lifted high only to be dashed,

and hear him later laughing fit to burst
and posturing as thunder or traffic.
They *are* hard to tell, by this medium,
from the grand and good ones (but how like life!)

because of course they really can't be seen
and that makes telling a difficult task,
so Helen-Keller-like in its demand
for varieties of subtle nuance.

XI. Rêves d'or

"The surest bet is to take no counsel
but to love notions in the mere abstract;
to hear 'us' as you would hear anyone,

intrigued by the form of the idea
and maybe the manner of the telling
but never taking it as gospel truth."

"And let's not start now with this silliness
of what-does-it-matter-since-fate-prevails:
for you *do* stand there in the yellow wood

and must choose between two diverging paths,
or many paths diverging from a point,
starting now and moving into ever."

"Most of us never begin to assess
the infinite ways we never followed,
various in essence and variform,

a vast web of eventualities
traced negative on the verso of life:
verging, converging and parting again,

or radiating from a single verb,
never ever to return or to meet."
Was it the yellow of the green spring growth,

was it the yellow of the changing leaves,
of summer sun flaming in foliage
and burning the wishbones of the branches?

Was it the rubbed round of the winter sun
lacquering a glare on the frozen snow,
or was it the yellow Indian silk

I wore the last time you made love to me?
The yellow of piss, the refracted rays
in the nubs of the white angora's eyes,

or the yellow of fear—were those woods fear?
Which yellow was it? It was "all of these."
It was the "yellow of your yellow hair."

But this eludes the question of counsel.
This evades—*n'est-ce pas?*—the valence of choice.

from *The Paris Review*

Wakefulness

◊   ◊   ◊

An immodest little white wine, some scattered seraphs,
recollections of the Fall—tell me,
has anyone made a spongier representation, chased
fewer demons out of the parking lot
where we all held hands?

Little by little the idea of the true way returned to me.
I was touched by your care,
reduced to fawning excuses.
Everything was spotless in the little house of our desire,
the clock ticked on and on, happy about
being apprenticed to eternity. A gavotte of dust motes
came to replace my seeing. Everything was as though
it had happened long ago
in ancient peach-colored funny papers
wherein the law of true opposites was ordained
casually. Then the book opened by itself
and read to us: "You pack of liars,
of course tempted by the crossroads, but I like each
and every one of you with a peculiar sapphire intensity.
Look, here is where I failed at first.
The client leaves. History matters on,
rolling distractedly on these shores. Each day, dawn
condenses like a very large star, bakes no bread,
shoes the faithless. How convenient if it's a dream."

In the next sleeping car was madness.
An urgent languor installed itself
as far as the cabbage-hemmed horizons. And if I put a little

bit of myself in this time, stoppered the liquor that is our selves'
truant exchanges, brandished my intentions
for once? But only I get
something out of this memory.
A kindly gnome
of fear perched on my dashboard once, but we had all been instructed
to ignore the conditions of the chase. Here, it
seems to grow lighter with each passing century. No matter how you
      twist it,
life stays frozen in the headlights.
Funny, none of us heard the roar.

from *The New Yorker*

FRANK BIDART

The Second Hour
of the Night

◊　◊　◊

On such a night

       after the countless

assemblies, countless solemnities, the infinitely varied
voyagings in storm and in calm observing the differences

among those who are born, who live together, and die,

     •

On such a night

      at that hour when

slow bodies like automatons begin again to move down

into the earth beneath the houses in which they
live bearing the bodies they desired and killed and now

bury in the narrow crawl spaces and unbreathing abrupt
descents and stacked leveled spaces these used

bodies make them dig and open out and hollow for new
veins whose ore could have said *I have been loved* but whose

voice has been rendered silent by the slow bodies whose descent
into earth is as fixed as the skeletons buried within them

•

On such a night

      at that hour in the temple of

delight, when appetite
feeds on itself,—

•

On such a night, perhaps, Berlioz wrote those pages

in his autobiography which I first read when my mother
was dying, and which to me now inextricably
call up

    not only her death but her life:—

"A sheet already covered her. I drew it back.

Her portrait, painted in the days of
her splendor,

    hung beside the bed—

I will not attempt to describe the grief that possessed me.

It was complicated by something, *incommensurate,*
tormenting, I had always found hardest to bear—

a sense of pity.

    Terrible, overmastering

pity swept through me at everything she had suffered:—

Before our marriage,
her bankruptcy.

(Dazed, almost
appalled by the magnitude of her sudden
and early Paris triumph—as Ophelia, as Juliet—
she risked the fortune fame had brought
on the fidelity of a public without memory.)

Her accident.

(Just before a benefit
performance designed to lessen, if not
erase her debts, a broken leg left her
NOT—as the doctors feared—lame, but visibly
robbed of confidence and ease of movement.)

Her humiliating
return to the Paris stage.

(After Ophelia's
death, which a few years earlier at her debut
harrowed the heart of Paris, the cruel
audience did not recall her to the stage
once, though it accorded others an ovation.)

Her decision, made voluntarily but forever
mourned, to give up her art.

Extinction of her reputation.

The wounds each of us
inflicted on the other.

Her not-to-be-extinguished, insane JEALOUSY,—
. . . which, in the end, had cause.

Our separation, after eleven years.

The enforced
absence of our son.

Her delusion that she had forfeited the regard of
the English public, through her attachment to France.

Her broken heart.

Her vanished beauty.

Her ruined health. (Corrosive, and growing,
physical pain.)

The loss of speech,—
. . . and movement.

The impossibility of making herself understood in any way.

The long vista of death and oblivion stretching before her
as she lay paralyzed for four years, inexorably dying.

—My brain shrivels in my skull
at the horror, the PITY of it.

Her simple tomb bears the inscription:

> *Henriette-Constance Berlioz-Smithson, born at*
> *Ennis in Ireland, died at Montmartre 3rd March 1854*

At eight in the evening the day of her death
as I struggled across Paris to notify
the Protestant minister required for the ceremony,

the cab in which I rode, *vehicle*
conceived in Hell, made a detour and

took me past the Odeon:—

it was brightly lit for a play then much in vogue.

There, twenty-six years before, I discovered
Shakespeare and Miss Smithson at the same moment.

Hamlet. Ophelia. There
I saw Juliet for the first and last time.

Within the darkness of that arcade on many
winter nights I feverishly
paced or watched frozen in despair.

Through that door I saw her enter
for a rehearsal of *Othello.*

She was unaware of the existence of
the pale dishevelled youth with
haunted eyes staring after her—

*There I asked the gods to allow her
future to rest in my hands.*

If anyone should ask you, Ophelia, whether the unknown
youth without reputation or position
leaning back within the darkness of a pillar

will one day become your
husband and prepare your last journey—

with your great inspired eyes

answer, *He is a harbinger of woe."*

•

On such a night, at such an hour

*she who still carries within her body the growing
body made by union with what she once loved, and now*

*craves or
loathes, she cannot say—;*

61

she who has seen the world and her own self and the gods

within the mirror of
Dionysus, as it were—

compelled to labor since birth in care of the care-
needing thing into which she had entered;—

. . . Myrrha, consigning now to

the body heavier and heavier within her
what earlier she could consign only to air,

requests

in death transformation to nothing
human, to be not alive, not dead.

II

Ovid tells the tale:—

                  or, rather, Ovid tells us that

Orpheus sang it
in that litany of tales with which he

filled the cruel silence after Eurydice
had been sucked back down into the underworld
cruelly and he driven back cruelly
from descending into it again to save her . . .

He sang it on a wide green plain
without shade,

               but there the trees, as if
mimicking the attending beasts and birds, hearing his song

came to listen: the alder, the yew, the laurel
and pine whose young sweet nut
is dear to the mother of the gods since under it
Attis castrated himself to become her votary and vessel . . .

Beasts; birds; trees; but by his will
empty of gods or men.

•

In each tale of love he sang,—
                              Ganymede; Apollo and
Hyacinthus; Pygmalion; Adonis avenged upon
Venus; the apples that Atalanta found irresistible,—

fate embedded in the lineaments of desire

(desire itself helplessly surrounded by what cannot be
eluded, what
even the gods call GIVEN,—)

at last, in bitter or sweet enforcement, finds

transformation (except for the statue
Pygmalion makes human) to an inhuman, un-
riven state, become an element, indelible,
common, in the common, indelible, given world . . .

The story of Myrrha, mother of Adonis, is of all
these tales for good reason the least known.

It is said that Cinyras, her father, had he been
childless, might have died a happy man.

*Famed both for his gold and for his beauty, Cinyras
had become King of Cyprus and of Byblus*

*by marrying the daughter of the king, Myrrha's
mother, whose father had become king by marrying the daughter*

*of the king, Myrrha's mother's
mother, Paphos,—*

*. . . child
born from the union of Pygmalion and the statue.*

When the eyes of Cinyras
followed, lingered upon her, Myrrha had the sensation
he was asking himself whether, in
another world, she could heal him.

Myrrha was Pygmalion and her father the statue.

He was Pygmalion and Myrrha the statue.

—As a dog whose body is sinking into quicksand
locks its jaws around a branch hanging
above it, the great teeth grasping so fiercely the stable world
they snap the fragile wood,—

. . . Myrrha looped a rope over the beam above her bed

in order to hang herself.

What she wants she does not want.

The night she could no longer NOT tell herself
her secret, she knew that there had never
been a time she had not known it.

It was there like the island

that, night after
night, as she

wished herself to sleep, she embellished
the approach to:—

the story has many beginnings, but one ending—

out of the air she has invented it, air
she did not invent . . .

•

In the earliest version whose making and remaking Myrrha
remembers,
     she and her father escape from Cyprus

in a small boat, swallowed, protected
by a storm that blackens sea and stars;

he has been stripped of power by advisors of the dead
old king, father of Myrrha's mother, Queen
Cenchreis, and now, the betrayers make Cenchreis

head of state,—

Cinyras in the storm shouts that they have made his
wife their pawn, and Myrrha shouts that many
long have thought
     they are HERS,—

. . . the storm, after days,
abandons them to face a chartless, terrifying horizon.

Then, the island.

In the version that Myrrha now
tells herself since both her father and mother as
King and Queen insist that with their concurrence

soon, from among the royal
younger sons who daily arrive at court as rivals for
her bed, she must choose a husband—

both for her own natural happiness, and
to secure the succession,—

. . . now she is too violated by the demand that she marry

to invent reasons why the story that she
tells herself to calm herself to sleep begins with
a powerless king standing next to his
daughter in a tiny boat as they stare out at
a distant, yearned-for, dreaded island . . .

On the island, later, she again and again relives
stepping onto the island.

Each of them knows what will happen here:—

   . . . she can delay, he can delay
because what is sweet about
deferral is that what arrives

despite it, is revealed as inevitable:—

she is awake
only during the lucid
instant between what she recognizes

must happen, and what happens:—

each of them knows that the coldest eye looking
down at them, here, must look without blame:—

now, the king
hesitates—

               he refuses to place his foot upon the shore:—

   . . . the illusion of rescue from what he is, what
she is, soon must recede, once on
land everything
not nature fall away,

                         as unstarved springs

divide them from all that
divide them from themselves:—

bulls fuck cows they
sired, Zeus himself fathered Dionysus-Zagreus
upon Persephone, his daughter:—

beasts and gods, those
below us and those above us, open
unhuman eyes

when they gaze upon what they desire
unstained by disgust or dread or terror:—

. . . Myrrha, watching him, now once again can close her eyes
upon sleep. She sees him

step onto the island. He has entered her.

•

Grief for the unlived life, grief
which, in middle age or old age, as goad

or shroud, comes to all,

early became Myrrha's
familiar, her narcotic

chastisement, accomplice, master.

*What each night she had given with such
extravagance,—*

. . . *when she woke, had not been given.*

Grief for the unlived life, mourning
each morning renewed as Myrrha

woke, was there

and not there, for hours merely
the memory of itself, as if long ago

she told herself
a story (*weird*

dream of enslavement) that seemed
her story, but now she cannot

recollect why listening she could not
stop listening, deaf to any other . . .

But soon she heard the music beneath every other music:—

what she could not transform herself
into is someone

without memory, or need for memory:—

*four steps forward then
one back, then three
back, then four forward . . .*

Today when Myrrha's father reminded her that
on this date eighteen
years earlier her mother announced that he
was the man whom she would in one month

marry,—

and then, in exasperation, asked what Myrrha
wanted in a husband, unsupplied by the young men cluttering his
court in pursuit of her hand and his throne,—

after she, smiling, replied, "You,"

blushing, he turned
away, pleased . . .

*Four steps forward then
one back, then three
back, then four forward:—*

today her father, not ten feet from where
once, as a child, she had in
glee leapt upon him surrounded by

soldiers and he, then, pretending to be overwhelmed
by a superior force fell backwards with
her body clasped in his arms as they rolled
body over body down the long slope
laughing and that peculiar sensation of his weight
full upon her and then
not, then full upon her, then not,—

until at the bottom for a half-
second his full weight rested upon her, then not,—

. . . not ten feet from where what
never had been repeated except within
her today after reminding her that today her mother

exactly at her age chose him,—

after she had answered his question
with, "You,"

blushing, he turned
away, pleased . . .

There is a king inside the king that the king
does not acknowledge.

*Four steps forward then
one back, then three
back, then four forward:*—

. . . the illusion of movement without
movement, because you know that what you
move towards

(malignant in the eyes of gods and men)

isn't there:—

doesn't exist:—

though the sensation of motion without
movement or end offers the hypnotic

solace of making not only each repeated
act but what cannot be repeated

an object of contemplation,—

. . . what by rumor servant girls, and slaves, as well as
a foreign queen

taste, for Myrrha alone

isn't there, doesn't exist,
malignant in the eyes of gods and men . . .

The gods who made us either
didn't make us,—

. . . or loathe what they have made.

*Four steps forward then
one back, then three
back, then four forward:*—

. . . but you have lied about your
solace, for hidden, threaded

within repetition is the moment when each step
backward is a step
downward, when what you move toward moves toward

you lifting painfully his cloak to reveal his
wound, saying, *"love answers need"* . . .

Approaching death, for days Myrrha more and more
talked to the air:—

My element is the sea. I have seen

the underside of the surface of the sea, the glittering
inner surface more beautiful than the darkness below it,

seen it crossed

and re-crossed by a glittering ship from which dark eyes
peering downward must search the darkness.

Though they search, the eyes
fix upon nothing.

The glittering ship swiftly,
evenly, crosses and re-crosses.

No hand reaches down from it to penetrate the final
membrane dividing those whose element
is the sea, from those who breathe in the light above it.

The glittering ship captained by darkness
swiftly, evenly, crosses and

re-crosses.

I have seen it. I cannot
forget. Memory is a fact of the soul.

●

Hippolyta, Myrrha's nurse, thanked the gods
she heard the thump of the rope

hitting the wooden beam, the scrape of
the heavy stool moved into place,

and clasped Myrrha's legs
just as they kicked away the light that held them.

—The creature plummeting resistlessly to the sunless
bottom of the sea was
plucked up, and placed upon the shore.

She slept. After a period of indefinite
duration Hippolyta's voice almost uninflected

woke her, saying that now her nurse must
know the reason for her action.

Failure had made her Hippolyta's
prisoner—; she

told her . . .

Head bowed deferentially, Hippolyta
listened without moving.

Hippolyta gathered up the rope, then
disappeared.

Myrrha slept. After a period of indefinite
duration Hippolyta's voice almost uninflected

woke her, saying that she had seen the King and
told the King that she could bring to him tonight a young

girl in love with him who wished to share
his bed, but who must, out of modesty, remain veiled.

Tonight the Festival of Demeter began, during
which the married women of Cyprus in
thanksgiving for the harvest, garlanded
with unthreshed
ears of wheat, robed in white, in secret
purification within the temple for nine days and
nights, abstained from their husbands' now-outlawed beds.

(Each year, Queen Cenchreis fulfilled with ostentatious
ardor the letter of the law.)

Hippolyta told Myrrha that when she
asked the King whether the King will

accept the girl, he asked
her age.

Hippolyta replied, "Myrrha's age."

The King then said, *"Yes."*

Listening to Hippolyta's words Myrrha
knew that tonight she would allow Hippolyta in
darkness to lead her veiled to her father's chamber.

The door that did not exist

stood open—; she would
step through.

Hippolyta once again
disappeared.

                    •

In her own room at last Hippolyta fell upon
her knees before her altar to the Furies.

Ten years earlier, when Menelaus and Odysseus
and Agamemnon's herald Talthybius
arrived in Cyprus seeking from the newly-crowned King
(Queen Cenchreis still wore mourning)

help for their expedition to humble Troy,—

. . . Cinyras, giddy not only with unfamiliar
obeisance to his power by men of power, but too much

wine, promised in six months to send sixty ships.

As a gift for Agamemnon, he gave his herald the breastplate
of the still-mourned King, gorgeously
worked with circles of cobalt and gold and tin, with two
serpents of cobalt rearing toward the neck.

Hippolyta and Myrrha overheard the Queen
next morning calmly tell the King that the great families who
chose the King's advisors had no intention of
honoring his drunken
grandiloquent bravado by funding sixty ships—

that if he persisted either the house of her
father must fall, or she would be forced
to renounce him and marry another, ending

the birthright of their daughter.

As a newcomer, a stranger on Cyprus, he owns
no man's loyalty.

—In six months, one ship sent by Cinyras
entered the harbor holding the Greek expedition;

on its deck were fifty-nine clay
ships with fifty-nine clay crews.

Serving on it were Hippolyta's
father and brother.

Cyprians applauded their new King's canny
wit, his sleight-of-hand and boldness; they felt

outrage when Agamemnon, as mere token of
his vengeance, sank the ship, its
crew strapped to its deck . . .

Now before the altar long ago
erected, Hippolyta implores the Furies:—

May the King of the Clay Ships
find the flesh within his bed

clay. Avenge in
torment the dead.

•

As Myrrha is drawn down the dark corridor toward her father

not free not to desire

what draws her forward is neither COMPULSION nor
                                                FREEWILL:—

or at least freedom, here *choice,* is not to be
imagined as action upon

preference: no creature is free to choose what
allows it its most powerful, and most secret, release:

I fulfill it, because I contain it—
it prevails, because it is within me—

it is a heavy burden, setting up longing to enter that
realm to which I am called from within . . .

As Myrrha is drawn down the dark corridor toward her father

not free not to choose

she thinks, *To each soul its hour.*

•

Hippolyta carrying a single candle led her through
a moonless night to the bed where
her father waits.

The light disappears.

Myrrha hears in his voice that he is
a little drunk.

She is afraid: she knows that she must not
reveal by gesture or sound

or animal
leap of the spirit that is hers alone, her animal

signature, that what touches him in ways
forbidden a daughter

is his daughter,—

. . . entering his bed, Myrrha must not be
Myrrha, but Pharaoh's daughter come by
law to Pharaoh's bed.

Sweeter than the journey that constantly surprises
is the journey that you will to repeat:—

. . . the awkward introduction of a foreign object

*which as you prepare to expel
it enters with such insistence*

*repeatedly that the resistance you have
marshalled against it*

*failing utterly leaves
open, resistless, naked before it*

what if you do NOT resist it CANNOT be reached:—

you embrace one of the two species of
happiness, the sensation of
surrender, because at the same instant

you embrace the other, the sensation of power:—

*. . . the son whose sister is his mother
in secrecy is conceived within
the mother whose brother is her son.*

Before leaving the bed of sleeping
Cinyras, Myrrha slowly runs her tongue

over the skin of his eyelid.

•

Cinyras insisted to Hippolyta that his
visitor must return a second night, then

a third—

if this new girl proves
beautiful, he will bind her to him . . .

No warrior, Cinyras is a veteran of the combats in
which the combatants think that what they

win or lose is love:—

at the well of Eros, how often he has
slaked the thirst that is but briefly
slaked—;
            he worries that though he still

possesses stamina, an inborn
grace of gesture, the eye of
command, as well as beautiful hands and feet,

thickenings, frayed edges to what he knows was his
once startling
beauty betray how often . . .

The sharp-edged profile still staring from the coins
stamped to celebrate his marriage

mocks him.

And now this creature who
seems when he is exhausted, is un-
renewable,

                to make love to his skin,—

. . . who touching its surface seems to
adore its surface so that he
quickens as if he is its surface.

—Myrrha was awakened by the bright lamp
held next to her face. It was held there

steadily, in silence.

The lamp was withdrawn, then
snuffed out.

She heard a sword pulled from its sheath.

Before the sheath clattered to the stone floor
she slipped from the bedclothes.

She heard the sword descend and
descend again, the bedclothes

cut and re-cut.

•

The gods, who know what we want not
why, asked who among them

had placed this thing in Myrrha.

Each god in turn denied it. Cupid
indignantly insisted that his arrows abhorred

anything so dire; Venus seconded her son.

Cupid then said that such
implacable events brought to mind the Furies.

The Furies when roused growled that in
a corollary matter they justly again and
again had been beseeched, but upon inspection

exertion by immortals was unneeded.

•

—Sheba's withered
shore . . . Scrub; rocks; deserted coast

facing the sea. Because there is no
landscape that Myrrha's presence does not
offend, she stares at the sea:—

across the sea

she fled Cinyras; encircled by the sea
lay the island that she spent childhood
approaching; from Cyprus the sea brought

NOT what she had expected, the King's
minions impelled by the injunction to
shut her, dirt shoved within her mouth, beneath
dirt silenced, exiled forever,—

but representatives of
the Queen, informing her of what had
followed her departure:—

when Cinyras found Hippolyta
bowing before an altar, he split her with his sword
from the nape to the base of the spine, then after
dragging the body to a parapet overlooking
rocks and sea, with a yell threw it over the edge;—

within hours what
precipitated Myrrha's disappearance was common
gossip;—

within days three warships
appeared in the harbor at Paphos, sent by
Agamemnon, conqueror of Troy.

Word came from them that the people of Paphos could
avoid destruction if, within three days,

Cinyras were delivered to them.

On the third day, as the King's advisors still
debated how to balance honor with prudence,

the King, standing on the parapet from which had
fallen Hippolyta's body,
                              looking out at the ships

leapt. Some said that the cause was
Myrrha; others, Agamemnon.

The eyes of the people of Cyprus
must find offense should Myrrha attempt return . . .

Cyprians are relieved that the Queen, not yet
forty, has decided to accept the unanimous

counsel of her advisors, and remarry.

·

—She still smells the whiff of something
fatuous when Cinyras as a matter of

course accepted her adoration.

Now Myrrha teaches her child by daily
telling her child, listening
within her, the story of Myrrha and Cinyras . . .

She failed because she had poured, *tried
to pour,* an ocean into a thimble.

Whatever lodged *want* within her had seen her
vanity and self-intoxication and married

her to their reflection.

The thimble was a thimble—and she had
wronged it . . .

She grew careless because she allowed
herself to imagine that if he once
saw her he must love what he had seen.

Bewildered, betrayed
eyes wait now to accuse her in death.

Her mother once told her:—

*A queen remains a queen only when
what she desires is what she is*

expected to desire.

She would anatomize the world
according to how the world

anatomizes DESIRE. As a girl she had taught

herself to walk through a doorway as if
what she knows is on the other side is
NOT on the other side, as if her father

were a father as other fathers (though
kings) merely are fathers—;
                                        will, calculation

and rage replaced in Myrrha what
others embraced as "nature" . . .

Her friends live as if, though what they
desire is entirely what they are
expected to desire, it is they who desire.

Not "entirely"; almost entirely.

—In the final months, when Myrrha again and
again told the child heavier and heavier within her
the story of Myrrha and Cinyras,

she stripped from it words like "ocean" and "thimble."

She was a sentence that he had spoken in
darkness without
knowing that he had spoken it.

She had the memory of taste before she knew
taste itself: *The milk*

that is in all trees. The sweet water that is beneath.

One fruit of all the world's fruit, for
her, tastes—;

she had failed because her fate, like
all fates, was partial.

Myrrha ended each repetition by telling the child
within her that betrayed, bewildered

eyes wait now to accuse her in death.

—Phoenicia; Panchaia; Sheba—

people everywhere lived lives indifferent to the death of
Cinyras—; suffocating, Sheba's
highlands thick with balsam, costmary,
cinnamon, frankincense—;

. . . there is no landscape that her
presence does not offend, so she is free to
prefer this forsaken shore swept by
humid winds, facing the sea.

Her body is dying.

That her body is dying, her labors not yet
finished, her child un-
born, is not what is bitter.

Myrrha addressed the gods:—

Make me nothing
human: not alive, not dead.

Whether I deny what is not in my
power to deny, or by deception

seize it, I am damned.

I shall not rest until what has been
lodged in me is neither

lodged in me,—nor NOT lodged in me.

Betrayed, bewildered eyes
wait for me in death.

You are gods. Release me, somehow, from both
life and death.

The gods granted her request. From her toes roots

sprout; the dirt rises to cover her
feet; her legs of which she never had been
ashamed grow thick and hard; bark like disease
covers, becomes her skin; with terror she
sees that she must
submit, lose her body to an alien
body not chosen, as the source of ecstasy is
not chosen—

        suddenly she is eager to submit: as the change

rises and her blood becomes
sap, her long arms long branches, she cannot bear

the waiting: she bends her face
downward, plunging her face into the rising

tree, her tears new drops glistening everywhere on its surface:—

fixed, annealed within its body
the story of Myrrha and Cinyras:—new
body not alive not dead, story
everywhere and nowhere:—

Aphrodisiac. Embalmers' oil. (Insistence of
sex, faint insistent sweetness of the dead undead.)
Sacred anointment oil: with wine an
anodyne. Precious earth-
fruit, gift fit for the birth and death of

prophets:—no sweet thing without
the trace of what is bitter
within its opposite:—

   . . . MYRRH, sweet-smelling
bitter resin.

                    •

Soon the child, imprisoned within the tree,
sought birth. Lucina, Goddess of Child-Birth, helped

the new tree contort, the bark
crack open,—

              . . . pretty as Cupid in

a painting, from the bitter
vessel of Myrrha and Cinyras Adonis was born.

We fill pre-existing forms, and when
we fill them, change them and are changed:—

day after day Myrrha told the child
listening within her her story . . .

Once grown to a man, beautiful as Cupid were
Cupid a man, Myrrha's son

                         by his seductive

indifference, tantalizing
refusals tormented love-sick Venus.

Ovid tells us that upon Venus Myrrha's
son avenged his mother.

His final indifference is
hunting (to Venus' horror) the boar

that kills him . . .

Venus did not, perhaps, in her own person
intervene in the fate of Myrrha and Cinyras,—
but children who have watched their parents'
blighted lives blighted in the service of Venus

must punish love itself.

                    •

*O you who looking within the mirror discover in
gratitude how common, how lawful your desire,*

*before the mirror
anoint your body with myrrh*

precious   bitter resin

III

On such a night, at such an hour,

when the inhabitants of the temple of
delight assume for each of us one
profile, different of course for each of us,

but for each of us, single:—

when the present avatar of powers not present though
present through him, different for each of us,

steps to the end of the line of other, earlier
inhabitants of the temple of
delight, different for each of us:—

when the gathering turns for its portrait

and by a sudden trick of alignment and light and
night, all I see

the same, the same, the same, the same, the same—

on such a night,

> *at such an hour*

. . . grace is the dream, half-
dream, half-

light, when you appear and do not answer the question

that I have asked you, but courteously
ask (because you are dead) if you can briefly

borrow, inhabit my body.

When I look I can see my body
away from me, sleeping.

I say *Yes*. Then you enter it

like a shudder as if eager again to know
what it is to move within arms and legs.

I thought, *I know that he will return it.*

I trusted in that none
earlier, none other.

                    •

I tasted a sweet taste, I found nothing sweeter.
Taste.
My pleasant fragrance has stripped itself to stink.
Taste.
The lust of the sweetness that is bitter I taste.
Taste.
Custom both sweet and bitter is
the intercourse of this flesh.
Taste.
The milk that is in all trees,
the sweet water that is beneath.
Taste.
The knife of cutting is the book of mysteries.
Taste.
Bitterness sweetness, eat that you may eat.
Taste.
I tasted a sweet taste, I found nothing sweeter.
Taste.
These herbs were gathered at full noon, which was night.
Taste.

                    •

. . . *bodies carrying bodies,* some to bury in
earth what offended earth by breathing, others

become the vessels of the dead, the voice erased
by death now, for a time, unerased.

•

infinite the sounds the poems

seeking to be allowed to S U B M I T,—that this

dust become seed

like those extinguished stars whose fires still give us light

•

This is the end of the second hour of the night.

from *The Threepenny Review*

A Week of Poems
at Bennington

◊   ◊   ◊

SUNDAY

What to Do with Objects

A little snow. Coffee. The bowled-over branches,
The wind; it is cold outdoors; but in the bed
It's warm, in the early lamp-light, reading poems.

These fingers, so rosy, so alive, move
About this book. Here is my wide-traveling palm,
The thumb that looks like my father's, the wedding ring.

It's time to prepare myself—as a friend said—
"Not to be here." It will happen. One day
The dish will lie empty on the brown table.

Toward dusk, someone will say, "Today
Some rooms were busy, but this room was not.
The gold knob shone alone in the dark."

No breath, no poems, no dish. And this small change
Will go unnoticed by the snow, the squirrels
Searching for old acorns. What to do with

All these joys? Someone says, "You take them."

MONDAY

When the Cat Stole the Milk

Well there it is. There's nothing to do.
The cat steals the milk and it's gone.
Then the cat steals you, and you're found
Days later, with milk on your face.

That implies that you become whoever
Steals you. The trees steal a man,
And an old birch becomes his wife
And they live together in the woods.

Some of us have always wanted
God to steal us. Then our friends
Would call each other, and print
Posters, and we would never be found.

TUESDAY

Being Happy All Night

—For Sven

It's as if the mice stayed warm inside the snow,
As if my cells heard laughing from the Roman vineyards.
Mice slept despite the cruel songs of the stars.
We laughed and woke and sniffed and slept again.

Some people inside my body last night
Married each other just in order to dance.
And Sara Grethe smiled so proudly the men
Kicked their heels on the planks, but kept the beat.

Oh I think it was the books I read long ago.
It's as if I joined other readers on a long road.
We found dead men hanging in a meadow.
We took dew from the grass and washed our eyes.

WEDNESDAY

With a Friend at Bennington

He wakes, reads some Frost, and soon is ready
To leave. "See you tomorrow." A long line
of feeling follows him out the door. His shoulders
Slope as usual in their way, carrying on them

Deaths and stories, a divorce, marital love
As pertinacious as a bulldog's mouth. Jane gone,
Who will hear the thin cough in the morning.
Hear the milk hitting the pail as his grandfather

Sings poems in the old barn, who will see
The forty drafts on yellow paper? Or notice him
Reading Francis Parkman till long after midnight.
"Stay, friend, be with us, tell me what happened."

THURSDAY

We Only Say That

"There are so many things to love around here."
We only say that when we want to hint
Something—the day after we notice a woman,
Who waves a hand with her female bravery.

We say, "The icicles are really brilliant today,"
Or "Let's all make fun of other people."
That would bring us closer, or "Martha brought
Her dog out into the morning snow."

Her hand reaches up to brush her neck,
Or she puts on her boots. A voice inside us
Says, "Oh a woman! Let's close the door.
Let's flirt and not flirt. Let's play cards and laugh."

FRIDAY

The Rebuke

Well I do it, and it's done.
And it can't be taken back.
There's a little wound in my chest
Where I wounded others, but

It will knit, or heal, in time.
That's what you say.
And some I wounded
Claim: "I am the better for it."
But I pull in my breath.

Was it truth-telling or
A thin man with a knife?
The wound will close, or heal
In time. That's what you say.

SATURDAY

Nothing Can Be Done

Don't tell me there's nothing that can be done.
The tongue says, "I know I can change things."
The toe says, "I have my ways."
The heart is weeping and remembering Eden.

Legs think that a good run will do it.
Tongue has free tickets; he'll fly to heaven.
But the buttocks see everything upside down—
They want you to put your head down there,

Remind the heart it was upside down
In the womb, so that when your mother walked
Upstairs—she knew where she was going—
You weren't going anywhere.

from *Agni*

GEORGE BRADLEY

In an Old Garden

◇　◇　◇

Some cloudy, colorless November day,
When leaves are down and odd uneven gray
Lines show up where recently a lush
Wall of impenetrable underbrush
Obscured all sign of such impediments
As constitute a fieldstone garden fence,
With autumn over, winter unarrived,
You stumble on whatever has survived
Of old New England farms: the border cairns
That mark an orchard gone to woods; a barn's
Mere outline; perhaps a hollow to surprise
The foot, telling how wells internalize
Themselves; and—look!—one sky-blue cupid's dart
That given time will learn its rime by heart.

from *The New Yorker*

From *Just Let Me Say This About That (IV)*

◊   ◊   ◊

The following excerpt is from a long poem cast in the form of a press conference. The three questioners are named Bird, Fox, and Fish, while the person being questioned, addressed only as "Sir," is either god, the president of the United States, everyone's father, or a combination of the three. He is, in Freud's phrase, someone to whom one tells one's story or refers one's problems "as to one who knows." (The questioners are indicated by italics, the speaker by Roman.) The questioners, though starting with inquiries about social and political matters, soon make it clear that what they really want to know is the value and meaning of life. In trying to explain its meaning, the speaker retells the story of Job in modern form, but the questioners recognize it immediately, so the speaker suggests instead that between them they come up with a plausible story to explain how an ordinary man, Mr. Fish for example, could suffer a run of bad luck, lose everything he has, and end up as a homeless bum on the streets. The culmination of Fish's unlucky streak comes one Christmas time at dusk when he is driving his three kids home from rehearsing the school pageant. He's had too much to drink, and when the car's tires hit an icy patch in the road, the vehicle skids down an embankment, takes out a chain-link fence in a gravel yard, flips once, and slides on its roof in soft snow onto the frozen surface of a quarry pond. At that moment the worst seems over, but when Fish's older son, who like the others is hanging upside down in his seat belt in the overturned car, frees himself and drops to the roof, the jolt sends the car roof punching through the ice, and "the screaming really starts." As the car sinks, Fish is thrown out, and freezing water pours in the open door pinning the kids in back where his son struggles to free his younger brother and sister from their belts. As the car goes under, Fish grabs the frame and, wrenching it desperately, tries to keep the car up, while out of the corner of his eye he sees his daughter's "blonde hair swirl across the window." Finally with "his lungs on fire for air" and the terrible cold "throbbing through / His temples while the car keeps going down / And going down, . . . Fish at last lets go." At this point the speaker averts his gaze:

Bird, have you ever thought how a pet's death
Is a pure sorrow? No human we've known long
Or been that close to seems, once they ground out

For good, ever to leave our odd hearts
Unmixed, it's just the way we are, but let
A little dog or cat go belly up

With X's on its eyes, and who'd believe
The grief. Mostly it's the gaze breaks
Your heart, that mute devotion struggling to say

How we're their all in all, their world's good weather,
How hands are made for petting, laps to curl in,
To tell in signs, those soft imperatives

Of tongue and tail, how wholly lost they'd be
Without our love or their true work to do
Of finding us when we get low so they

Can make it right: "Are you sad? That's
No good. I can help. Can't I help?"
That's just the way they talk, Bird, like the simple,

Gentle souls they are, to spoil whose trust
Must be that sin without forgiveness except
That they forgive, so much like kids of three

Or four whose parents are their gods but better,
Fox, because they don't grow up, move off,
Forget to write or phone and then when you

Get old and start to slobber, take your power of
Attorney so if you slip and fall and break
A hip, they can slap you in a home

That quick! some sad old folks' encampment full
Of tepid gruel and walkers, slack mouths and trembling
Hands, and that pervasive smell of urine

Drying in empty rooms where radios play.
No, Bird, I've known some blood-dumb biters in my day
But no dog or cat who'd do that. You know,

Sometimes I think that's what the old Egyptians
Meant: giving their gods feral heads,
Not just to hint that we're as far from gods

As animals from men but that a dog
Or cat's sweet single-hearted love of its
Own master seems to mirror in reverse

What we expect from gods, that recognition
Of each one's uniqueness (so we don't
Get lost among the numbers) and the care

That thought implies. Of course, historically speaking,
Boys, that's sentimental hooey, seeing
It takes another two, three thousand years

To get a god in love with stiffs and losers,
One whose eye is on the sparrow so
You know he watches me. So shoot me, Fox,

If I'm a sentimentalist at heart
But all I know's I never had so strong
A sense of love's omnipresence as this once,

Standing at my window one blue winter
Afternoon, watching snowflakes fall
And dusk come on, I heard the little girl

Named Amy down the block, barely six
And crying now because her spaniel puppy'd
Slipped out of the yard that noon (a thing

As blonde as she and just as innocent of
The world) to leave her kicking down the alley
Through the snow in rubber boots and hooded

Yellow slicker calling "Piper! Piper!"
While mother looked on helpless from the steps,
Unable to console the heartbreak in her voice,

That baffled note of pain you only get
When loss is still a language we're not used to
And our first failure caring for a thing

Weaker than ourselves who trusts us wholly
Still strikes us like a thunderbolt, and so,
Imagining her puppy wandering scared

In snowy yards, its floppy ears caked stiff
From trailing through the drifts, and starting now,
Because he's very cold, to make those little

Yipping noises meaning for all we know
In dog talk, "Amy, help me, please. Oh, find me
Soon, soon," Amy goes calling "Piper, Piper"

To bring her headstrong puppy back, and, Bird,
You know, I thought if half the problem most folks
Have imagining there's something larger

Than themselves whose will is love is just
To picture its homely presence in their lives,
Those folks could well do worse than think of Amy's

Anxious search and how, when days grow cold
And it gets dark enough to miss our way,
No dog's so lost an innocent loving heart

Can't find him out at last and bring him home.
I wonder if that's what Fish thought, Fox, staring
Blindly at the thermos in his hand

As someone threw a blanket round his shoulders,
Cold and dazed in that bleak lunar glare
Of tow truck headlights now the divers' work

Was done, the cable on the car's rear axle
Sawing through the ice as the wrecker's winch
Tightened and whined and Fish blankly watching

Wreathes of steam rising from the thermos
So's not to look again at what lies helpless now
Beneath three blankets, stunned that he

Can see at all after what he'd seen,
Damp hair plastered against their delicate foreheads
Like animals whose limbs are lightly downed

Or that gray mournful sleekness of drowned kittens,
A faint blue in the hollows of shut eyes
Brought down to violet at the broken throat,

The tiny thread of blood from Teddy's ear,
And, Fox, I think Fish thought then not about
What power in this world could still forgive

Or find him in that wide abyss where he
Was headed but what he'd tell his wife when they
First met and she, guessing what had happened

From his eyes, started screaming like an
Animal in pain, "Oh god, Bill, what've
You done, oh jesus, what've you done with my children?"—

A scream that he'd hear echoing inside
For years and years, shrieking like a whirlwind
That sweeps up his home and marriage, job

And friends and spins them off into the endless
Dark until, for just one moment, maybe
Twenty years after, Fish awakens,

Sitting on the sidewalk, back propped against
A building, wakes up in sunlight with the dazzling
Sense they'd all come back, his wife and kids,

His work, his old, warm former life, then smells
The dried vomit on his clothes and sees
The empty pint, stuck in a paper sack,

And knows it's just an aching dream of longing
For all the things he's lost and won't get back.
So how's that, boys, for giving Fish a yarn

That makes his bumhood seem a riff he'd earned.
I think it has its moments, though keep in mind,
Penn Station's full of stinking bums in winter,

They can't all have killed their kids, which is
To say, Bird, for my taste the tale's a trifle
Moist, not that sentimental things

Aren't true, they can be, often are, you bet,
It's just that as a rule to trust their being
So can't do you any sort of good,

If you see what I mean. Besides I could've told
His story lots of ways—I think you'll own
I'm something of a raconteur—well, now,

Suppose I'd made Fish someone who's in love
With degradation, its drowsy, downward sense
Of certainty once a man's lost

His place and found he likes the feel of being
Lighter than a gob of spit, made Fish
A kind of imp of the perverse testing

The lonely self's lower depths. What was it,
Fox, they called those guys years back who travelled
Through our big midwest in summer jumping

Head first in folks' septic tanks and cesspools,
Paid meals to muck them out? Um, honey-jumpers—
That's it. Well, just suppose I'd made Fish here

A honey-jumper of the human spirit,
Ripe and reeking in the gasping noon
Of existential anguish, so to speak,

You'd think that might explain a drunken bum
Found crumpled in the men's room of some seedy
Railway station outside Moscow or in Paris,

But, boys, we speak plain English, you and I,
Much like dogs and cats, what have we
To do with degradation or dementia,

Appalling penchants for self-humiliation,
Detention, starvation (and several other -ations
I could mention, plus some -entions, if I

Weren't such a gentleman), no, boys,
Told that way, I can't advise your taking
Fish's tale to heart—too French, much too . . .

French, or else too Russian. But look here, what's
It matter how convincing in its daily
Grit his life is, Bird, if Fish's case

Like Joe's ends up with some miraculous
Reversal, six kids returned where he once
Had three, his car repaired, a younger wife

Who works, the foreman canned, a night school degree?
That just won't wash. You see, what gives a life
Its weight, what makes it mean, if that's the right

Expression, 's just its sense of being final.
You know how, Fox, you're teaching kids a game
Across a board, the younger ones'll move,

See they've blundered, smile their porpoise smiles
And say, "Please, Daddy, can't I take it back,
"Can't I, Daddums, huh?" Well now, you know,

They're small and cute and look a lot like you,
So what's a dad to say; they take it back.
But when they pull that stunt the hundredth time,

You've got to grab a handful of their hair
And wipe the board off with their squealing faces.
No, Bird, you can't do that. You're adult,

And everything you teach them has to show
That being grown up means you play the hand
You're dealt—if you see, Fish, what I mean?

*Oh, sir, I catch your drift, at least where I'm
Concerned. No one has to take a dump
In my straw hat for me to get the joke.*

*What is this place, a small town barber shop
Where Fish plays stooge for every vicious prank?
Supposing, as you say, these tales are made*

*To show us how the real world goes and what
It means to be adult, still in your stories
I'm the one who always takes the lumps.*

*I know I'm no great shakes, no one for scaling
Heights, mine's the low road, always was,
I can live with that. I wonder if at last*

*That's what makes you hate me so? Because
I'm happy where I stand, eat dirt and ask
For more and still hang on no matter what,*

Simple, sincere, with a sense of who I am,
Knowing I'm passive-aggressive, anal-retentive,
Type B, kindly, common, mortal man.

Yes, Fish, and I'm a ding-dong daddy from Dumas.
What bus did you get off, bud, coming here like
Francis of Assisi with bird-crap on your shoulder?

Honest, you short guys slay me. Got a wire
Here for you somewhere says, "RELAX, YA MUTT,
YOU'RE NOT GOOD ENOUGH TO BE THAT HUMBLE."

It's all the dumb stuff that comes from reading
Books, worse yet, from writing lives in books
Till even short guys think life's like a book,

Hauled from oblivion's silent well, set up
On shelves beyond the body's fall, compressed
By angel fingers of narration so it

Makes sense (and what makes sense has value, right?),
Then borne aloft through memory's flawed heaven
Until "All flesh is grass" translated reads

"All fat is newsprint wrapped in gleaming cowhide."
Oh sure, Fox, it's pathetic, but in this low
Line of work, what's not? You see the symptoms

Daily, boys—that's if you watch the talk shows—
The plain folks' painful longing for the light
As if a spotlight's dingy wafer gave

In fifteen minutes fame a brief foretaste
Of what it's like to be immortal, of how
It feels to have a life worth saving, and earned

Not by being true or good, not by
Even being humble, but by some self-
Demeaning revelation, real or feigned,

Or just repeated till believed, that fuels
A witches' kitchen masked as therapeutic
Chat, a grim parental hunt played out

By victims and survivors. I must say it's
Enough to make one long for simpler times,
Days the camera's gaze got turned on crowded

Stands at football games and always found
Two drunken truckers, shirtless in zero weather,
One painted red, one painted blue, in wigs

And skirts and plastic pig snouts shouting, "*We're*
Number one!" their middle fingers raised,
Until the camera zoomed in for a close-up

When Mr. Blue pulled down his plastic snout
And, grinning, mouthed, "Hi, Mom! Hi, Dad!" and, boys,
I'll bet his folks were proud and that's no joke,

'Cause Mr. Blue's brother's in the pen
(Twenty to life: extortion, racketeering)
And last time he was seen on screen two marshals

Had him under the arms, lifting him into
A van, with his coat thrown over his head, and as
They judge such matters in the street, I'd say

No way Blue ain't got that sucker beat.
But whether you go for witches or for goons,
You come away convinced the sense of self

And its survival had its start in childhood
Memories of being held within a
Parent's gaze, that look that first conveyed

The notion they were someone separate, special,
Safe from harm as long as daddy watched,
Until as they grew up that gaze was swallowed

Whole, and came back as the soul. It's why
Most final fantasies anticipate
Reunion, a thought brought home to me here just

The other day. You know how at the Giant
Standing in the check-out line, hemmed in
By tabloids stuffed in racks, big headlines breezy

As their colored covers—ALIENS ATE
MY SISTER, WOMAN GIVES BIRTH TO PUPPY, TRAGIC
DEATH IN DWARF-THROWING CONTEST—there's always

One or two'll tout some after-death
Event whose opening shot—a massive heart
Attack, electric shock, near drowning, motorcycle

Wreck—sends the victim soaring
Out above his body feeling odd
Finding that he's somewhere slowly walking

Through a tunnel filled with mist that ends
In brilliant light where his whole family wait,
And as they pat his back or pump his hand

Or kiss him shyly on the cheek he feels
His being flooded with such bliss he can't
Believe the black paramedic pounding on

His chest intends to bring him back from this
To his old humdrum life and leave him gasping there,
Beached in a cold backwater of regret.

Of course, these stories have a point the hacks
Who write them always want to poke right in
Your eye: uncanny how the imagery

That quasi-stiffs come up with—misty tunnel,
Blinding light, spry chorus of defuncts—
Recurs in most accounts of hearts jump-started

Back to Main Street, almost as if, you'd say,
Some layer that they passed through in common grounded
This resemblance, almost as if some *there*

Were really there (unlike Oakland, unlike
Downtown Philly), the grubs who sling this stuff
Not seeing what these fatal wannabes

All share besides a brush with death's the fact
Of being born, its imagery transposed
(Front for back, in that unbuttoned state

That waits on getting zapped) to solve a lack
Of final figuration. Recall this came up
Earlier when I said our universe

Was like some fearful sphere with no outside.
And why's that, boys, except it mimes the shape
Of mind (that other, odder globe no one

Breaks out of breathing), why also at breath's border
Imagining gets subtly turned around,
Unable to project its own immense

Conclusion, falls back upon a fable of
Return, of death as bright rebirth within
The circuit of the stars. Besides, time's shown

Creeds of cosmic sense do best if based upon
The family, gain ground when their main motive's
That ache for what is ours we call nostalgia.

Still, love is strong, Fox. Who's to say its warmth
Can't last amid night's glittering machine
And find its long way back to those we love?

At least that's how most folks have got to figure
If, come nights, they want to get to sleep.
But you and I, boys—we've known the world, felt

Its worth, found love, and found it out, bought dear
In its back streets a clear-eyed wisdom too
Terrific to repeat for those less knowing

Than ourselves, felt the staring emptiness
of noon melt the will, the cold
Despair at three A.M. stick in the stomach's

Pit so tight no amount of heaving
Pries it loose, kneeling naked, sick and
Shaking, on any icy bathroom floor,

Found life will never be like our best dreams
And love, for all its power in this world,
When faced with time's relentless wheel, fails and

Freezes in the space between the stars.
Besides, what sort of person wants to spend
Eternity with Mom and Dad and Sis

And Bud, with Spot the dog and Puff the cat?
I see the light, Fish, dawning in your eyes.
It's true: scientific studies funded by

These selfsame tabloids show (besides the fact
YOUR UNDERWEAR CAN KILL YOU WHILE YOU SLEEP)
That folks with out-of-body, after-death

Reunions to relate are almost always
Orphans, yes, poor, little, please-more-soup-sir
Urchins grown up wanting what they've never

Had, then let them get their lights punched out,
They fantasize a family. I find, Fox, there're
Some mysteries not too difficult to explain.

from *The Southwest Review*

ANNE CARSON

TV Men: Antigone (Scripts 1 and 2)

◇　◇　◇

Antigone likes walking behind Oedipus
to brake the wind.
As he is blind he often does not agree to this.
March sky cold as a hare's paw.
Antigone and Oedipus eat lunch on the lip of a crater.
Trunks of hundred-year-old trees forced
down
by wind
crawl on the gravel. One green centimeter of twig
still vertical—
catches her eye. She leads his hand to it.
Lightly
he made sure
what it was.
Lightly left it there.

[Antigone felt a sting against her cheek. She motions the soundman
out of the way and taking the microphone begins to speak.]

There is nowhere to keep anything, the way we live.
This I find hard. Other things I like—a burnish
along the butt end of days
that people inside houses never see.
Projects, yes I have projects.
I want to make a lot of money. Just kidding. Next
question. No I do not lament.

God's will is not some sort of physics, is it.
Today we are light, tomorrow shadow, says the song.
Ironic? Not really. My father is the ironic one.
I have my own ideas about it.
At our backs is a big anarchy.
If you are strong you can twist a bit off
and pound on it—your freedom!

Now Oedipus has risen, Antigone rises. He begins to move off,
into the wind,
immersed in precious memory.
Thinking *Too much memory* Antigone comes after.
Both of them are gold all along the sunset side.
Last bell, he knew.
Among all fleshbags you will not find
one who if God
baits
does not bite.

[For sound bite purposes we had to cut Antigone's script from 42
seconds to 7: substantial changes of wording were involved but we
felt we got her "take" right.]

Other things I like: a lot of money!
The way we live, light and shadow are ironic.
Projects? yes: physics. Anarchy. My father.
Here, twist a bit off.
Freedom is next.

from *The Paris Review*

Symbol of the Faith

◇ ◇ ◇

Deliberate anachronism is an artistic device available to
cultures in a late stage of their development.
—HUGO VON HOFMANNSTAHL

The crescent moon, as always too exact
And too high-burnished for a neutral fact
Of nature, in our Christian sky of calm
Is warlike science fiction of Islam.

∾

I am a Janissary Corps Jules Verne,
Not myself Ottoman, though what I earn
Is from the Sultan. So I chronicle
His far experiment that you know well,

Although as using other properties.
The period, as you will recognize,
Is after real gunpowder, though before
That powder was dependable. My Corps,

So many thousand strong, upon a high
Plateau in Anadolu, of a ply
Of Balkan forests and of pliant horn
From all the oxen in our column torn,

And bonded for a tensile covering
(The hide, cut into strips, we twist for string)
Is forming, like a template of the Ark,
A huge crossbow. Into the moonless dark

It will release, no arrow for a Djinn,
But yet another bow, one smaller, thin,
Of profile airfoil, that will bear a third,
To be released by clockwork. You have heard

How stars unnatural point out the birth
Of prophets and how stars that fall to Earth
Are stepping stones to Heaven as they part.
Jerusalem, thy rock is met by art.

By jacks the size of trees the bow is raised;
The windlass turns and it is drawn. Apprised
In Istanbul that his design is done,
Sinan himself comes out to count it down.

The sounding string forms shock waves in the air;
The lesser bows climb out of sight. Cold, bare,
To emptiness returns the plain below.
But, shining in the ice of space, our bow.

from *Southwest Review*

HENRI COLE

Self-Portrait as Four Styles of Pompeian Wall Painting

◊   ◊   ◊

FIRST STYLE

To become oneself is so exhausting
that I am as others have made me,
imitating monumental Greek statuary
despite my own feminized way of being.
Like the empire, I was born of pain—
or like a boy, one might say, for I have
become my father, whom I cannot fathom;
the past is a fetish I disdain.
Since they found the bloodless little girl,
with voluptuous lips, buried in me,
I am unsentimental. I do not see
the gold sky at sunset but blackbirds hurled
like lava stones. I am like a severed
finger lost in the wreckage forever.

SECOND STYLE

Unable to care for people, I care
mostly for things. At my bitterest,
I see love as self-censorship.
My face is a little Roman theater
in perfect perspective—with colonnades
and landscapes—making illusionistic

reference to feelings I cannot admit.
Painted in Dionysiac yellows and reds,
my unconscious is a rocky grotto
where flies buzz like formalists.
Despite myself, I am not a composite
of signs to be deciphered. In the ghetto—
where Jews, prostitutes and sailors once lived—
I am happiest because I am undisguised.

THIRD STYLE

Tearing away at an old self to make
a new one, I am my most Augustan.
I grieve little. I try to accustom
myself to what is un-Hellenized and chaste.
I let my flat black dado assert itself
without ornament. Can it be, at last,
that I am I—accepting lice clasped
to me like a dirty Colosseum cat?
On a faded panel of Pompeian red,
there's an erotic x-ray of my soul:
a pale boy-girl figure is unconsoled,
pinned from behind at the farthest edge
of human love, where the conscience is not whole,
yet finely engraved like a snail's shell.

FOURTH STYLE

If great rooms declare themselves by the life
lived in them, each night I am reborn
as men and boys stroll among the ruins,
anonymously skirting the floodlights,
sinking into me tenderly, as they do
each other during their brief hungry acts.
"As brief as love," they used to say, Plato
and his kind, exiling man from happiness,
but I am more than a cave whose campfire,
swelling and contracting, is all that is real.

Tomorrow, when I am drunk on sunlight,
I will still feel the furtive glances,
the unchaste kisses and the wet skin
imprinting me until I am born again.

from *The New Republic*

Lines Composed Over Three Thousand Miles from Tintern Abbey

◊   ◊   ◊

I was here before, a long time ago,
and now I am here again
is an observation that occurs in poetry
as frequently as rain occurs in life.

The fellow may be gazing
over an English landscape,
hillsides dotted with sheep,
a row of tall trees topping the downs,

or he could be moping through the shadows
of a dark Bavarian forest,
a wedge of cheese and a volume of fairy tales
tucked into his rucksack.

But the feeling is always the same.
It was better the first time.
This time is not nearly as good.
I'm not feeling as chipper as I did back then.

Something is always missing—
swans, a glint on the surface of a lake,
some minor but essential touch.
Or the quality of things has diminished.

The sky was a deeper, more dimensional blue,
clouds were more cathedral-like,
and water rushed over rock
with greater effervescence.

From our chairs we have watched
the poor author in his waistcoat
as he recalls the dizzying icebergs of childhood
and mills around in a field of weeds.

We have heard the poets long-dead
declaim their dying
from a promontory, a riverbank,
next to a haycock, within a copse.

We have listened to their dismay,
the kind that issues from poems
the way water issues forth from hoses,
the way the match always gives its little speech on fire.

And when we put down the book at last,
lean back, close our eyes,
stinging with print,
and slip in the bookmark of sleep,

we will be schooled enough to know
that when we wake up
a little before dinner
things will not be nearly as good as they once were.

Something will be missing
from this long, coffin-shaped room,
the walls and windows now
only two different shades of gray

the glossy gardenia drooping
in its chipped terra-cotta pot.
Shoes, socks, ashtray, the shroud of curtains,
the browning core of an apple.

Nothing will be as it was
a few hours ago, back in the glorious past
before our naps, back in that Golden Age
that drew to a close sometime shortly after lunch.

from *Poetry*

ALFRED CORN

Jaffa

◇   ◇   ◇

Tel Jaffa's Mandate era clock tower
no longer pays much attention
to wavewashed rocks offshore, where travelers
late as the first century rowed out
to inspect the sea monster's ribcage
and rusty remnants of the broken

manacles that helped Andromeda keep
her father's word. Our sunburns sympathize
with the young sacrifice's skin, exposed
to killing UV rays—briefly dimmer
when a fleeting silhouette eclipsed their whitehot
source, and Perseus in wingèd sandals

skated the crest of an uphrust thermal,
Cap of Darkness and Medusa's head
bundled together in his leather pouch.
So Hellenism swept into Asia Minor,
the event commemorated in bleached bones

that felt it coming as a liquid green
reptilian eye took in his sword's advance,
bronze stabbing downward with the noonday light.
Fetters soon to corrode relaxed, surrendered.
The royal gazette detailed plans for a wedding.

On the *Aladdin*'s stucco terrace, pink
and gold hibiscus framing the seaward view,
we raise a glass. Asked why the tower clock
hands don't move, a mustached waiter adjusts
dark glasses and admits he doesn't know.

from *New England Review*

Echo

◇　◇　◇

Lovers check each other—"How are you?"—
when love is going, but before it's gone.
"Oh, I'm better. The nausea's settled down.
The mad howling stopped the other night."
Some rueful laughter on the other end.
"Me, too," she whispers, in her quiet voice,

"me, too." He thinks: I love her quiet voice.
"Yesterday, at the market, I saw you"—
she catches, laughs. It's hard for love to end.
It's hard to wake up, certain that it's gone.
He says, "I thought about you all last night,
but I'm better. The nausea's settled down."

They never say that love has settled down,
that it no longer uses its sweet voice
to carry them in boats across the night.
If you deny love, love will deny you;
the nighttime of its daytime voice is gone,
as you will be. It's hard for love to end.

But any love is difficult to end;
all endings seem to whisper, then lie down—
an old man dying by the fire, soon gone,
as if he'd never lived. Her quiet voice,
that only yesterday spoke just to you,
will soon become a whisper in the night,

then disappear forever from the night.
And there's no preparation for that end.
She laughs again. "I want to be with you."
He understands. He puts the phone back down.
How will he live without her quiet voice?
What will he do, when she's finally gone?

Within a week the moving van is gone.
He works all day, and dreads the quiet night.
The day will come when he'll forget her voice;
he has no need for longing for that end.
He'd settle now for keeping dinner down.
He hears again: *I want to be with you.*

He stares into the pool of night, her voice
behind him, gone. He monitors the end:
he lies down, hears the faint refrain: "... *with you* ..."

from *The Antioch Review*

TOM DISCH

What Else Is There

◇   ◇   ◇

So much remains we haven't seen
Painted: the snow, now, at 5:19—
  A kind of lavender, while the sky
  Still retains its twilight dye,
The blue that refuses to be green.

And then there's beef, with its obscene
Relevance to who we are and what we mean.
  Bones, offal. No knowing why
    So much remains

Unnoticed, unremarked, behind a screen
Of seemliness. We serve a machine
That serves our purposes: the eye.
  It sees the day, and thinks it cannot lie.
    So much remains.

from *Poetry*

The Difference Between Pepsi and Pope

◊   ◊   ◊

I have this blind spot, a dark line, thin as a hair, that obliterates
a stroke of scenery on the right side of my field of vision
so that often I get whole words at the end of sentences wrong
like when I first saw the title of David Lehman's poem
"The Difference Between Pepsi and Coke" and I misread
"Coke" for "Pope." This blind spot makes me a terrible driver,
a bad judge of distances, a Ping-Pong player that inspires giggles
from the opposite team.
              I knew a poet who dressed up as a cookie
and passed out a new brand in a crowded supermarket.
The next day he gave the Pepsi Challenge to passersby
in a mall.
              I felt old-fashioned admitting to this poet that I prefer Coke,
that wavy hyphen that separates its full name Coca~Cola.
Like the bar let down in the limbo dance, the Spanish tilde comes down un
not even a lowercase letter can squeeze under it.
I searched for that character recently, writing to David Lehman,
telling him about an electronic magazine, the address of which
had this ~ in it. I couldn't find it, although I stared
at my computer keyboard for more than a few minutes.
I only noticed it today in the upper left hand corner, above the tab,
the alternate of `, if you hit the shift key. I wonder if I also have a blind spot
in my left eye. I wonder if the poet who dressed as a cookie
is happy in his new marriage. I wonder if you can still get a bottle of Tab
anywhere, that awful soda my forever-dieting aunt used to drink,
with its pink logo, its "a" all swirls, looking like @.

Yesterday,
when my husband was waiting at an intersection, he said, *Is anyone coming?*
I looked from the passenger seat and said confidently, *We can make it.*
Then we were almost run off the road. I said
I'm sorry I'm sorry through the exchange of honks and fists
and couldn't believe when my husband forgave me so quickly.

Not only that,
but I'm a bad proofreader, I thought to myself as I made a mental list
of ways that I felt inadequate. One friend also recently noted that maybe I
talk too much about myself, so I told her the Bette Midler joke,
Enough about me, what do YOU think of me? which doesn't *really*
bring me back to David Lehman and his poem, but does make me realize
how far away I strayed from my original point
which was that I thought his poem would be funny because of the title,
not the real title, but my mistaken one. I started to guess his poem
in my head: Pepsi is bubbly and brown while the Pope
is flat and white. Pepsi doesn't have a big white hat. The Pope
can't get rid of fender rust. Pepsi is all for premarital sex.
The Pope won't stain your teeth.

But "The Difference
Between Pepsi and Coke" is a tender poem about a father
whom the speaker reveres and I wonder if David Lehman's own father
is alive or dead which is something I often do—wonder
how much is true—when I read a poem by someone I like
which I know is not the right way to read a poem even though
Molly Peacock said at her reading that she is the "I"
in all of hers and doesn't use the word "speaker" anymore.

Still,
I feel like a Peeping Tom, although this is really about what I can't see,
my blind spots, and how easy it is for me to doubt my decisions,
how I relate to the father in Lehman's poem who "won't admit his dread
of boredom" and panics and forgives. How easy it is to live for stretches at a time
in that skinny dark line, how easy it is to get so many things all wrong.

from *Salt Hill*

Like God,

◇   ◇   ◇

you hover above the page staring
down on a small town. By its roads
some scenery loafs in a hammock of
sleepy prose and here is a mongrel
loping and here is a train pulling into
a station in three long sentences and
here are the people in galoshes waiting.
But you know this story and it is not
about those travelers and their galoshes,
but about your life, so, like a diver
climbing over the side of a boat and
down into the ocean, you climb, sentence
by sentence, into this story on this page.

You have been expecting yourself
as the woman who purrs by in a dress
by Patou, and a porter manacled to
the luggage, and a matron bulky as
the *Britannia,* and there, haunting
her ankles like a piece of ectoplasm
that barks is, once again, that small
white dog from chapter twenty.
These are your fellow travelers and
you become part of their logjam of
images of hats and umbrellas and
Vuitton luggage, you are a face
behind or inside these faces, a
heartbeat in the volley of these
heartbeats, as you choose, out of all

the passengers, the journey of a man
with a mustache scented faintly with
Prince Albert. "He must be a secret
sensualist," you think and your awareness
drifts to his trench coat, worn, softened,
and flabby, a coat with a lobotomy, just
as the train arrives at a destination.

No, you would prefer another stop
in a later chapter where the climate is
affable and sleek. But most of
the passengers are disembarking, and
you did not choose to be in the story
of the white dress. You did not choose
the story of the matron whose bosom
is like the prow of a ship and who is
launched toward lunch at The Hotel Pierre,
or even the story of the dog-on-a-leash,
even though this is now your story:
the story of the man-who-had-to-
take-the-train and walk the dark road
described hurriedly by someone sitting
at the cafe so you could discover it,
although you knew all along it would
be there, you, who have been hovering
above this page, holding the book in
your hands, like God, reading.

from *Boston Review*

Movietime

◇   ◇   ◇

They can't wait. ("We couldn't wait," they'll say.)
And that's not the only thing the lovers can't do.
They seem unable to get their clothes off in time,
or to catch the breath they're losing in each other's mouth.
Oddly, they've lost the knack of getting into a bed
without keeling over onto the floor in a tangle
of bedclothes and other clothes. (Fabric can be so stupid!)
If only they could get out of each other's way
or at least into each other's ways in the right way.
And they can't slow down, and clearly can't go fast enough
to catch up to what they're feeling—maybe if something had
some texture, but things slide by, going far too fast.
Can't they sort of go back to point zero and start over?
Really, they seem like strangers who can't get acquainted
and who, by trying harder, get stranger and stranger.
God only knows what they *can* do; probably it's just
whatever this is they're doing now crashing into each other
at this impromptu intersection they've just created.
If nothing happens soon, we're afraid they'll start *honking.*
Can't *someone* stop a sec to gasp, "Pardon me" or "After you?"
Well, let's hope it's all clearer to them than it is to us
("Can't we *please* have a *little* more light?" we find we're praying)
—even though we've been in that position ourselves,
in those positions, in a dark room some suddenly wild night
with scream after scream about to push past everything.

It seems, then, profoundly artful (while perfectly banal)
for the camera to leave them to their breathless inventories
and ferocious ineptitude they're getting better at

—by cutting to an all-night deco beanery
and its fat, lone diner, a placid and famous detective,
who s sitting there and simply, competently eating.
Seeing food on the screen of this dark, musty movie house
isn't exactly the most appetizing thing in the world.
Still, his fork's unerring in finding the way to his mouth,
his spoon never winds up depositing chowder in his ear.
Feats of coordination we can say we, too, have mastered.
So, we especially enjoy seeing his gestures glide
between sheer slobbery and icky, self-conscious prissiness.
A common achievement, commonly taken too lightly.
Of course, what's-his-name actually (if that's the word) doing this
is even more famous, so the interplay of disguise
and guise (that actor sampling what, and while, this gumshoe eats,
for example): this teases and fascinates on its own.
To suspend our disbelief would be to lose the "beauty part,"
this magical uncertainty of "takes" doubled and trebled.
Now the sensitive, round, good-natured face looks troubled.
From under his eyebrows, the camera peers deeply into
a too clear water glass and jumbo portion of tapioca,
a soiled, creased paper napkin; it swings around, up,
and scans the blue tracery of neon in the mirrors.
So many, many clues—and not a single crime in sight!
When camera pulls away, that's him there in the middle of
the mess, calmly, reassuringly to us, ruminating.
What was total alien jumble is starting to reveal
to him certain underlying kinships: it's coming together.
His smile says it all: Digestion doing fine, thank you.
He taps a finger on the Formica—oh ever so lightly.
With chaos, it implies, you take your time, *you take your time.*
Okay, we'll wait around with him, we can be patient, too.
One A.M. Two A.M. And everything is going slower.
Out there, something set in motion is slowing down.
He's standing up—must be time to go. But go where? Do what?
He pays the bill, so slowly we can count out change clinking
over the cashier's ritual, "Button up, Buddy, it's cold tonight."
"Bud," maybe. No one's called him *"Buddy"* since Pappy died.
"How come?" his face asks with such eloquent perplexity
we're cracking up, we're rolling around. He's beautiful!
(And, hey, did you glom on to the size of that tip he left?)

Outside, morning paper under his arm, he's walking away,
doing that endearing, flatfooted toddle of his.
Oh my, we knew it, he's one of those *graceful* fatties!
On the deserted street, he stops a second, short of breath
(poor guy, we think, this *isn't* acting!), and is almost around
the corner and lost from view, when we realize

how happy we are with all these tiny textures of being
and time the fat guy has generously treated us to
—so many moments to talk over and appreciate,
bits of personality we'll rescue from time's rush-rush
(and from the damned plot always trying to do itself in).
Which is why we like to beat the crowd by leaving early
—before masks drop and the whole thing runs smack into its ending,
and, stunned, everything is itself, nothing more, nothing else.
Because, isn't this what movies are for?—offering large
and variegated surfaces of hard-to-figure-out depth
to our revery's minute, pleasurable inspection,
to savoring and recollection and repetition,
so that our minds move around more than the movie does,
quickly from moment to moment, but slowly within it.

Strolling home on the peaceful, lamplit, empty avenue,
we try out a wide waddle, a pigeon-toed toddle—and then
remember that right about *now* the lovers are rousing
and whispering across the world rifting between them
what, arm in arm, you and I, it so happens, are murmuring,

"Was it good for you?" "Mmmm. And you? Was it good for you?"

from *The Kenyon Review*

EMILY FRAGOS

Apollo's Kiss

◇   ◇   ◇

Devise Cassandra. Become her, in possession,
and the world becomes perfect. For even gods
crave perfection. Desire her like a man
and like a man be refused in all your desire.
Surrender: Beg a first and last kiss and pray
she will acquiesce, her virtue stirred.
Then, breathe into her mouth the powered
prophecy and for all you are losing
—the deprivation she will give and give—
release her half-gifted as you are, half-mortal.

In the courtyard, animals are captured
by their hind legs, held up on haunches,
throats slashed. She walks on burning
stones. Swift, it is slaughtering season.

from *Chelsea*

Mass in B Minor

◇   ◇   ◇

Lord, have mercy on Bach the accused,
found guilty of tampering with the hymns.
Guilty also of smuggling a subversive,
a *girl,* into the choir loft to sing.

Have mercy on Bach,
whose choir practice ended in despair,
which is to say, in fisticuffs,
the Bach who brawled in the street for his art.

He wrote for money, who wrote for You.
Have mercy. Good Teuton,
he wrote a groveling letter to the Elector
and enclosed the Kyrie and Gloria.

Johann Sebastian: on the concert program
the high fence of his name had been erected,
guard towers charred in the same Black Letter
as the book my father brought back from the war.

He pronounced its title for us: *Mein Kampf.*
And slid the enemy sword with just the scrape
of a grace note back into its scabbard.
A flag too heavy to unfold—

when had the swastika been removed?
The pencilled names of the fallen
lay in the mass grave of a small notebook.
Christ, have mercy.

Have mercy on Bach, whose Sanctus saved no one,
not even the damned. Crystalline, cyclonic,
the Kyrie seeped through the chapel,
becoming what we breathed,

the prayer entering the body first.
The man next to me was just back from Poland.
"Let us arrange your taxi to Auschwitz,"
the sign in his hotel had read,

the flesh made word to dwell among us.

from *New England Review*

Weird River

◊　◊　◊

We sit down on the rocks above a river,
Like three crows in a ruin. Star Asper burns
In the pure heaven. The voice of the Star
Utters one law: *You must account for everybody.*
The night is cold and getting colder. Dawn,

Far away.—Suddenly the first crow asks,
"How shall I start?" The burning Star replies,
"Look down. What do you see?" The first crow says,
"It's cold enough to snow." "You can't *see* cold,"
Says the Star. "OK, I see a girl washing

A corpse," says Crow One. "Also, a big dog."
—By this time, the other crows are getting restless.
They want to say something. But the night wind
Is cold and makes a loud sound.—"Was this ruin
Ever whole and a flourishing house . . . ?"

Whispers the second crow under his breath.
The burning Star sighs. He can hear small sounds.
"This place was always a ruin, where gather
All souls in flocks toward the wild migration
From life to life in the same world." Star Asper

Smiles down on the tumult at the dark river.
Then the second crow, having found a hollow
In the ruined wall, quickly falls asleep
And cries in his dreams.—Crow Three says, "Look, Star,
One law is too many. We can't do it."

"Then I'll add another law," says Star Asper
In a great voice. *No other book than YOURS!*
—The dog howls at the light. Frightened by the
Dog, the three crows fly away. And rosy Dawn,
In tears, is heard to say: "Weird river, flow on."

from *Partisan Review*

To Cupid

◇　◇　◇

You make desire seem easy.
　　　　　　　　　　So it is:
Your service perfect freedom to enjoy
Fresh limitations. I've watched you in person
Wait for the light and relish the delay
Revving the engine up before you spurt
Out of the intersection.

　　　　　　　　　　　How all your servants
Compose their amorous scripts—scripts of confinement,
Scripts of displacement, scripts of delay, and scripts
Of more delay. Your own Fabrice so hankered
After the distance of his prison cell
He managed to regain it, for the sake
Of viewing her, the jailer's daughter, daily—
But at a window, but among her birds.
Of course they could not touch. In later life
They touched, they did touch, but in darkness only.

When I switched off my light I was dog-tired
But for some minutes held off sleep: I heard
The pleasant sound of voices from next door
Through windows open to the clement darkness.
A dinner for the couple one floor up,
Married today. I hardly had the time
Before falling away, to relish it,
The sociable human hum, easy and quiet
As the first raindrops in the yard, on bushes,
Heard similarly from bed. Chatting, the sounds

Of friendliness and feeding often broken
By laughter. It's consoling, Mr. Love,
That such conviviality is also
One more obedience to your behest,
The wedding bed held off by the wedding feast.

Good will within delay within good will.
And Cupid, devious master of our bodies,
You were the source then of my better rest.

from *The New Yorker*

Again, The River

◇   ◇   ◇

for Geneviève Pastre

Early summer in what I hope is "midlife,"
and the sunlight makes me its own suggestions
when I take my indolence to the river
and breathe the breeze in.

Years, here, seem to blend into one another.
Houseboats, tugs, and barges don't change complexion
drastically (warts, wrinkles) until gestalt-shift
dissolves the difference.

Sentence fragments float on a wave of syntax,
images imprinted in contemplation,
indistinct impressions of conversations
which marked some turning.

Food and drink last night with a friend—we've twelve years
history of Burgundy and good dinners
and as many books off the press between us
toasted together.

Writing is a difficult form of reading.
Paragraphs that roll away from their moorings
seem like passages to another language
half-comprehended.

Sometimes thought is more like a bad translation.
Hazy shapes resistant to sentence-structure
intimate—but what do they mean, exactly?
Texture, sound, odor

(dockside, urinous, up on green slopes, roses
in full bloom like elegant girls of forty)
imprint images in aleatoric
absence of order.

Isolated words can unlock a story:
what you ate, she felt when she heard the music,
what's brought back by one broken leaf, whose sticky
sap on a finger

named a green, free season to city children.
Now, daylight's duration is equinoctial:
spring is turning swiftly to summer; summer's
ripeness brings endings.

I can feel a change in the weather coming.
When I catch a glimpse of myself in mirrors,
I see someone middle-aged, with my mother's
sallow complexion.

Whom do we write books for? Our friends? Our daughters?
Last night's dinner companion has two daughters,
women in their thirties with strong opinions.
My child is younger,

might say there won't be books in the "2000's,"
just "hard copy" "downloaded" from computers.
Children won't haunt library aisles, as I did,
tracking their futures.

(What about the homeless man reading science
fiction on the steps of St. Paul, a tattered
paperback, a galaxy on the cover
he was approaching?)

Houses are precarious or unsettling.
We who left them young, and applaud our daughters'
rootlessness still scrutinize wind-chapped faces
of pavement-dwellers.

"Every woman's one man away from welfare"
—he may be a college trustee, a landlord
or a bland, anonymous civil servant
balancing budgets.

My friend's postcard goddesses, morning teapot,
Greek and Latin lexicons, Mac computer,
fill the magic cave of a room she works in
which she'll be leaving

when her lease is up (as provincial theater
troupes strike sets, pack trunks), lares and penates
ready to be set on a desk and bookshelves
in closer quarters

where she'll reestablish haphazard suppers
on her Cévennes grandmother's round oak table.
Where will I be? Too many airline tickets
away to answer.

(I lead two lives superimposed upon each
other, on two continents, in two cities,
make believe my citizenship is other
than that blue passport's.)

But today there's wind on the Seine; a tugboat
with embroidered curtains and gardened windows
looks like home as it navigates the river
toward other moorings.

from *Ploughshares*

Pomegranate Variations

◊ ◊ ◊

> *Then sucked their fruit globes fair or red:*
> *Sweeter than honey from the rock,*
> *Stronger than man-rejoicing wine,*
> *Clearer than water flowed that juice;*
> *She never tasted such before,*
> *How should it cloy with length of use?*
> —CHRISTINA ROSSETTI, "Goblin Market"

And thanks to Eavan Boland's "Pomegranate"

I

Most know the name. But since so many claim
ignorance of its color, nature, shape,
how can I do less than bring one in?

Next week, therefore, one makes its way to class.
I peel off the chartreuse
pricetag; plunge in the dull

knife I've brought with me in my bag—not plunge,
rather gouge, pry, saw
and finally penetrate beneath the rind.

Lo and behold, the inside
looks nothing like the outside.
As a door is closed

upon a child still rosy from the bath,
pale partitions separate
clusters of ruby seeds.

Juice stains the silly knife, the paper napkins,
and the palmprint-clouded plastic platter
which I now hand to the student on my left

nearest the door. "Here," I tell him. "Take
this, touch, taste it." "Which part do I eat?"
he asks. I say, "The seed."

II

I brought the pomegranate in because
(why else?) we'd read a poem called "Pomegranate,"
whose speaker, first the girl Persephone,
later on as mother turns to Ceres.

Love and blackmail are the gist of it.
Ceres and Persephone the names.
And the best thing about the legend is
I can enter it anywhere. And have.

I brought the poem in because the textbook
chapter on Symbolism and Allegory
demanded fleshing out, as a globed fruit
asks for sun and rain. An antidote

to dryness, these twin spheres of tart pink water
yielding their juices to each lonely tongue,
first the pomegranate in the poem,
then the pomegranate on the plate.

Weeks passed, and I kept pulling words from them.
Not that they didn't have words already,
but to bring forth and test them, to expose them . . .
Words they discovered in their mouths like tongues,
blunt words, raw words, words to stash, to hoard,
and finally to build on. Words aren't children:
use them three times, they're yours forever.
Ignore them: you're the poorer, they are not.
Abuse them: you sound silly, they survive.

Behind shut doors we're safe,
I said. Now out with it.
And they began to speak
and set speech down and write.
But sweetness stuck their words
together. Week by week
this honey soured to curse:
fuck and *shit* and *cunt.*
Testing the air, the water?
Measuring one another?
Spite for the world they had inherited,
poverty of the wordhoard they could claim?

I listen, ruthless; prod each wavering
impulse to grab and hold on to a name.

Call it a fruit. Call it the body's language,
renascent itch that says I am alive.
Sour sharpness, rose and green, a light like sunset
before a storm. The usual fresh crop
of eyes and lips. The usual
appetite for fruit: some touched, some tasted.
The one who said, "What do I eat?"
pretended to be poisoned when he tasted,
mimed a violent tumbling from his chair.

The door is shut. We glance at one another.
"Send it around," I say. The hoary spell:
Swallow a seed, you cannot leave this place.
Phantom figures on the page take shape:
Sheila's father playing cards with the devil;

Steve's carpenter ecstatic in the middle of nowhere,
happy as Christ, Mike ventures, in the desert
(even if Steve spells the word "dessert");
Janice's mother under whose tutelage
even Apollo would crunch.

I am not exempt. I eat a seed.
In Ormos once a pomegranate tree
stood in a back garden by the sea
where there also grew a lemon tree,
beans, and prickly okra six feet tall.

Picking that okra one hot summer dawn,
I suddenly made out a chameleon
motionless on the stalk, a violent green.
Did I cry out? Drop my basket? Run?
I was twenty-one.

V

The fruit we hand around is recollection,
trapped in this leathery russet fringed sphere
small enough to fold a hand around
of what had never really been known:

information, memory, or rumor
floating till now unanchored as a breath
now named, grown dense, made able to be held—
and yet, as if it is too hot to hold,

or else too heavy, passed from hand to hand,
sweet-sour globelets locked inside, sensations
in cells enough for all of us to share,
synecdoche and globed idea of autumn,

mortality's pink slip,
ticket to a certain season . . . Wait!
The hour is over. Tentatively someone
from outside tries the door.

VI

The dream began and ended
on green blade of hill
severing a sunlit bowl
my mission was to fill.

Laps; vessels; upturned faces.
What do we do with our hands
asked Homo Habilis as they straightened up
if not to mark the paths our minds have made?

Ache in the hand from writing.
The sweet solution thinning, thinning, thinning,
the savor going watery and null.
With time so short, why hold back anything?

Already they are pressing at the door.
Ache in the jaw from talking.
Not that desire or energy are gone,
but see, this plethora of red partitions,

doors, desks, decorums, panels, skins, shells, rinds,
walls that hold in the secret of the fruit
which at a magic word spills out its sap,
scarlet, intoxicating, onto white.

from *The Kenyon Review*

Letter with No Address

◇　◇　◇

Your daffodils rose up
and collapsed in their yellow
bodies on the hillside
garden above the bricks
you laid out in sand, squatting
with pants pegged and face
masked like a beekeeper's
against the black flies.
Buttercups circle the planks
of the old wellhead
this May while your silken
gardener's body withers or moulds
in the Proctor graveyard.
I drive and talk to you crying
and come back to this house
to talk to your photographs.

There's news to tell you:
Maggie Fisher's pregnant.
I carried myself like an egg
at Abigail's birthday party
a week after you died,
as three-year-olds bounced
uproarious on a mattress.
Joyce and I met for lunch
at the mall and strolled weepily
through Sears and B. Dalton.

Today it's four weeks
since you lay on our painted bed
and I closed your eyes.
Yesterday I cut irises to set
in a pitcher on your grave;
today I brought a carafe
to fill it with fresh water.
I remember bone pain,
vomiting, and delirium. I remember
pond afternoons.

               My routine
is established: coffee;
the *Globe;* breakfast;
writing you this letter
at my desk. When I go to bed
to sleep after baseball,
Gus follows me into the bedroom
as he used to follow us.
Most of the time he flops
down in the parlor
with his head on his paws.

Once a week I drive to Tilton
to see Dick and Nan.
Nan doesn't understand much
but she knows you're dead;
I feel her fretting. The tune
of Dick and me talking
seems to console her.

               You know now
whether the soul survives death.
Or you don't. When you were dying
you said you didn't fear
punishment. We never dared
to speak of Paradise.
At five A.M., when I walk outside,
mist lies thick on hayfields.
By eight the air is clear,

cool, sunny with the pale yellow
light of mid-May. Kearsarge
rises huge and distinct,
each birch and balsam visible.
To the west the waters
of Eagle Pond waver
and flash through popples just
leafing out.

              Always the weather,
writing its book of the world,
returns you to me.
Ordinary days were best,
when we worked over poems
in our separate rooms.
I remember watching you gaze
out the January window
into the garden of snow
and ice, your face rapt
as you imagined burgundy lilies.

Your presence in this house
is almost as enormous
and painful as your absence.
Driving home from Tilton,
I remember how you cherished
that vista with its center
the red door of a farmhouse
against green fields.
Are you past pity?
If you have consciousness now,
if something I can call
"you" has something
like "consciousness," I doubt
you remember the last days.
I play them over and over:
I lift your wasted body
onto the commode, your arms
looped around my neck, aiming
your bony bottom so that

it will not bruise on a rail.
Faintly you repeat,
"Momma, Momma."

You lay
astonishing in the long box
while Alice Ling prayed
and sang "Amazing Grace"
a cappella. Three times today
I drove to your grave.
Sometimes, coming back home
to our circular driveway,
I imagine you've returned
before me, bags of groceries upright
in the back of the Saab,
its trunk lid delicately raised
as if proposing an encounter,
dog-fashion, with the Honda.

from *Ploughshares*

The Cretonnes
of Penelope

◇   ◇   ◇

How stupid Penelope's suitors must have been,
Each morning as they elbowed for a place
Near her, and cocked their wits, eyeing each other,
Never to notice yesterday's tapestry
Had disappeared, like every day's before.

They kept maneuvering, and they kept score,
Each trying to get the better of his brother.
So each day's small creation went unseen
Unless some maid in waiting saw that face
Glancing from corners of the tapestry.

She wove a glimpse of him in every scene
She patterned on the vanishing tapestry.
Nor did it have to be obliquely traced
To fool the fools not looking any more,
Who couldn't tell one figure from another.

But if this game was all, she wanted more,
One friend (it wouldn't have to be a lover)
Who saw how the resourceful tapestry's
Long lesson in how never quite to mean
Inscribed the careful lines upon her face.

At night when she ripped up the tapestry
She felt she'd run a marathon in place.
Her sole delight was her most painful chore.
She knew she couldn't make it new again.
But when the sun came up she started over.

from *The Paris Review*

ANTHONY HECHT

Rara Avis in Terris

◇   ◇   ◇

For Helen

Hawks are in the ascendant. Just look about.
　Cormorants, ravens, jailbirds of ominous wing
Befoul the peace, their caws
　　　　　　　　　raised in some summoning
　　To an eviscerating cause,
　　Some jihad, some rash all-get-out
　Crusade, leaving the field all gore and guano
　Justified in hysterical soprano

　By balding buzzards who brandish the smart bomb,
　　The fractured atom in their unclipped talons.
Ruffling with all the pride
　　　　　　　　　of testosteronic felons,
　　They storm the airwaves with implied
　　Threats and theatrical aplomb
　Or cruise the sky with delta stealth and gelid
　Chestful of combat-decorative fruit salad.

　It's the same in the shady groves of academe:
　　Cold eye and primitive beak and calloused foot
Conjunctive to destroy
　　　　　　　　　all things of high repute,
　　Whole epics, Campion's songs, Tolstoi,
　　Euclid and logic's enthymeme,
　As each man strives and focuses his labor
　Industriously to deconstruct his neighbor.

And that's not the worst of it; there are the Bacchae,
The ladies' auxiliary of the raptor clan
With their bright cutlery,
                              sororal to a man.
        And feeling peckish, they foresee
        An avian banquet in the sky,
Feasting off dead white European males,
Or local living ones if all else fails.

    But where are the mild monogamous lovebirds,
    Parakeets, homing pigeons, sundry doves,
Beringed, bewitching signs
                              of the first, greatest loves
        Eros or Agape gently defines?
        God's for the ark's small flocks and herds,
    Or Venus incarnate as that quasi-queen
    Of France known as Diane de la Poitrine.

    They are here, my dear, they are here in the marble air,
    According to the micro-Mosaic law,
Miraculously aloft
                    above that flood and flaw
        Where Noah darkly plies his craft.
        Lightly an olive branch they bear,
    Its deathless leafage emblematic of
    A quarter-century of faultless love.

from *The New Republic*

DARYL HINE

The World Is Everything That Is the Case

◇   ◇   ◇

Ludwig Wittgenstein

Embodying the liar's paradox,
  Why did he have to reinvent the wheel?
  Unable, he said, to lie or cheat or steal,
Or understand it when a lion talks,
How to construe a language game that mocks
  Significance, too scrupulous to feel
  That others are indubitably real,
Puzzled the solitary chatterbox.

Ultimate mystery, another's pain
  Even the saint that caused it might refuse
    To recognize, like a strange native place.
What does it profit anyone to gain
  His own imaginary soul, and lose
    Forever everything that is the case?

from *Poetry*

EDWARD HIRSCH

The Lectures on Love

◇　◇　◇

1. CHARLES BAUDELAIRE

These lectures afford me a great pleasure,
so thank you for coming. My subject is love
and my proposition is a simple one: erotic love,
which is, after all, a fatal form of pleasure,
closely resembles a surgical operation, or torture.
Forgive me if I sound ironic or cynical
but, I'm sure you'll agree, cynicism
is sometimes called for in discussing torture.

Act One, Scene One: The score is "Love."
The setting of a great operatic passion.
At first the lovers have equal passion
but, it turns out, one always seems to love
the other less. He, or she, is the surgeon
applying a scalpel to the patient, the victim.
I know because I have been that victim
though I have also been the torturer, the surgeon.

Can you hear those loud spasmodic sighs?
Who hasn't uttered them in hours of love?
Who hasn't drawn them from his (or her) lover?
It's sacrilegious to call such noises "ecstasy"
when they're really a species of decomposition,
surrendering to death. We can get drunk
on each other, but don't pretend being drunk
puts us in a sudden death-defying position.

Why are people so proud of that spellbound
look in the eyes, that stiffening between the legs?
Example One: She ran her hand down my legs
until I felt as if I'd been gagged and bound.
Example Two: She no longer gave me any pleasure,
nonetheless, I rested my hand on her nude body
almost casually, I leaned over and tasted her body
until her whole being trembled with pleasure.

The erotic is an intimate form of cruelty
and every pleasure can be used to prostitute
another: I love you, so I become your prostitute
but my generosity is your voluptuous cruelty.
Sex is humiliation, a terrifying game
in which one partner loses self-control.
The subject concerns ownership or control
and that makes it an irresistible game.

I once heard the question discussed:
Wherein consists love's greatest pleasure?
I pondered the topic with great pleasure
but the whole debate filled me with disgust.
Someone declared, *We love a higher power.*
Someone said, *Giving is better than receiving,*
though someone else returned, *I prefer receiving.*
No one there ever connected love to power.

Someone actually announced, *The greatest pleasure
in love is to populate the State with children.*
But must we really be no better than children
whenever we discuss the topic of pleasure?
Pain, I say, is inseparable from pleasure
and love is but an exquisite from of torture.
You need me, but I carry the torch for her . . .
Evil comes enswathed in every pleasure.

2. HEINRICH HEINE

Thank you, thank you ladies and gentlemen.
I have had myself carried here today
on what we may call my mattress-grave
where I have been entombed for years
(forgive me if I don't stand up this time)
to give a lecture about erotic love.

As a cripple talking about Eros,
a subject I've been giving up for years,
I know my situation (*this time
he's gone too far!*) is comical and grave.
But don't I still appear to be a man?
Hath not a Jew eyes, etc., at least today?

I am an addict of the human comedy
and I propose that every pleasure, esp. love,
is like the marriage of the French and Germans
or the eternal quarrel between Space and Time.
We are all creeping madly toward the grave
or leaping forward across the years

(Me, I haven't been able to leap in years)
and bowing under the fiendish blows of Time.
All that can distract us—gentlemen, ladies—
is the splendid warfare between men and women.
I don't hesitate to call the struggle "love."
Look at me: my feverish body is a grave,

I've been living so long on a mattress-grave
that I scarcely even resemble a man,
but what keeps me going is the quest for love.
I may be a dog who has had his day
(admittedly a day that has lasted for years)
but I'm also a formidable intellect of our time

and I'm telling you nothing can redeem Time
or the evident oblivions of the grave
or the crippling paralysis of the years

except the usual enchantments of love.
That's why the night hungers for the day
and the gods—heaven help us—envy the human.

Ladies and gentlemen, the days pass into years
and the body is a grave filled with time.
We are drowning. All that rescues us is love.

3. MARQUIS DE SADE

This is the first time I have given a lecture
on my favorite subject—the nature of love—
so thank you for courageously inviting me.
I hope you won't regret having invited me
when you hear what I think about erotic love.
These are provisional notes *towards* a lecture

since what I've prepared are some observations
which, forgive me, I will not attempt to prove
but which I offer as subjective testimony.
What I *will* claim for this evidentiary testimony
is its forthright honesty, which I cannot prove.
I offer you the candor of my observations,

and I trust I will not shock you too much
(or too little) by revealing the deep abyss
at the heart—the vertiginous core—of love.
We will always desecrate whatever we love.
Eroticism stands on the edge of an abyss:
Sex is not enough until it becomes too much.

Love is erotic because it is so dangerous.
I am an apostle of complete freedom who believes
other people exist to satisfy my appetites.
I am not ashamed to pursue those appetites
and I have the will to enact my cruel beliefs.
The greatest *liaisons* are always dangerous.

Exhibit Number One is an innocent specimen.
My niece has a face aureoled by grace,
a guileless soul, and a lily-white body.
I like to masturbate all over her body
and to enter behind while she says grace.
Her humiliation is a delicious specimen.

Exhibit Number Two takes place in church.
I send my valet to purchase a young whore
and he dresses her as a sweet-faced nun.
(Do I have any compunction about this? *None.*)
In a pew I sodomize the terrified whore
until she becomes a member of my church.

It takes courage to be faithful to desire—
not many have the nerve. I myself feed
from the bottom of a cesspool for pleasure
(and I have fed from her bottom with pleasure).
I say whosoever has the courage to feed
from the ass of his beloved will sate desire.

Please don't leave. My doctrine is *isolism:*
the lack of contact between human beings.
But strangle me and you shall touch me.
Spit in my face and you shall see me.
Suck my cock and you taste a human being.
Otherwise we are the subjects of isolism.

Forgive me if I speak with too much freedom.
I am nothing more than an old libertine
who believes in the sanctity of pleasure.
Suffering, too, is a noble form of pleasure
like the strange experience of a libertine.
I would release you to a terrible freedom.

4. MARGARET FULLER

Thank you for attending this conversation on love.
I am going to argue in the Nineteenth Century

a woman can no longer be sacrificed for love.
The Middle Ages are over, ladies and gentlemen,

and I am going to argue in the Nineteenth Century
we are not merely wives, whores, and mothers.
The Middle Ages are over, gentlemen. And ladies,
we can now be sea captains, if you will.

We are not merely wives, whores, and mothers.
We can be lawyers, doctors, journalists,
we can now be sea captains, if you will.
What matters to us is our own fulfillment.

We can be lawyers, doctors, journalists
who write ourselves into the official scripts.
What matters to us is our own fulfillment.
It is time for Eurydice to call for Orpheus

and to sing herself into the official scripts.
She is no longer a stranger to her inheritance.
It is time for Eurydice to call for Orpheus
and to move the earth with her triumphant song.

She is no longer a stranger to her inheritance.
She, too, leaves her footprints in the sand
and moves the earth with her triumphant song.
God created us for the purpose of happiness.

She, too, leaves her footprints in the sand.
She, too, feels divinity within her body.
God created us for the purpose of happiness.
She is not the betrothed, the bride, the spouse.

She, too, feels divinity within her body.
Man and Woman are two halves of one thought.
She is not the betrothed, the bride, the spouse.
The sexes should prophesy to one another.

Man and Woman are two halves of one thought.
They are both on equal terms before the law.

The sexes should prophesy to one another.
My love is a love that cannot be crucified.

We are both on equal terms before the law.
Our holiest work is to transform the earth.
(My love is a love that cannot be crucified.)
The earth itself becomes a parcel of heaven.

Our holiest work is to transform the earth.
Thank you for attending this conversation on love.
The earth itself becomes a parcel of heaven.
A woman can no longer be sacrificed for love.

5. GIACOMO LEOPARDI

Thank you for listening to this new poem
which Leopardi has composed for the occasion;
he regrets he cannot read it here himself
(he is, he suggests, but a remnant of himself),
especially on such an auspicious occasion.
He has asked me to present you with this poem:

Poetry Would Be a Way of Praising God if God Existed

> Deep in the heart of night
> I stood on a hill in wintertime
> and stared up at the baleful moon.
> I was terrified of finding myself
> in the midst of nothing, myself
> nothingness clarified, like the moon.
> I was suffocating inside time,
> contemplating the empty night
> when a bell rang in the distance
> three times, like a heart beating
> in the farthest reaches of the sky.
> The music was saturated with stillness.
> I stood listening to that stillness
> until it seemed to fill the sky.
> The moon was like a heart beating
> somewhere far off in the distance.

But there is no heart in a universe
of dying planets, infinite starry spaces.
Death alone is the true mother of Eros
and only love can revivify the earth.
Look at the sky canopied over earth:
it is a black sea pulsing without Eros,
a world of infinitely dead, starry spaces.
Love alone can redeem our universe.

6. RALPH WALDO EMERSON

Thank you for coming to this lecture on love.
I have been told that in public discourse
my true reverence for intellectual discourse
has made me indifferent to the subject of love,
but I almost shrink at such disparaging words
since I believe love created the world.
What else, after all, perpetuates the world
except enacted love? I savor the words.

The study of love is a question of facts
and a matter of dreams, a dream that matters.
Lovers are scientists studying heavenly matters
while their bodies connect the sweetest facts.
Please don't blush when I speak of love
as the reunion of two independent souls
who have drifted since birth as lost souls
but now come together in eternal love.

There can be no love without natural sympathy.
Let's say you're a hunter who excels at business
(I'm aware this may be none of my business)
but for me it doesn't arouse much sympathy.
Let's say, however, you drink tea in the morning
and like to eat apple pie for breakfast;
we both walk through the country very fast
watching the darkness turn into early morning

and this creates a mutual bond between us
that leads to a soulful sharing of sabbaths.
The heart has its jubilees and sabbaths
when a fiery lightning strikes between us.
I do not shy away from the subject of sex
which is, after all, a principle of the universe
(it is also, alas, a principle of my verse)
since we are bound to each other through sex.

Look how the girls flirt with the boys
while the boys slowly encircle the girls.
The village shops are crowded with girls
lingering over nothing to talk with boys.
Romance is the beginning of celestial ecstasy,
an immortal hilarity, a condition of joy:
civilization itself depends on the joy
of standing beside ourselves with ecstasy.

Love is a bright foreigner, a foreign self
that must recognize me for what I truly am;
only my lover can understand me as I am
when I am struggling to create myself.
So, too, I must love you as you truly are—
but what is that? Under your cool visage
and coy exterior, your advancing age,
I sense the young passion of who you are.

The lover comes with something to declare—
such declarations affirm the nature of love.
Here is what the lover says to his love
in the heat of passion, this I declare:
My love for you is a voluptuous world
where the seasons appear as a bright feast.
We can sit together at this delicious feast.
Come lie down with me and devour the world.

7. COLETTE

My young friends, this is the final lecture,
though not the last word, on the subject of love,
so thank you for listening. It is my pleasure
to address a passion I know something about
(which is something, forgive me, I can't say about
all the previous lecturers)—not just pleasure,
but the unruly depths we describe as love.
Let's call our tête-à-tête, "A Modern Lecture."

My mother used to say, "Sit down, dear,
and don't cry. The worst thing for a woman
is her first man—the one who kills you.
After that, marriage becomes a long career."
Poor Sido! She never had another career
and she knew firsthand how love ruins you.
The seducer doesn't care about his woman,
even as he whispers endearments in her ear.

Never let anyone destroy your inner spirit.
Among all the forms of truly absurd courage
the recklessness of young girls is outstanding.
Otherwise there would be far fewer marriages
and even fewer affairs that overwhelm marriages.
Look at me: it's amazing I'm still standing
after what I went through with ridiculous courage.
I was made to suffer, but no one broke my spirit.

Every woman wants her adventure to be a feast
of ripening cherries and peaches, Marseilles figs,
hothouse grapes, champagne shuddering in crystal.
Happiness, we believe, is on sumptuous display.
But unhappiness writes a different kind of play.
The gypsy gazes down into a clear blue crystal
and sees rotten cherries and withered figs.
Trust me: loneliness, too, can be a feast.

Ardor is delicious, but keep your own room.
One of my husbands said: is it impossible

for you to write a book that isn't about love,
adultery, semi-incestuous relations, separation?
(Of course, this was before our own separation.)
He never understood the natural law of love,
the arc from the possible to the impossible . . .
I have extolled the tragedy of the bedroom.

We need exact descriptions of the first passion,.
so pay attention to whatever happens to you.
Observe everything: love is greedy and forgetful.
By all means fling yourself wildly into life
(though sometimes you will be flung back by life)
but don't let experience make you forgetful
and be surprised by everything that happens to you.
We are creative creatures fuelled by passion.

Consider this an epilogue to the lectures on love,
a few final thoughts about the nature of love.
Freedom should be the first condition of love
and work is liberating (*a novel about love
cannot be written while you are making love*).
Never underestimate the mysteries of love,
the eminent dignity of not talking about love.
Passionate attention is prayer, prayer is love.

Savor the world. Consume the feast with love.

from *The Paris Review*

The Job Interview

◇   ◇   ◇

with André Breton, 1957

The question, Monsieur Gracq advised, had best
be asked, and answered, in the Old Lion's den:
would I, duly scrutinized, be allowed
    to translate *Nadja*?

Factors in my favor: I did speak French
—the one parlance necessarily shared—
and my links to certain Proscribed Figures
    were, to him, unknown.

Bravely enough, therefore, I proceeded
through the Place Blanche and up the Rue Fontaine,
though in my heart (or in some other place)
    I knew the danger:

Breton's legendary loathing of queers . . .
Ever since Jacques Vaché had overdosed
on opium in a Nantes hotel, naked
    with another man,

Surrealism's pope had unchurched men
of my kind, condemned our "perverted race"
to a paltry outer darkness, claiming
    he could sense, could *smell*

an intolerable presence . . . Fee fo fum.
Climbing his stairs, I wondered if I gave
off the emanations of turpitude:
        would he detect me

by the scent of my "disgusting practice"?
Was I entitled to conceal from him
—indeed *could* I conceal the taint which made
        whatever talent

I might have merely an interference,
an imposture? A scuffle of slippers,
and the author of *Nadja* let me in
        past the museum

of surreal objects, himself another
museum of sorts, who had shown epigones
how to read, how to live, and how to love.
        Some epigones.

Others had failed,—rejections, suicides;
Of which no hint discolored our encounter,
affable to a fault. Perhaps the three
        decades since Nadja

had revealed to the world her Accidents
of Sublimity had blunted Breton's
erotic stipulations; and I was so
        pusillanimous

as to keep my *tendencies* to myself,
where they fluttered helplessly enough:
of course I knew in my heart that the one
        surrealist act

—O coward heart! would be to challenge this
champion of liberation, this foe of all
society's constraints, but I could do
        nothing of the kind,

nor need I have. O reason not the need:
I left the Master of the Same New Things
with every warrant of his trust in me
      as his translator

(*Traditorre—tradutore!* in fact,
if not in French), and forty years have passed
since that traduced encounter. Where are we?
      Nadja in English is still

in print, and lots of people still hate queers.
I allay that heart of mine with the words
Breton wrote to the first of his three wives
      (Simone, a Jew like me):

criticism will be love, or will not be.

from *The New Republic*

The Hanging Gardens

◊ ◊ ◊

Gone: The Palace of Forty Columns. Gone:
The Garden of Heart's Ease, The Garden of Roses.
Gone: The Garden of the Shah. And even
The Garden of the Throne is nothing now
but rubble unreflected in brown rain
drying in the ruined reflecting pool. Gone,
the hanging gardens built for a homesick queen
who missed the meadows of her childhood mountains.

A child pondering my old Book of Wonders,
I daydreamed of gardens floating over the desert
in never-ending bloom—green stepping-stones,
each lush with lilies and bromeliads.
I thought they were wizardry not work
in the dry land of tamarisk and camel thorn.
Amytis knows. And doesn't want to know.
The gardeners hide from her. The cypresses
are lovely, yes, and the waterlilies too—
lovely the date palms lining the waterways,
and the blooming water hyacinths—but I,
because I'd read my Book of Wonders, knew
their purpose was to shade the channeled water.

As Amytis at nightfall ascends her garden,
turning tier on tier in the cooling dusk
in the present tense of our imagining,
she doesn't touch the waterlilies. They'll part,
uncovering the lead-lined troughs—reeds, tar.
Through gaps in ivy and purple clematis,

she sees and doesn't see the slaves' palm prints
fired in rough brick. Beside the river, she'd watched
young slaves slap wet clay into bricks, then pile
dry brush on them. Before they lit the piles,
one slave—she'd seen him and she hadn't seen him—
strolled the haphazard rows, pressing his palms
into the soft brown river clay, and twisting.
(I've seen him do this. Why can't Amytis?)

Down the false mountain, dammed, channeled, pumped
Euphrates water cascades like a mountain stream,
murmuring like a mountain stream, purling
and chuckling over artful, moss-draped stones,
but when she isn't careful Amytis hears
the *shaduf's* splash, and creaking, laden rise.
If her mind drifts, she'll hear the steady clomp,
the muted huffing of the ox against its yoke,
the capstan's squeal, the slip and drag, the rasp
and slop of chain pumps forcing water up the mountain.
Freed, it plunges, rippling like a stream,
shaded with ferns, protected by blue cedars,
and, along the streambed, cultivated moss
is painted with spoiled milk and brushed like velvet.

All planned: each brown bloom plucked and carried off,
and every barren spot is soon adorned
with a new rarity: white myrtle, rosy
oleander with its almond scent,
narcissus, bonarets from Scythia—
a thoughtful gardener calculating her
bedazzlement.
                        Impatiently, she prowls
the rooftop garden of her upmost terrace,
watching the blurred red sun disintegrate
and slide below the crenellated walls
of her dry kingdom. The first stars separate
from the harsh sunlight overdazzling them,
and her eyes open and she begins to see
what she has come to see.

She ascends an artificial mountain, descends
an otherworldly garden. Each paradise
adores its wolf, its snake, its scorpion.
She savors possibility: assassins
beneath the roses, demons in the willow.
Now, anything can happen, although it never does,
and I, a torchbearer, arise from the tall grass,
ignite my torch and join the path. She follows.
The upward path is now the downward path
and on the way down—backward, dark—black leaves,
wind-lashed in flaring torchlight, lunge at us,
beat at their twigs. And when the leaves rip free,
pelt toward us, tangle in her hair, she laughs
and leaves them there—laughs, and follows me.
But not me really and not the torch,
but torchlight as it slides
across white blossoms, changing them to moons—
blue, luminous and unattainable:
torchlight and nothing. An ache for paradise
says my new Book of Wonders, pages filled
with new research and fresh equivocation
spilling from the past and past-perfect tenses:
a pile of dubious rubble in the desert.
A name that may have been a mistranslation.
A garden that was built by another, later king
for a concubine. Or wasn't built at all.
Or that was, at best, a mound of mud
planted with short desert trees and brush.
And through the wavering possibilities
I see her and I do not see her walking
the rectilinear spiraling ziggurat
uphill at dusk, downhill in moonlight;
walking through her own absence; picking her way
discreetly through rubble in the desert; circling
a mound too closely planted for her to climb;
walking the rectilinear spiraling ziggurat,
uphill at dusk, downhill in the moonlight
of a word Herodotus misunderstood.
Or understood. I see her and I do not see her.

from *River Styx*

169

The Word "Answer"

◊   ◊   ◊

*"Prayer exerts an influence upon God's action, even
upon his existence. This is what the word 'answer' means."*
—KARL BARTH, *Prayer*

1

Lightning walks across the shallow seas,
Stick figures putting feet down hard
Among the molecules. Meteors dissolve
And drop their pieces in a mist of iron,
Drunk through atomic skin like dreamy wine.
The virus that would turn a leaf dark red
Seizes two others that would keep it green.
They spread four fingers like a lizard's hand.
Into this random rightness comes the prayer,
A change of weather, a small shift of degree
That heaves a desert where a forest sweated,
And asks creation to return an answer.
That's all it wants: a prayer just wants an answer,
And twists time in a knot until it gets it.

2

There's the door. Will anybody get it?
That's what he's wondering, the bath's still warm;
And by the time he towels off and puts on

His pajamas, robe, and slippers and goes down,
They'll be gone, won't they? There's the door again;
And nobody's here to answer it but him.
Perhaps they'll go away. But it's not easy,
Relaxing in the tub, reading the paper,
With someone at the front door, ringing and pounding,
And—that sounds like glass—breaking in.
At least the bathroom door's securely bolted.
Or is that any assurance in this case?
He might as well go find out what's the matter.
Whoever it is must really want . . . something.

3

We ask for bread, he makes his body bread.
We ask for daily life, and every day,
We get a life, or a facsimile,
Or else we get a tight place in a crowd
Or test results with the prognosis—bad.
We ask and what is given is the answer,
For we can always see it as an answer,
Distorted as it may be, from our God.
What shall we ask for then? For his return,
Like the bereaved parents with the monkey's paw,
Wishing, then wishing again? The last answer,
When we have asked for all that we can ask for,
May be the end of time, our mangled child,
And in the doorway, dead, the risen past.

4

With this prayer I am making up a God
On a gray day, prophesying snow.
I pray that God be immanent as snow
When it has fallen thickly, a deep God.
With this prayer I am making up a God
Who answers prayer, responding like the snow
To footprints and the wind, to a child in snow

Making an angel who will speak for God.
God, I am thinking of you now as snow,
Descending like the answer to a prayer,
This prayer that you will be made visible,
Drifting and deepening, a dazzling, slow
Acknowledgment, out of the freezing air,
As dangerous as it is beautiful.

from *Connecticut Review*

Stanzas on a Hidden Theme

◇   ◇   ◇

I

There is a gold light in certain old paintings
That represents a diffusion of sunlight.
It is like happiness, when we are happy.
It comes from everywhere and from nowhere at once, this light,
    And the poor soldiers sprawled at the foot of the cross
    Share in its charity equally with the cross.

II

Orpheus hesitated beside the black river.
With so much to look forward to, he looked back.
We think he sang then, but the song is lost.
At least he had seen once more the beloved back.
    I say the song went this way: *O prolong*
    Now the sorrow if that is all there is to prolong.

III

The world is very dusty, uncle. Let us work.
One day the sickness shall pass from the earth for good.
The orchard will bloom; someone will play the guitar.
Our work will be seen as strong and clean and good.
    And all that we suffered from having existed
    Shall be forgotten as though it had never existed.

from *The New Yorker*

The Orchard

◊   ◊   ◊

I saw the dog in a dream. Huge white
Boney creature. Big as a horse. At first
I thought it was a horse. It was feeding
On apples. As a horse might. Though not
With a horse's patience. For it was starving.
Its hipbones were empty bowls. The horse
Wolfed down the apples. Without breathing.
Without looking up. The way a dog wolfs
Down meat. And then it growled. And I saw
That the horse *was* a dog. But the apples
Were still apples. Windfall from the orchard
Above the lake. Pitiful place. The few trees
There grow black and yellow. And the thin grasses
Stagger down to the abandoned north field,
Which floods in winter and then freezes—
Blue ground, marbled with red and white,
Like a slab of meat—and when the far deer
Cross over it, and the birds cross over it,
It is as if the memories held within
The meat were rising from it. Or it is like
Flies crawling. . . . I saw the dog in a dream.
And then, days later, just before dawn,
I climbed to the orchard. And there he was.
The same dog. Chewing on a dead doe.
And it was troubling. I thought I might
Still be dreaming—as was the case
When for many months I could not sleep
And I lost the power to tell the figures
In my dreams from those we call real.

I thought the scene might have been staged
For me. By my mind. Or by someone
Who could read my mind. Someone
Who was having a good laugh
At my expense. Or testing me
In some way I could not understand.
Beneath the black and yellow trees,
The dog's skin seemed abnormally white
And the blood on his broad muzzle shone
Like wet paint. I closed my eyes. Not because
The ghostly creature was now biting
At the neck of the doe, the way
Those dark creatures who drink blood
And live forever do—since the river
Of blood flows forever, the streams
Of an eternal city, forever running,
Forever carrying their musky loads
Of blooming and expiring words
And figures, a thousand thousand
Yellow lights forever flickering off
And on in the black liquid, gold,
Sweet liquid, fallen—I closed my eyes.
Not out of distaste. But to see if the dog
Would disappear, the way the mist
Had thinned and vanished as I climbed
The hill. But the dog was still there
When I opened them. Staring straight at me.
He lifted his large paw. Placed it
On the doe's chest, and started to rip
At her belly. There was the sound
Of cloth tearing. And what did I do?
I picked up an apple. I wanted to see
If the dog—when the apple struck his side
And he fell—would rise in a second form,
And then a third. As dream figures do.
Dog. To horse. To man. Or I wanted to see
If the apple would pass through the dog
As through a ghost. And if the dog
Like the best of ghosts would turn
And instruct me in my confusion.

175

Or I wanted to bring the scene down
To size. The way the bright lights
That clank on at the end of the play
Show the mad king to be nothing
But a skinny man holding a costume
Of cloth and paste. I wanted the dog
To be just a stray, gnawing on a bone.
Or maybe I wanted none of these things.
Maybe I wanted what the hunter
Wanted when he struck the doe. Maybe
I wanted a piece of the dog's feasting,
The way the hunter wanted a piece
Of the doe's improbable swiftness.
The gun fires. The smell of burnt powder
Sprays up. A knotted string of birds
Unspools across the white sky. And deep
In running blood a man thrusts his hands.
I wanted something. But I did not throw
The apple. It was a small fruit. The size
Of a child's hand. Black and yellow. Riddled
With worms and misshapen. I put my teeth
To it. I took a bite. Chill flesh. Rank.
The dog kept feeding. I was not bothered
By the blood. The last of the red leaves
Scudded about me. And a few drops fell
From the dark sky. There is blood
Everywhere. The trees shed it. The sky.
There is no end. And isn't it pretty?
We say. Isn't it pretty? Amn't I?
Isn't the starving dog? Isn't the doe?
Even half-eaten? She gave her body
To the dog. The fallen body looked
So heavy. It looked like it weighed
Ten thousand pounds. More than the lake
Or the frozen field. The doe dreamed
Of her death and it came to pass.
She courted the hunter and he shot her.
And she fell. And then the man stood
Over her. A white shadow. Laughing.
And then the dog stood over her. A black

Shadow. Laughing. And the dog came close.
The way a lover might. Had the doe
Been human. And he put his mouth to her.
As a lover might. Had he been human.
And her chastened flesh was a chalice.
And she was peaceful. And there was bliss
In this. And some horror. Around her
The thorns shone black and yellow.
And the fallen fruit lay black and yellow.
And black and yellow are the colors
Of the orchard's hive when it masses
And the queen in a fiery constellation
Is carried to new quarters. The wind
Stirred in the orchard. The dog bit
Into the doe's chest. And the apple
In my hand, against my lips, small,
Misshapen, the size of a child's fist,
Full of worms, turned suddenly warm
And soft. And it was as if, on that hill,
While the dog fed and the lake lay
Frozen, I was holding in my hand,
Against my lips, not a piece of fruit,
Not a piece of bitter, half-eaten fruit,
But the still warm and almost beating
Heart of some holy being—just lifted
From the dead body. And the heart
Was heavy. And wet. And it smelled
As it would smell forever. Of myrrh.
And burning blood. And gold.

from *New England Review*

Roman Hours

◊　◊　◊

1. *The Horologium of Augustus*
13 B.C.

We
are led into
a courtyard off Via di Campo
Marzio #48, past a man in a little shop

who
is fixing shoes,
down to the basement and across a
sort of catwalk to a shaky ladder, at the foot of which we

see,
through a meter
of standing water, the bronze letters
set in travertine which say Ε Τ Η Σ Ι Α Ι Π Α Υ Ο Ν Τ Α Ι, that is,

"The
Etesian winds
stop," as they do on the Aegean
at the end of summer, when the sun is in Virgo. It was a

dream
of emperors,
teaching even the sun at last to
walk orderly between monuments and anniversaries which

are
the expression
of a self both invisible and
immortal, one identical with the world of natural law,

now
beyond the griefs
of cracked and linear time, ablaze
in the incised tangle of the analemma, being rather

part
of time itself,
untouchable, having transcended
dynastic art, a shadow walking between the Mausoleum

of
Augustus and
the Ara Pacis, on whose threshold
there stood, on the Emperor's birthday, this solar affirmation

that
the past, given
the pattern of the divine, had been
made present; that the future, being certain, was also present.

Deep
beneath modern
pavements, the pinched grace of these lines still
remembers the moment the wind's breath died on the water's face; the

shade,
the touch of it,
cast by a human head lost in thought,
to whom it occurred that the one way to godhead was through absence.

2. *The Meridian of Santa Maria degli Angeli*
A.D. 1703

A crumb of light
high on the southern wall
of a pagan frigidarium
supposedly built by Christian slaves
under the Emperor Diocletian
(but there were ways out
to forswear libel flee profane)
and now become a church

That pure ellipsis trembles
by which one thing becomes another
moving leisurely in a double focus
across the marble inlay of a floor
wrought with signs of the zodiac
Clouds swim across
as it lights the hooves of an amiable ram
done in giallo antico

In the heavens as on earth
what is taken for observed truth
is not quite the same thing as law
The historian writes *As the lives*
of the faithful became
less mortified and austere
they were every day less ambitious
of the honors of martyrdom

Beyond the heliacal hole
is the ineffable core
toward which the motes climb and climb
A few people wait far below
impatiently as if knowing

they must respect this motion
but no longer knowing quite why
and at 12:17:45 exactly

by my watch (legal time not solar time)
the solar macula crosses the bronze rail
it walks between Resurrection and Resurrection
silent traveler considering one by one
the sequence of bronze letters
TERMINUS PASCHAE
considering the disordered world
humans have made of paradise

3. The Janiculum Cannon
A.D. 1847

It was Pius IX who decided
    that the bark of a howitzer should
replace the exuberant riot
    of the city's church bells, their uncoordinated

ringing, and therefore establish
    the hour of noon for the rabble.
The shakoed soldiers push
    the monster from its cave in the hill,

count backwards in Italian,
    and the crowd flinches and recognizes
once again the voice of extinction
    by which it may tell the hours.

At the puppet theater nearby, Pulcinella
    is beaten around the head with a stick
by the Devil for the third time today.
    The children are silent and do not blink.

The cannon was elsewhere during
    the period of the Second World War,
the population finding
    other ways to fill its appetite for gunpowder;

nor again until 1959
    (lest the custom seem precocious,

or the dead too soon forgotten)
    did that stroke of outrageous noise

strip the tender green from each branch
    and announce its message to all
in accents of intolerant bronze.
    Through the smoke in its acrid blue coil,

we thank you, Papa, we thank you,
    who taught us to make the sky
way over by the Pincio
    clap its hands in reply.

from *The Yale Review*

Second Time Around

◊   ◊   ◊

You're entangled with someone more famous than you
Who happens to vanish.
You marry again in haste, perhaps to a nurse
Or your late wife's good friend,
Someone whose name will never appear in print
Except, perhaps, in your entry for Who's Who;
Someone obliging and neutral, not too good looking
To whom you say, "Darling, the supper was excellent."
Free, now, of that brilliant aura, that physical dazzle
That you always acknowledged, insisting
You relished her fame, believing you meant it,
And love her you did, but you're so relieved she's gone.

How sweet to embrace the mundane, endorse the ordinary,
In its starchy smock or its ruffled apron,
Saying, "Bronwyn—or Carole, or Elsie—
Suits me down to the ground." The ground.
There's to be no more celestial navigation;
It's the end of smart missives, of aerial bombardment.
One can relax, and slump into being human.

Sometimes you sift through her papers
When you're bereft of ideas,
Though of course ideas are not what stimulates art:
It's snapshots of people in old-fashioned bathing suits,
The man she saw by the road with the three-legged dog,
That week in Venice when it never stopped raining, the odor
Of freshly washed hair when she dried it in sunlight . . .
Something she lightly sketched in that needs fleshing out;

Could you? Should you? You put it to one side.
With a minor effort of will you stop thinking about her,
And decide instead to update your vita,
Or work some more on that old piece
On Descartes that has always given you trouble.
And Bronwyn, or Elsie, or Carole
Comes tiptoeing into your study with a nice cup of coffee.

from *Michigan Quarterly Review*

Ballade

◇ ◇ ◇

EN L'AN SOIXANTE-ONZIEME DE MON AGE

We who have ten years to live, approximately,
Are having a good talk at this party.
Ten years of good health, if we're lucky—
O foot on the moving stair!

EN L'AN QUARANTE-HUITIEME DE MON AGE

Whoever wants to make love to all of them
Women I mean—whoever wants to see all the shows—
Flowers, dramas, dog—come forward now
And eat this cheese and see if it will make you want more.

EN L'AN CINQUIEME DE MON AGE

It's okay, pillaging
And loving mud. Knowing my tranquility
Is hard due to constant desire
For education, I steam through a winter's young fires.

EN L'AN QUINZIEME DE MON AGE

Girl with ruffles in your hair
And tussles in your dress
And flamingos for bouche
And gladiolas for clasps gosh we're idiots.

EN L'AN VINGT-DEUXIEME DE MON AGE

I watch this fuel
Burning down
And think I'm an expert
On zooming life.

EN L'AN TRENTE-HUITIEME DE MON AGE

A book comes out. And then another. I'm gratified
Like a house robber. I am planning another side-
Ways book and then another. I go abroad and
Write a play, called "Husband Blubber"

EN L'AN SOIXANTE-DEUXIEME DE MON AGE

Lying on the operating table
I wrote a letter to myself in code
And, while the morphine was wearing off,
I had a strange vision of Goldilocks.

EN L'AN DIX-HUITIEME DE MON AGE

Oh eighteenth year! Truly you are like a jewelry box.
You open and shut with a pam! I know it's over.
Everything is over. The ballgame. My friendship. My romance.
Before my next birthday it seems as though twenty years pass.

EN L'AN TRENTE-DEUXIEME DE MON AGE

Appearances are just getting used to it here
The way we are hoping they carved it.
I'm flouncy said Jenny and talked to knees
Until the first bee waves really came right out of it.

EN L'AN SOIXANTE-QUATRIEME DE MON AGE

I lost you, flowers. I lost you, lovely V,
Neckline of straw and flowers, I lost your key. I lost my key.
It could have been everything that I lost
If I had died this year.

EN L'AN SOIXANTE-TREIZIEME DE MON AGE

I am polite to women and puppies
And cross with cads. I have a lot of years and decades in me
And they divide me like Sunday ads
It's the Big Sale of the Week, when I can speak in song.

EN L'AN ONZIEME DE MON AGE

Occurring and curving and curving and occurring
The dynamic street on which I live
Is blending graciously this evening with another street
On which two whom I play football with live.

EN L'AN QUATORZIEME DE MON AGE

I much prefer the arrondissement
To this terrible year.
My dog becomes hysterical
I come home to opened doors.

EN L'AN TRENTE-SIXIEME DE MON AGE

My daughter is five years old.
Can you imagine, five?
For five years she has been growing
She has been roving, she has been improving, she has been being alive.

EN L'AN VINGT-HUITIEME DE MON AGE

Give me some more poetry and I'll get you some more whiskey
I can drink all night and I can sleep well all morning
I am typing out more poems than there are paintings by Wassily
Kandinsky
And, as you know, that's quite a lot.

EN L'AN SIXIEME DE MON AGE

If I pause on my way past the statue of Abraham Lincoln
That sits in front of our school
It is to easily pick up a snowball
And when I throw it to try to nick you on the ear.

EN L'AN CINQUANTE-SEPTIEME DE MON AGE

The worst things that happened
Did not happen before
But happen this year
Like the crack of a gun.

EN L'AN TRENTIESME DE MON AGE

I'm writing like François Villon but not really.
There's no doom in it. I'm not being tried for my life.
I have a thousand years in which to write
A wonderful seamlessness has just come up in my poetry.

from *The Yale Review*

The Secret Amplitude

◇　◇　◇

I

Perhaps the hardest feeling is the one
Of unrealized possibility:
Thoughts left unspoken, actions left undone

That seemed to be of little consequence
To things considered in totality;
And yet that might have made a difference.

Sometimes the thought of what one might have done
Starts to exhaust the life that it explains,
After so much of what one knew has gone.

I guess that all things happen for the best,
And that whatever life results remains,
In its own fashion, singularly blest.

Yet when I try to I think about the ways
That brought me here, I think about places
Visited, about particular days

Whiled away with a small handful of friends,
Some of them gone; and about the traces
Of a particular movement, that ends

In mild effects, but that originates
In the sheer "wonder of disappointment,"
Ascending in an arc that resonates

Through the heavens, before a dying fall.
I don't know what Wittgenstein might have meant
By *nothing is hidden,* if not that all

The aspects of one's life are there to see.
But last month, coming back on the *métro*
From the basilica of St. Denis,

My sense of here and now began to melt
Into a sensation of vertigo
I realized that I had never felt.

II

Start with the condition of the given:
A room, a backyard, or a city street.
Next, construct an idea of heaven

By eliminating the contingent
Accidents that make it seem familiar.
Spanning these polarities—the stringent

Vacuum and the sound of a lawnmower—
Find the everyday experiences
Making up our lives, set on the lower

Branches of the tree of knowledge. Is *this*
What people mean by living in the world?
A region of imaginary bliss,

Uncontaminated by reflection,
Rationalized by the controlling thought
Of simple beauty, of the perfection

Of the commonplace through acquiescence?
Think of a deeper order of beauty,
A kind of magnificence whose essence

Lies in estrangement, the anxiety
Of the unrecognized, in resistance,
And in the refusal of piety.

Nothing comes of nothing: what ideals
Alter is the look of things, the changing
Surfaces their argument reveals

To be illusory. Yet one still *tries,*
Pulled inward by the promissory thought
Of something time can never realize,

Both inexhaustible and self-contained;
Of something waiting to be discovered
In the dominion of the unattained.

III

I always think about it in a way
So inflected by the thought of places,
And of my distance from them; by other

People, and the measure of another
Year since they departed, that they get hard
To separate, like the thought of a day

From the day itself. I suppose the proof,
If there is one, is by analogy
With the kind of adolescent "knowledge"

I had on those afternoons in college
When I'd go to New York, and the evening
Deepened, and then the lights came on. Aloof,

Yet somehow grounded in the real, it's
Like an abstract diagram of a face,
Or the experience of memory

Drained of its vivifying imagery
—Of Geoff's cigars, for instance, or Willy's
Collision with the pillar at the Ritz—

Until the pure experience remains.
For over time, the personal details
Came to mean less to me than the feeling

Of simply having lived them, revealing
Another way of being in the world,
With all the inwardness it still sustains,

And the promise of happiness it brought.
So it began to take over my life—
Not like some completely arbitrary

Conception someone had imposed on me,
But more and more like a second nature;
Until it became my abiding thought.

IV

How much can someone actually retain
Of a first idea? What the day was,
Or what the flowers in the room were like,

Or how the curtains lifted in the breeze?
The meaning lies in what a person does
In the aftermath of that abundance,

On an ordinary day in August
In the still air, beneath a milk-white sky—
As something quickens in the inner room

No one inhabits, filling its domain
With the sound of an ambiguous sigh
Muffled by traffic noises. Underneath,

The movement starts to recapitulate
Another season and another life,
Walking through the streets of Barcelona,

Its alleys and its accidents combined
Into an arabesqure of feeling, rife
With imprecision, blending everything

Into a song intended to obscure,
Like the song of the wind, and so begin
To repeat the fallacy of the past:

That it was pure, and that the consummate
Endeavor is to bring it back again.
Would it make any difference? Each breath

Anticipates the next, until the end.
Nothing lasts. The imperative of change
Is what the wind repeats, and night brings dreams

Illuminating the transforming thought
Of the familiar context rendered strange,
The displacement of the ordinary.

V

I hadn't been to Paris in six years.
My hotel room was like a pleasant cell.
On the plane I'd been bothered by vague fears

Of being by myself for the first time,
Or recognizing the sound of the bell
Of St. Germain des Prés, or a street mime

At Deux Magots, and being overwhelmed
By the sensation of being alone.
Even with a friend, from the distant realm

Of Rome, I couldn't shake the impression
Of exile, as though I'd come to atone
For some indescribable transgression—

A state of anonymity, without
Anonymity's deep sense of pardon.
We ate, and walked about, and talked about

The true nature of the sentimental.
Later, as I imagined the garden
Of the new Bibliothèque Nationale

Drowsing in its shade of information,
I felt the peace of insignificance,
Of a solitude like a vocation

To be inhabited, to be explored
With the single-minded perseverance
Of a blind man whose sight had been restored.

Everything seemed so mindless and abstract,
Stripped of the personality I knew.
The evening was like a secret compact,

And though it was May, the night air felt cold.
The sky was black. The sky was gold and blue
Above an Eiffel Tower lit with gold.

VI

What is the abstract, the impersonal?
Are they the same? And whence this grandiose
Geography of a few emotions?

Think of an uninhabited landscape,
With its majesty rendered otiose
By a stranger's poverty of feeling;

Then contemplate that state without a name
In which something formless and inchoate
Stirs in an act of definition, like

A thought becoming conscious of itself,
For which the words are always late, too late.
The motion spreads its shape across the sky,

Unburdened by causality and death.
Where is that paradise? Where is that womb
Of the unreal, that expansiveness

That turned the mountains into vacant air,
The empty desert to an empty tomb
On Sunday, with the body set aside,

The sense of diminution giving way,
Through the oscillations of the sublime,
To an infinite expanse of spirit?

If only one could know, at this remove,
The private alchemy, obscured by time,
By which an inhospitable terrain

Became an open space, "a fresh, green breast"
Of a new world of such magnificence
That those who entered were as though reborn,

And everything they heard and saw and felt
Melted into shape and significance;
And what that secret amplitude was like.

VII

But is there even anything to know?
Linger over the cases: the dead friends,
And what the obituaries omit

And one can only imagine: what *it*
Must have felt like at the end, suspended
Between two impossible tasks, as though

The burden of each day were to rebut
A presumption of disillusionment
And a sense of hopelessness, deflected

By the daily routine, yet protected
By the cave of the imagination;
Until at last the inner door slammed shut.

When did it all become unbearable?
The question begs the questions of their lives
Asked from the inside, taking for granted

Their very being, as though enchanted
By the way the settings, in retrospect,
Make up the logic of a parable

Whose incidents make no sense, and by how
Time tries to project a kind of order,
And the terrifying clarity it brings,

Into the enigma of the last things—
A vodka bottle lying on the floor,
An off-hand remark ("I'll be going now")—

With everything contained, as in a proof,
In a few emblems of finality:
The bullet in the mouth. The sharp report

That no one else can hear. The sharp report
That only someone else *could* hear. The long,
Irrevocable transport from the roof.

VIII

If God in Heaven were a pair of eyes
Whose gaze could penetrate the camouflage
Of speech and thought, the innocent disguise

Of a person looking in the mirror;
If a distant mind, in its omniscience,
Could reflect and comprehend the terror

Obscured by the trappings of the body—
If these possibilities were real,
Everything would look the same: a cloudy

Sky low in the distance, and a dead tree
Visible through the window. The same thoughts
Would engage the mind: that one remains free

In a limited sense, and that the rough
Approximation of eternity
Contained in every moment is enough.

What sponsors the idea of a god
Magnificent in its indifference,
And inert above the shabby, slipshod

Furnishings that constitute the human?
What engenders the notion of a state
Transcending the familiar, common

Ground on which two people walked together
Some twenty years ago, through a small park?
The benches remain empty. The weather

Changes with the seasons, which feel the same.
The questions trace out the trajectory
Of a person traveling backwards, whose name

Occupies a space between death and birth;
Of someone awkwardly celebrating
A few diminished angels, and the earth.

IX

It's been nine years since the telephone call
From Mark, and a year since the one from John.
And it's as though nothing's *changed,* but that all

The revisions were finally over.
And yet now more than half my life is gone,
Like those years of waiting to discover

That hidden paradise of the recluse
I was always just about to enter—
Until it came to seem like an excuse

For the evasion of intimacy.
At Willy's memorial last winter,
Edward Albee spoke of his privacy,

And how at last he wandered up the stairs
To a "final privacy." And perhaps
The illusions that keep us from our cares

Are projections of our mortality,
Of the impulse inside the fear it maps
Onto the sky, while in reality

The fear continues underneath. I guess
That despite the moments of resplendence
Like the one in Paris, it's still the less

Insistent ones that come to rest within.
I don't know why the thought of transcendence
Beckons us, or why we strive for it in

Solitary gestures of defiance,
Or try to discover it in our dreams,
Or by rending the veil of appearance.

Why does it have to issue from afar?
Why can't we find it in the way life *seems?*
As Willy would have said—*So, here we are.*

from *Southwest Review*

About Her

◇   ◇   ◇

I. AT SIXES AND SEVENS

What I cannot remember
about that day that time
was simply gone (*Simply? A*
drop from a height, a blow
to the head, made my brain whirl)
Comes calling now—Lost Soul—
to haunt   Lost twin I longed for
all the days of my life
Long gray afternoons we played
together, made up songs
drew, read books   She and I
identical
        (*And lethal*)

I did not know her power
where she came from, how she got
so strong   It seems she came one
day when I was thirty-one
Came with the illness to take
care of me   Take these pills she'd
say, a lot of pills   How changed
she was!   Knowing better than
I what could not be taken:
The intolerable: Life
a cul-de-sac
        Then *she* was

gone seven years   My flesh
my blood   I did not know
her, recognize her tread
Wiser, she knew where to
keep hid   Nearly a year
she lived invisibly
Out of thin air one day
she took me over   Where?

                                        No

matter   My trust was a
sister's trust—the youngest—
unaware sisterhood
is sometimes murderous

II. RRRROSE

She hates me wants to see me dead and stops
at nothing—mimics taunts and jeers, wielding
the lines of my palm, wearing my clothes
this twin   The girl I never was

> *Name her   Turn on light after light*
> *Sharply limned, first she will split*
> *then burn beneath your mind's focus*

An old French teacher—hairy legs, seamed hose—
in what? 8th grade? insisted I was Rrrrose
My own first name unutterable she said
in *that* language   I couldn't breathe   Instead
turned up my nose, took a tropistic turn
toward the midnight sun—first via German—
where, guttural or trilled initially,
R could exist and flourish and be me

I want to believe I am not alone
without *her*   That there exists some Other
with a different mien—not smirking
not looking blankly on as I drop down
and down   Be she Sister, Healer, or Some-
one in my image, who comes through the mirror

III. REPRODUCTION

Is she *ma mort,* the one whose gloves cut
through the mirror?   Cocteau's Princess—
no queen—just another messenger
poets want to take for their own
Death?

        Is she minute, a seed still green
and "warm with night, dug from the soil-
bed of *my* heart, from which *my* Death shall
germinate"?   Will I like Paula
Becker "eat its kernels"?

                       Childless by
choice, neither do I want to take
death in *and* bear it, nor walk pregnant
into the afterlife

             Sister,
spit and image, there is so little
we rule: The forces of Fate are
steadfast   Death adheres to the fertile
Kore's chastity did not save her
The choice was narrow and costly: Shun
the strange red fruit or patiently
wander the underworld forever

"Let us mourn together" Rilke
wrote in his Requiem for Paula
"that someone took you out of your
mirror"   For now she would paint no more—
no more portraits, fruits, self-portraits
with amber beads—leaving nothing
behind but mourners
                 (Her child lived)

Does it all start in the mirror, *der
Spiegel,* the noun of looking and
seeing, the pool of self-hate and self-
love, reflecting all things evil
and good?   Did Narcissus see in the

water a beloved dead twin
sister?

       Do all our makings go on
there, not through the window but in
the mirror?   And if so, can you help
me?   Sister?

from *Poetry*

Ontological

◇   ◇   ◇

for Elfie Raymond

If it were not so bright,
Not so dark;
If there had been another hour,

Another storm,
Something to keep track of
Or something to hold at bay;

If there had been no bird
On the barest tree,
With one bitter crumb in its mouth,

One little speck;
If the honey surrounding that crumb
Had not been sweet,

If the evening had been less silent,
Humming one note
Without leaving any name,

Calling me to a field whose sickle moon
Made it clear
That nothing would speak;

If the way to the field
Had been less glorious,
A drop of dew beside a milkweed seed,

A ladybug scampering toward light,
And flowers on fire
Swaying among tall grasses—

A river of paper lanterns at dawn;
If the current did not carry
The scent of cyclamen,

Wild as grief
Spilling its horn of plenty,
Outlasting the final kiss of day.

from *The New Criterion*

PHILIP LEVINE

Drum

◇   ◇   ◇

Leo's Tool & Die, 1950

In the early morning before the shop
opens, men standing out in the yard
on pine planks over the umber mud.
The oil drum, squat, brooding, brimmed
with metal scraps, three-armed crosses,
silver shavings whitened with milky oil,
drill bits bitten off. The light diamonds
last night's rain; inside a buzzer purrs.
The overhead door stammers upward
to reveal the scene of our day.
                              We sit
for lunch on crates before the open door.
Bobeck, the boss's nephew, squats to hug
the overflowing drum, gasps and lifts. Rain
comes down in sheets staining his gun-metal
covert suit. A stake truck sloshes off
as the sun returns through a low sky.
By four the office help has driven off. We
sweep, wash up, punch out, collect outside
for a final smoke. The great door crashes
down at last.
                    In the darkness the scents
of mint, apples, asters. In the darkness
this could be a Carthaginian outpost sent
to guard the waters of the West, those mounds
could be elephants at rest, the acrid half light

the haze of stars striking armor if stars were out.
On the galvanized tin roof the tunes of sudden rain.
The slow light of Friday morning in Michigan,
the one we waited for, shows seven hills
of scraped earth topped with crab grass,
weeds, a black oil drum empty, glistening
at the exact center of the modern world.

from *Michigan Quarterly Review*

Making Love

◊   ◊   ◊

Why make? I used to wonder.
Is it something you have to keep on
making, like beds or dinner, stir it up

or smooth it down? Sex, I understood,
an easy creaking on the upholstered
springs of a man you meet in passing.

You *have* sex, you don't have to make it,
it makes *you*—rise and fall and rise again,
each time, each man, new. But love?

It could be the name of a faraway
city, end of a tired journey you take
with some husband, your bodies chugging

their way up the mountain, glimpsing
the city lights and thinking, If we can
keep it up, we'll make Love by morning.

I guess it was fun for somebody,
my grandmother once said. By then
I was safely married and had earned

the right to ask, there in the kitchen
beside the nodding aunts. Her answer
made me sad. In her time, love meant making

babies, and if I had borne twelve
and buried three, I might see my husband
as a gun shooting off inside me, each bullet

another year gone. But sex wasn't my question.
Love was the ghost whose shape kept
shifting. For us, it did not mean babies,

those plump incarnations the minister
had promised—flesh of our flesh,
our *increase*. Without them, and twenty years

gone, what have we to show
for the planing and hammering, bone
against bone, chisel and wedge,

the tedious sanding of night
into morning—when we rise, stretch,
shake out the years, lean back,

and see what we've made: no ghost,
it's a house. Sunlight through the window
glazing our faces, patina of dust

on our arms. At every axis, mortise
and tenon couple and hold. Doors
swing heavy on their hinges.

from *The Gettysburg Review*

J. D. McCLATCHY

Descartes's Dream

◊   ◊   ◊

He felt a sudden weakness on his right side
And leaned over to his left to walk the streets
But, sensing he made a foolish figure, straightened up
Only to be spun around by a violent wind
And, as he sought shelter in the college chapel,
Rushed by a man in black he thought he'd known.
Who learns to doubt everything can see
The world's painted dropcloth drawn on strings
Past the grimy window of a *train de vie.*
I will my arm to move but the flesh abides.

Clockmaker, coolie, collaborator—
He will depend on nothing, not the servant
Girl with her small breasts, not the duke's
Armies or the thrumming wheel of logic.
In the quadrangle the others all stood upright
Talking with the friend he'd slighted.
Friend? Whom to trust and whom to shun?
Sudden thunder. Fiery sparks are streaming
Through the room. They come from the friend's mouth.
Truth is whatever darkness we choose to ignore.

He opened the book he found on an upper shelf.
Old tags he recognized but couldn't name.
Someone called to him from the quadrangle.
If he wished to find his friend, here was a gift
To give him, he said, and held out a curious melon,
The seeded song of nature, its germs of light.
He wanted to show the book now to the man

But as he turned the pages the words slid
Into tiny portraits, copperplate engravings
Of the servant girl, the duke, his mother, himself.

Bodies, those false witnesses, serve the light,
Which would not shine unless it broke against them.
The weight of the falling planet presses into
His eyelids. Suddenly, both the man and the book
Disappeared. The weight lifted. Reason
Again held the reins of the bolting blood-horse.
How far must we get away from the earth to see it
Properly? How long must we go without knowing
Before we discover that everything leads back
To something as simple and dreadful as the night?

from *Southwest Review*

HEATHER McHUGH

Past All Understanding

◊   ◊   ◊

Gasworks Park, 1996

A woman there was balancing her baby
back-to-back. They held each other's hands,
did tilts and bends and teeter-totters on
each other's inclinations, making
casual covalency into
a human ideogram,
spontaneous Pilobolus—
a spectacle at which
the estimable Kooch
(half Border and half Lab)

began to bark. He wouldn't stop. The child slid off
the woman's back; now they were two
who scowled and stared. You looked,
I started to explain, like one
big oddity to him. (They weren't appeased.) He barks at
crippled people too. (Now they were horrified.) Meanwhile a wind

rose at the kiosk, stapled with yard jobs, sub-clubs, bands somebody
named
for animals. The whole park fluttered up and flailed, and Kooch,
unquenchable,
perceived the higher truth. By now the uproar was enough
to make the bicyclists bypassing (bent beneath their packs),
an assortment of teaching assistants (harried, earnest, hardly earning)—

and even some white-haired full professorships all come to a halt,
in the wake of the wave of their tracks.
What brouhahas! What flaps!
To Kooch's mind, if you
could call it that,
the worst was
yet to come—

for looming overhead, a host of red and yellow kites appeared
intent on swooping even to the cowlicks of the humans—Were
these people blind—the woman in pink, the man in blue, who paused
there
in his purview, stupidly, to shake their heads? He thinks
we're in danger, I tried again
to reason with my fellow-man.
But now the dog

was past all understanding; he was uncontainable. He burst
into a pure fur paroxysm, blaming the sky for all that we
were worth, holding his ground with four feet braced
against an over-turning earth. . . .

from *Denver Quarterly*

Chalk-Circle Compass

◊   ◊   ◊

First comes conscience—
care about the circle,
guilt about the oblong
or the wobble.

Then comes the innocent
to the board to parse the arc,
sketch the wedge,
to breathe onto the slate

as if wholesomeness could set
it free, as one would pat
a bubble from a baby after milk.
A rustic udder,

an orb with fingers,
is a poor example
of geometry. Only
if one were teaching awe

would one approve the hand-drawn
oddball
this arm's-length wooden compass
cannot give to the world.

Only if circumference went feral
or was, originally, a wild thing,
would you try your rough unaided hand
at a ring worth teaching.

But you could draw them both, teach
love for unmatching eyes
on the blackboard—one bearing
personality's squint,

the other seeing so well through history
it never fills with history's litter,
the sterling circle,
the one whose tearless shape

hurts the child enough
to—long after the examination—
stay somewhat ideal
in her, in him, like

just what it is, a ripple.

from *Poetry*

W . S . M E R W I N

The Chinese Mountain Fox

◇   ◇   ◇

Now we can tell that there
must once have been a time
when it was always there
and might at any time

appear out of nowhere
as they were wont to say
and probably to their
age it did look that way

though how are we to say
from the less than certain
evidence of our day
and they referred often

through the centuries when
it may have been a sight
they considered common
so that they mentioned it

as a presence they were
sure everyone had seen
and would think familiar
they alluded even

then until it became
their unquestioned habit
like a part of the name
to that element it

had of complete surprise
of being suddenly
the blaze in widened eyes
that had been turned only

at that moment upon
some place quite near that they
all through their lives had known
and passed by every day

perhaps at the same place
where they themselves had just
been standing that live face
looking as though it must

have been following them
would have appeared with no
warning they could fathom
or ever come to know

though they made studied use
of whatever system
logic calculus ruse
they trusted in their time

to tell them where they might
count on it next and when
if once they figured right
as though it traveled in

a pattern they could track
like the route of some far
light in the zodiac
comet or migrant star

but it was never where
they had thought it would be
and showed the best of their
beliefs successively

to be without substance
shadows they used to cast
old tales and illusions
out of some wishful past

each in turn was consigned
to the role of legend
while yet another kind
of legend had wakened

to play the animal
even while it was there
the unpredictable
still untaken creature

part lightning and part rust
the fiction was passed down
with undiminished trust
while the sightings began

to be unusual
second-hand dubious
unverifiable
turning to ghost stories

all the more easily
since when it had been seen
most times that was only
by someone all alone

and unlike its cousins
of the lowlands captive
all these generations
and kept that way alive

never had it been caught
poisoned or hunted down
by packs of dogs or shot
hung up mounted or worn

never even been seen
twice by the same person
in the place it had been
when they looked there again

and whatever they told
of it as long as they
still spoke of it revealed
always more of the way

they looked upon the light
while it was theirs to see
and what they thought it might
let them glimpse at any

moment than of the life
that they had rarely been
able to catch sight of
in an instant between

now and where it had been
at large before they came
when the mountains were green
before it had a name

from *The Yale Review*

ROBERT MEZEY

Joe Simpson [1919–1996]

◊   ◊   ◊

Joe Simpson was a man I scarcely knew.
I saw him when he came to see his father.
Our talks, if they were talks, were brief and few.
And yet I think I knew the man, or rather,
I knew something about him. From his eyes
A certain light (though uncertain to me)
Seemed to precede him through the world of lies,
Flickering shadows where he could not see
What might await, what writhing shapes of pain,
What narrow passages, where only faith,
That cannot know what it is faithful to,
Can find the right path to the gates of death,
A path he followed, and did not complain,
A path that might lead nowhere, as he knew.

from *The New Yorker*

Artisan and Clerk

◇ ◇ ◇

Like ghosts leaving their bodies those factories
were leaving us. Their black hulks were lying here,
complex and empty—but we heard that they

were in fact still living, elsewhere. Their souls
had flown to a heaven called Brazil and there
had taken new bodies, glorious, in a new world.

The caged and vented fires there, we heard, the power
of the renovated hammering, the titanic outputs,
the inexhaustible eternity of the materials

and the labor of that world were beyond our imagination,
and the way those mills shone beside plunging rivers
fresher and wider than our oceans here,

the way they stood in the shade of primitive trees and eyes.
And we were shaken by a further rumor: of a flaw
in the world, in being itself, and even deeper—

a flaw in salvation. It was said that those ghosts,
even beatified, were eating heaven—that despite
infinity, they would soon consume it all,

have nothing left, and start on their own bodies.
Was this, then, what awaited us? Not likely. We
were condemned. They sat us down with the manual that said,

"If you are seeking work for fifty hours each week,
then seek for one hundred. Forget sleep. Work
at having no work harder than you ever worked at work:

then you will find work faster and when you find it
you will have learned how to work. Remember,
all who seek will find, and so, think what it means

that you are still seeking. Remember, there's work for all,
but unless you try harder than the others
they will get it and there will be none for you.

Take their work and it will teach them to work harder.
You will have what you desire, so think what it means
that you are unemployed and want to die and do not dare."

I remember that when I wrote this manual we were happy.
It was a difficult, long-drawn-out job,
what with the committee, the management, the board,

and even the shareholders demanding to approve each word,
and in total agreement fighting over the drafts,
differences without distinction, hoping to compose

by mindless opposition something perfectly insipid and bold.
Months, years went by, I was paid well
for my work to be erased, and when we could

we huddled together in the depths of the house.
We had and raised our child, we fought and cried,
watched the birds in the garden at the seed

the manual paid for, though they were free in the wild
to take their glory elsewhere
and find what seed they would.

Then it was all over, the warring factions
were satisfied, the self-help manual
for the unemployed was finished and so was I.

And now that, to help me, they put it in my hand,
I have to contemplate the perfection of my work—
no future book can equal its inescapable clarity—

and its uselessness—neither I nor anyone
will ever find work again. Our child, for instance:
when we were employed we trained him at dire expense

with the greatest artists, and he had already created
his famous series of workers, changed into light and money,
circulating through the elongated noplace

of fiber optics. But now he draws graffiti on walls,
dodging the police, for who can afford canvas?
Or he breaks windows, scrapes stones over marble façades,

writes manifestos on stolen fastfood paper napkins,
identifying himself with the subtle, relentless
markings and destructions of the wind and rain,

for no one is going to buy him any other press
and lithographic stone, no bank is going to invite him
to carve the divine history with all

its demonic grotesques on the new cathedral's door.

from *The Yale Review*

The Right Empowerment
of Light

◊   ◊   ◊

In the right empowerment of light, pictures taken
are so well washed I get 4- x 6-inch rectangles
of light's domination.

In a photo of rural Japanese radishes that light finishes
with translucence, vegetables become slender lanterns
destined to appear as specialty of the house, but how to serve
the light, how to slice it; how to bite it, swallow it
without the chest lighting up, ribs becoming frame
for a lamp shade?
In church you chew on His death; you don't sample
His infinity. What is the etiquette?

In the film about the infant emperor
the royal feces was collected in brass
jade and gold
and gave off light
in the kingdom so there was no opposition
to the production of milk by his wet nurse
for his lifetime that gave off light
in the beam of piss that in the sand
formed veins of gold.

I want to say it's radioactive: that last summer,
his sisters in the house first time in years,
I walked into the room rebellion with me
yet my father lit up, they said.

223

There is divine light.
There is also arrogance, the other
radiance.

from *Michigan Quarterly Review*

Enchanted Rock

◊　◊　◊

I could sit all day on this esplanade—
always come back here when my trips are done.

Sit with their nectar, claim it for heart's calm,
make it into phrases all afternoon.

Fountain ledges braided by fluted granite,
comforting hexagons of civic stone.

Harbor like the beginningless and the endless.
Heart's calm like the colossal clouds of June.

Suppose there were steps down into the Hudson,
for sacred bathing, like a Banaras ghat.

Suppose I could have done with all the honey,
hived in a notebook, like a sacred writ.

June would become July, and mere immersion
make everything look sacred in the heat.

Immersion would become the liberation.
Triumph lie in the not phrasing it.

Like student hours, half a life ago,
cloud-watching through my carrel's tinted glass.

There to please the fathers, ravel the texts,
 come up with secrets no one else could guess.

In the book dust, the air-conditioning,
I can admit there was a kind of bliss.

The archives acquired by the Texas billions.
The boyish expectation of success.

But best was time off at Enchanted Rock,
two hours west of Austin, acres huge,

magma massed over the green steaming plain.
I would sit in full lotus on my ledge,

meditate some secret about Spirit,
how it rides it out, age after world age.

Soar with the heat waves and the thunderheads.
Then climb down to a chute at the Rock's edge,

plunge in its torrent, roar, shiver in silence
on the warm granite, by a tamarisk.

All the time in the world to amaze the fathers
by absolute acquittal of each task.

In the meantime, sitting in princely ease,
my thoughts like rifffles, and my flesh like musk,

I had disappeared into a spell of sweetness
about which they would never know to ask.

Now it is the fathers have disappeared.
Enfeebled. Disesteemed. Estranged. Or dead.

Their love, when all is summed, was never grudging,
nor the debt ever adequately paid.

A youth will seem ungrateful, or insouciant,
I shrug it off because he's just a kid.

And was there any secret about Spirit
I could have, even had I tried, betrayed?

Now the fathers are nowhere to be seen.
And so I see them in colossal clouds

tall all summer out over the harbor.
Their blessedness bestrides the esplanade's

serenity the livelong afternoon.
Ebbs and floods with the estuary's tides.

Floats in the limpid spaces between worlds,
undemanding as Epicurus' gods.

Would the clouds look different after immersion?
Back in the endless and the beginningless?

In the meantime I sit and think of the Rock,
that its sweetness was, that its spell took place.

It is like the sun sunk in these fountain ledges
(their film over the granite an abyss).

Now it is a disc under the cloud cover.
Now it is a dazzle I couldn't face.

from *The Yale Review*

Flamingos

◇   ◇   ◇

1

My quarrel with your quorum, Monsignor
Flamingo, is that you scant the rubicund
in favor of a fatal petal
tint. I would rather bask
in riots of the roseate
than measure your footfalls'
holy protocols beside the head-
board of a drowsy demiurge.
I think God snores in rose
leaves of serenity, not in your
clatter of cadaverous vermeils.

2

I find flamingos beautiful Tartuffes
who entice as they distance me.
When they display their billiarding,
adolescent sprawl of knees I
remember the parochial
school girls in pink cashmeres, their rosy
kneecaps polished by novenas.

Flamingos have the silhouettes
of parking meters. They have no epaulettes
and yet seem always in uniform—
little, stilted *caudillos*! They swarm
in unruffled ripples of defiling pink.
They mimic ballerinas and yet stink.
Flamingos are dirty in their purity,
blazon Venezuelas of lewd suavity.
Beneath their transcendent, backbent
legs flamingos are somnolent
and lubricious birds whose stiff tutus
amuse
the spoonbills and anhingas who erect
nests of fish skin to reflect
the imperial smut of the sky.
                    I feel a samba roll
under my eyelids when flamingos stroll
oceanward at sundown and clap their stubs of wings
in gawky, rank, hierophantic posturings.

4

When the Lord God created the flamingos, He
fell into despondency. He knew
that roseate feathers on such skeletons
elicit incredulity. He gloomed
for days, obsessive as a poet who
discovers a covert love affair between
obstreperous syllables and then,
cracking grandeur from the egg of shame,
sets these
diametric desperadoes in a pas de deux.

5

Only in Miami is supreme
loneliness apparent in flamingo dawn.
The squalor of the place is cruelly pink.
There are pink curtains on the lousy shacks.
The impulse to adorn deepens the nakedness.
There, flamingos all the color of a bone
scavenge in vermillion stateliness.
Their pink flocks forage in that loneliness.

from *The Gettysburg Review*

Views of La Leggenda della Vera Croce

◇ ◇ ◇

How will I ever get this in a poem,
When all I have to do is type *AREZZO*
And the name sidles up along a station platform—

The train I'm riding in begins to slow—
And—though I swore I wasn't getting off this time—
I know a train comes every hour or so

To wherever I'm headed—Perugia? Rome?—
And suddenly I'm rushing off the train,
Depositing my bag, crossing the waiting room,

And striding up the Via Monaco again
As if I couldn't see each fresco perfectly,
Couldn't see them, now, against this screen . . .

But in a minute, they'll array themselves in front of me:
Soldiers, horses, placid ladies, kings
All patient, in their places, not spinning crazily

Like the first time I saw them: unearthly beings
Breathing luminous pearl-green instead of air,
Horses and ladies-in-waiting flapping wings

Stolen from the eagle on the soldiers' banner,
Their brocaded sleeves and bridles grazing spinning walls,
Hats twirling, armor flying, coils of hair

Unraveling into whirling manes and tails—
And that was before the winged arm's appearance. . . .
When the *Times* ran an article about Stendhal's

Famous nervous breakdown from the art in Florence,
Half a dozen friends sent it to me.
I suppose these tales of mine require forbearance.

Not that I had a breakdown, though I was dizzy,
Closed my eyes, leaned against a wall
And told myself that there was time to see

Each panel—one by one—down to each detail,
Hats, sleeves, daggers, saddles, bits of lace;
I studied every panel: *Adam's Burial,*

St. Helena's Discovery of the Cross,
Solomon Meeting Sheba, The Annunciation,
The Dream of Constantine, The Torture of Judas,

Whose other name I learned from a machine
Which, with the help of a hundred lire coin,
Supplies a telephone with information;

I did it for a laugh; I chose Italian.
I thought I heard *The Torture of the Jew*
And was so stunned I played the thing again

(My Italian was, after all, fairly new
And the woman on the tape spoke very quickly
But she did say *The Torture of the Jew*—

In Italian it's *ebreo*—quite matter-of-factly)
The Torture of the Jew Who Wouldn't Reveal
The Location of the True Cross—I got it exactly—

Put in a lot of coins to catch each syllable
(I also heard the English, which said Judas),
All the while not looking at the rope, the well;

Instead, I chose a saintly woman's dress,
An angel's finger pointing to a dream,
A single riveting, incongruous face—

What was I supposed to do? They were sublime.
The Inquisition wasn't exactly news
And, while I did keep my eyes off that one frame,

I wasn't about to give up on those frescoes.
In fact, I saw them again, a short while after
And soon after that—in those heady days

Trains cost almost nothing and a drifter
Could easily cover quite a bit of Italy,
Though I tended to stay in Tuscany. The light was softer,

And—probably not coincidentally—
It had a higher density than any other place
Of things that could dazzle inexhaustibly

And I was insatiable, avaricious
For what—even asleep—a person can't see
From a slim back bedroom in a semi-detached house

Like every other house in its vicinity
On a site whose inhabitants had been wiped out
To make room for spillover, like my family,

From the very continent I would have dreamed about
If I'd had even an inkling of the mastery
Of what its subtlest inhabitants had wrought

When they weren't doing away with people like me . . .
See how Solomon, listening, leans his head?
How the tired horseman leans against a tree—

How the guard beside the emperor's makeshift bed
Can't resist the sorcery of sleep—
So only we can catch the angel's finger pointed

At the dreamer's head, the horse's sudden leap
As if straight from that vision, to the battle scene:
Christianity's triumph over Europe . . .

I love the wing, the arm, the dreaming Constantine,
The moonlight casting shadows on the tent—
It *is* moonlight—though there is no moon—

Pale, as always, silvery and slant;
It's coming from the angel's pointing arm
Which I didn't even notice that first moment—

All I saw was undiluted dream—
I didn't really care what it was for—
Beside, we fared no better under pagan Rome

Which hadn't stopped me from going there—
I might not even have thought about Jerusalem,
If I hadn't found myself staring straight at her.

I was wandering lazily around the Forum
Without even a guidebook or a map.
I didn't care which stones were the gymnasium,

Which pillars hunched together needing propping up
Paid tribute to which boastful, scheming god,
Amazing, I suppose, that all that stuff could keep—

The advantage of stone, I guess, over mud and wood—
But the things I like best are always beautiful—
I don't admire antiquities as I should—

I lack the imagination for them. Still,
In my own haphazard way, I was thorough;
I did cover everything, though I'd had my fill;

Walked through every arch, every portico,
And—there—in the middle of the Roman Forum
Was my own first *menorah,* stolen years ago

My altar, carved with rams' horns on its rim—
(If you want to find them, they're in the Arch of Titus,
On your right, as you face the Colosseum;

Splendid reliefs the *Blue Guide* says;
It's the only arch acknowledged with a star)
Soldiers were parading them, victorious,

Transporting them—if only I knew where—
What was I doing at these celebrations,
When I'd fasted over this, year after year,

Chanting the entire book of *Lamentations*
In candlelight, sitting on the floor?
How she's become as a widow, that was great among nations. . . .

The torture of the Jew couldn't compare.
After all, wasn't it a work of fiction?
This was actual footage from a war,

Which had always been—forgive me—an abstraction,
Despite—or because of?—all the people killed
Trying to save the Temple from destruction,

The few survivors forced to watch as every field
Around Jerusalem was plowed with salt,
Then brought to Rome in chains, for all I knew to build

This very chronicle of their defeat.
Still, if you take the long view, here I am
And Titus isn't anywhere in sight.

Besides, I'd hate to sacrifice a ram—
Or whatever's required—bullock, turtledove—
I much prefer the chance to chant a psalm

When I need a quick, relatively foolproof, salve
Or have managed to entangle myself yet again
In a muddle only God would ever forgive

(Like this breeziness about the Temple's destruction,
This complete inability to feel its loss,
Not to mention my ridiculous and total passion

For Piero's *Legend of the True Cross,*
My worry that I've never loved Jerusalem so well
As when it looks just like Arezzo in his frescoes)

It's not a matter of faith—though it should be—
But the chance to infiltrate with my own voice
All that unadulterated majesty;

Don't be too shocked, I'm often blasphemous;
It's a deal I have with God; at least I pray.
Though He may have a plan—I'm not impervious—

In which I'm expected to wake up one day,
Go to synagogue, recite the psalms
And convince myself with every word I say.

Beggars can't be choosers; these are godless times;
Let Him hold on to His illusions.
Besides, maybe I do have a few qualms

About my persistent heretical allusions
To Someone who is—after all—a Deity . . .
You'll find I'm a jumble of confusions.

Besides, I'm not sure God much cares for piety—
My guess is—since David was His favorite—
That He's partial to passion, spontaneity

And likes a little genuine regret.
True, David lost his ill-begotten child—
But what did the pious ever get?

Unless you buy that dictum in the Talmud
That the reward for the commandment is the commandment,
In which case, nothing's ever withheld,

But that may not be what the rabbis meant.
And who am I, at the end of a mangled century,
To talk about God, reward and punishment?

Especially from this vantage point, in Italy,
And that's where we are, gaping, in Arezzo—
Though there are lots of places we could be:

Florence, Santa Maria Novella, the piazza
Where they rounded up the Jews to ship them east . . .
Or reading some *well-known facts* about matzah

In a just-published newspaper in Bucharest
(How it must contain the blood of Christian children)
Or even at a swim meet, as Europe's finest

Actually do a synchronized routine
About the Nazis and the Jews and win the cup.
Why not Ostia Antica, in the ruin

Of the oldest known synagogue in Europe?
Go yourself, take the Rome Metro, Linea B;
Otherwise, you'll think I'm making this up.

They found it building a road in 1960.
At first, it looks like any Roman basilica:
Columns with ornate capitals, a stairway

And then you notice bits of Judaica
On some of the columns—*lulav, etrog, shofar*
And, after a while, looking down, the swastika

Patterned in the black-and-white mosaic floor—
I know, I know, it was an obvious design—
Bold, easy to lay out—you see it everywhere—

But to me, it's a harrowing premonition:
We should never have set foot on such a continent;
How could we have failed to see this omen,

Which, even in retrospect, will not look innocent
Of what it would inevitably mean?
As if no Jewish building on the continent—

Not even under layers of earth—escaped that sign,
But, still, it's third century (let's call it C.E.
Since my Lord is, after all, an older one)

And there—carved in the marble, for all to see:
Are a few of my most beloved eccentricities:
The *shofar,* with its desperate cacophony

And the *etrog* and *lulav*—pure frivolities
Of gathered citron, willow, myrtle, palm
Shaken in the air to jumbled melodies

Of a congregation belting out a psalm,
Then circling the room chanting hosanna.
Call it piety. Call it delirium—

Citron, willow, myrtle, palm, hosanna—
No one's even certain what they mean—
Unless it's sheer loveliness, sheer stamina—

Some say the citron's a heart, the palm branch, spine,
The willow leaf's two lips, the myrtle, eye
(Does every group of plants concoct a human?)

But this came after the commandment—some rabbi,
Improvising, finding similarities,
But I say God devised it purely whimsically—

(*And ye shall take you . . . the fruit of goodly trees,
Branches of palm trees, and the boughs of thick
Trees and willows of the brook . . .*), merely to tease

The solemn air in which they were to frolic . . .
Maybe God prefers synagogues as I do:
Dismantled, as in Ostia, bucolic,

A few columns and mosaics in a meadow,
The grass and weeds so high you think you're lost.
He can slip out, that way, incommunicado;

One day in seven isn't enough rest.
Not that I claim to understand His ways;
I'd fail, if He put me to a test

Of anything but willingness to praise . . .
But still, I would think the UJA
Or World Jewish Congress would be able to raise

Enough funds to pave a little pathway
From the rest of Ostia Antica to the synagogue . . .
For older people, for instance, it's a long way

(Since, as usual, the local Roman demagogue
Banned synagogues within the city wall)
And some of them might be cheered to see an *etrog,*

A *lulav,* a *shofar* on an ancient capital,
The way, when I'm standing on the *bimah,*
Chanting ancient columns from a scroll

And come to, say, *they called the place Be'er Sheva
And so we call it to this very day*—
I feel a kind of wild reverse amnesia—

Having forgotten—and suddenly remembered—all eternity
Proof, beneath my narrow silver pointer
That there will be no end to this very day. . . .

But I'm forgetting the swastikas on the floor,
The distance from town, the torture of the Jew,
The round-up in Florence, the Judean war,

Who Italy's allies were in World War II
Before their final-hour about-face,
How—if you make your way to Urbino,

To enter the double turrets of the palace
That looks like something Piero once dreamed up
To house his enigmatic masterpiece

(*The Flagellation*—the reason for your trip),
You will also have to forget the Paolo Uccello.
Or walk right by it. Don't even stop.

Don't let the helpful guide attempt to show
The beauty of its composition, frame by frame,
How the tiny golden circle that appears to glow

Between the stately woman's finger and thumb
Is the sacred host—stolen from the altar—
Purchased by a Jew for a hefty sum—

How the red stream, in the next frame, on the floor
Is blood from the host burning in his fireplace
As soldiers with spears and axes throng his door.

One child sobs, one grabs his mother's dress;
The blood has seeped outside, through stone and mortar
And into the next frame's version of the stateliness

Of a clerical procession to the altar:
Incense. Psalter. Cross. *The Host Returned.*
Next, the woman, out in a field somewhere,

Is met by an angel and what? forgiven? warned?
Before the soldiers hang her from a tree . . .
Then the Jew, with wife and children, is burned;

The flames near one child's head, the other's knee
(All four are tied are together to the stake).
But we don't see the Christian woman die;

In the final frame she's on a catafalque,
A pair of devils grabbing at her feet
For what the angels, at her head, will not forsake

Without at least putting up a fight.
(My money's on the angels, but it's close.)
The guide calls it Uccello's greatest insight

To leave us with something so ambiguous—
A spiritual struggle . . . iniquity.
You see, I didn't heed my own advice;

I actually asked the guide to tell the story—
And a crowd gathered round to listen in.
No one blinked an eyelash but me . . .

Perhaps they didn't notice the children
Burning, in that fifth frame, at the stake . . .
It is, after all, a night-time scene;

The Jew is wearing red, the children, black.
Besides, in Europe, burning Jewish childen
Aren't all that difficult to overlook,

What with the complex struggle over sin
And so much never-ending beauty—
And even I, who see them, still take in

The two Pieros, the Raphael, the ideal city
Which unreal Urbino still resembles. . . .
Is there anything more despicable than ambiguity?

How could I not have left the palace in shambles?
Or, at least, burned the painting publicly?
I'm not interested in symbols

With two breathing boys right in front of me
Burning with their parents on a palace wall
For anyone who comes along to see

Or rather not see—since they're invisible
To all but specially trained eyes—
Tie a rope around me. Throw me in a well—

I'm sick of this unnatural disguise.
Sick of turning away. Sick of everything—
I need—as in Arezzo—to close my eyes—

To stop these flames and likenesses from spinning
From the painted to the identical real landscape
But it's worse with my eyes closed; now they're careening

Around my tight-shut eyelids' burning map—
That red you get when you shut your eyes in sunlight
Consuming the entire extent of Europe—

A continent notoriously profligate
Of knees, heads, fingers, elbows, thighs.
Wasn't *this* Uccello's greatest insight:

That if you gradually habituate the eyes
They will be capable of watching anything?
I wonder if this came to God as a surprise.

Could He actually have known about this failing
And still gone ahead with our creation?
You can't, after all, have everything;

We're pretty good at visual representation,
Not to mention all those people who could sing
And care for sheep while arguing with a vision . . .

He's certainly done His share of watching
And nonetheless managed to survive.
Unless He hasn't. But I'm not touching

That one. Besides, when you work out how to live
Your one puny life on this unnerving earth,
It's so much more appealing to believe

In some strategic artistry, some worth,
As if bitterness were a fleeting misconception.
I do have a fondness for the truth,

But am willing to make, in this case, an exception,
Which has been, more or less, my people's way.
We've learned to be remarkable at self-deception

What with the Messiah's long delay . . .
Just look at the Jew in the fresco in Arezzo,
Why have I avoided him until today?

Clearly he's faking it—the first Marrano—
(According to the legend he's accepting Jesus)
That's not how rapture looks to Piero—

The over-the-top bliss is preposterous.
The Jew was probably desperate to get dry . . .
He hasn't got a clue about the location of the cross;

He can't even manage his own inventory.
Where's his holy ark? his candelabrum?
Why are these bits of ash dredging the sky?

Where's his citron, willow, myrtle, palm?
What's that splinter in his upturned eye?

from *Western Humanities Review*

Ode to Meaning

◇　◇　◇

Dire one and desired one,
Savior, sentencer—

In an old allegory you would carry
A chained alphabet of tokens:

Ankh Badge Cross.
Dragon,
Engraved figure guarding a hallowed intaglio,
Jasper kinema of legendary Mind,
Naked omphalos pierced
By quills of rhyme or sense, torah-like: unborn
Vein of will, xenophile
Yearning out of Zero.

Untrusting I court you. Wavering
I seek your face, I read
That Crusoe's knife
Reeked of you, that to defile you
The soldier makes the rabbi spit on the torah.
"I'll drown my book" says Shakespeare.

Drowned walker, revenant.
After my mother fell on her head, she became
More than ever your sworn enemy. She spoke
Sometimes like a poet or critic of forty years later.
Or she spoke of the world as Thersites spoke of the heroes,
"I think they have swallowed one another. I
Would laugh at that miracle."

You also in the laughter, warrior angel:
Your helmet the zodiac, rocket-plumed
Your spear the beggar's finger pointing to the mouth
Your heel planted on the serpent Formulation
Your face a vapor, the wreath of cigarette smoke crowning
Bogart as he winces through it.

Torsion, a cleavage
Stirring even in the arctic ice,
Even at the dark ocean floor, even
In the cellular flesh of a stone.

Gas. Gossamer. My poker friends
Question your presence
In a poem by me, passing the magazine
One to another.

Not the stone and not the words, you
Like a veil over Arthur's headstone,
The passage from Proverbs he chose
While he was too ill to teach
And still well enough to read, *I was*
Beside the master craftsman
Delighting him day after day, ever
At play in his presence—you

A soothing veil of distraction playing over
Dying Arthur playing in the hospital,
Thumbing the Bible, fuzzy from medication,
Ever courting your presence.
And you the prognosis,
You in the cough.

Gesturer, when is your spur, your cloud?
You in the airport rituals of greeting and parting.
Indicter, who is your claimant?
Bell at the gate. Spiderweb iron bridge.
Cloak, video, aroma, rue, what is your
Elected silence, where was your seed?

What is Imagination
But your lost child born to give birth to you?

Dire one. Desired one.
Savior, sentencer—

Absence,
Or presence ever at play:
Let those scorn you who never
Starved in your dearth. If I
Dare to disparage
Your harp of shadows I taste
Wormwood and motor oil, I pour
Ashes on my head. You are the wound. You
Be the medicine.

from *The Threepenny Review*

The Closing, the Ecstasy

◊   ◊   ◊

A last considerable rift runs between us.
This might close it.
In a dim warm room
I'd sit in my chair, you'd stand precisely
Six feet away, our eyes would meet
(Granting we've shared the remainder that matters),
You'd shuck your clothes to the ultimate thread
And wait in the narrow bar of sun
That pierces the bullseye window above you,
Firing the white incalculable change—
Racking the slender wedge of your torso
Till truth leaks from it, then smokes, then streams.

First, glare and dark, an assorted turbulence—
Every notch of the visible spectrum,
The hot unfolding of new prime colors—
Boils out from the boundary line
Of where you end and, pouring toward me,
Frees my dubious eyes to see you
Shift through further unforeseen spectra
In headlong metamorphoses
(Every order of bristlecone pine
And Joshua tree, the endless forms
Of usable water and potent creature,
Chiefly the higher animals): becoming
In sequence an unbridled horse,
A famished leopard, the brute Cape buffalo,
Predators, raptors, lone storks and cranes,
Scores of other huge existences—

Each an aspect of both your self
And the single pulse of eager blood
Which beats at the crux of every life
That's drawn and held my eyes and care.
Then, in reach of my arm, the black-maned lion
Rears in a locked intent to spring.

★

Though each shape nods to mark my presence,
Each offers speedy death or blindness
Till I concede my fear, astonished
Thanks and trim expectant glee
At the promise I'm all but sure I read
In the fierce unfolding of your hid nature
My luck accrued through patient watch
To witness this sequestered warning
In quiet domestic space as common
As kitchen doors or table lamps
A luck from which I fail to run.
So while the triggering light withdraws,
You sink again to human form.
Far your most imposing phase.

The sight suffices; the rift grinds shut.
Yet one final feasible act—
None watching but we in this safe room
In brown still air—might seal the gap
Beyond a chance of widening
If you'll persist in the dare you've launched.

Start at the crown of your tall head
And—downward pointing with a dry forefinger
From brow to eyes to nipples, navel,
Your intricate tripartite groin—
Teach me the secret name of each part
In whatever language (Mandarin, Macedonian,
Tlingit) serves to chart the phenomena,
Concealed coordinates and heights,
Of nothing finer than a tended body

Near apogee: trusty guidance
Is what I've lacked. Adroit as a mellow
Turkish masseur, I know the uses
Of every cell.
                    And that topography suffices,
A grid for stringing memory,
Unless I choose the sizable risk
Of moving toward you or you toward me.
The mildest touch from these strong hands,
That held off death, could trace the path
You've named down your whole tender length:
Awarding more than negligible pleasure,
A canny homely durable ecstasy
If I can also bring your mind in this same hand.
That sober progress may convince
Your skin to flourish. In moments, minutes,
Hours, decades, shafts and vanes
May sprout and complicate and strengthen
Down your arms, every grade
Of color known in jungle birds,
Till—at the scary edge of burning—
You're more than rigged to take free flight
On wings sufficient to bear a ship
Or stay as the messenger I've persuaded
And you've agreed to be, here on.

We welcome each. This will not recur
Unless both our tenacious wills
Or the thrust of whatever eye may watch
From however high in the pitch of blue
Demand again this shared hazard
So gorgeous, profligate, selfless, new—
Not elsewhere known on Earth or under.

from *Poetry*

March

◇   ◇   ◇

Seeing the March rain flood a field
Then runnel from sight, as the wind
Kicks up a bare-limbed fury of trees
And a single crow flies north-northeast
Into gray distances from which
One bruised cloud goes driven grimly
After another so the whole sky
Blunders in a stampede of shapes
So changeable they disprove shape,
And then the rain again, in which
The clouds come down but differently
This time, driven like nails blunted
And lost with hitting the ground
Till how many will it take
To fill the field then disappear,
As what we call a change in season
Blusters, or storms, or goes dead still
With us left standing underneath
To wonder or ignore such change
From overhead to sometimes underfoot
And going on regardless where we go,
Who we were, what we ever said or did.

from *Connecticut Review*

Four Corners, Vermont

◇   ◇   ◇

October sun, blue sky
burning the fields sienna,
even the governor upstate
raking a lawn, his kingdom
of this world. That afternoon
on Main Street, at the four
corners, the cop was trying
to push a small bat with
the butt of his pistol from
the window-box by the door
of the Putnam Hotel, an
unused window-box
where the bat, mistaken, caught
by daylight, had fluttered down
like a fallen leaf. Three
townsmen, not doing much
but holding their own, keeping
up on the news, kept watch.
The policeman laughed, tucking
his pistol back in its
holster. The teenage bellhop
so far with nothing to do
has pitched the bat out now.
It quavers to the walk
by the rail of the hotel stairs.
The bellhop and a man
wearing a jack shirt, worn
and too small for his arms,
stomp at it, grinding their heels

between the palings. The boy
runs back inside. It is
Norman Rockwell-ish, this
tableau the passers-by
are watching. Soon the boy
is back and kneeling with
a fork. The leaves have fallen
but the day is warm; even
the governor tidies his lawn.
The boy will jab at the black
remnant, the tines will ring
out, hitting the pavement
again; again. Everyone
in the land must know his place,
any beast
of the field his lair, his own.

from *The New Republic*

The Coat

◇   ◇   ◇

Not night now, not the night's
one chilling vocable
of sharp air, not the cross
parental babble of it
burning your infant ear,
not anything you say
in answer, no good, not fair,
the fiercest syllables
that turn, as soon as spoken,
into steam that lifts away,

no, none of these is the
beloved in the story.
There's no beloved, none,
except the coat you wear,
the heavy coat you've clung
so long, so hard to that
the only warmth you sense
now is the warmth that seeks
an arctic bitterness
to hoard itself against.

Here you are easiest
where only phantom shapes
across the honeyed vagueness
of the window pass—
easiest where no lock
is turned, no door is opened,
no one at all to find

in your greeting that the coat
that kept you warm outside
has brought the cold in with it.

from *Ploughshares*

ROBERT B. SHAW

A Geode

◇   ◇   ◇

What started out a glob of molten mud
hawked up by some Brazilian volcano
back in the Pleistocene is now a rock
of unremarkable appearance, brown
as ordinary mud and baseball-size.
Picking it up produces the surprise:
besides a pleasant heftiness, a sound
of sloshing can be noticed. Vapors caught
within its cooling crust were liquified,
and linger still: a million-year-old vintage.
Although one might recall the once ubiquitous
snowstorm-in-a-glass-globe paperweights,
this offers us no view inside to gauge
the wild weather a shake or two incites.
Turbulence masked by hard opacity . . .
If we could, which would we rather see?—
age-old distillate, infant tears of the earth,
or gem-like crystal of the inner walls
harboring them like some fair reliquary?
To see the one we'd have to spill the other.
Better to keep it homely and intact,
a witness to the worth of hiddenness,
which, in regard to our own kind, we call
reticence, and in terms of higher things,
mystery. Let the elixir drench unseen
the facets that enshrine it, world without end.

from *The Hudson Review*

Ambiguity's Wedding

◇   ◇   ◇

after E. D.

Bride of Awe, all that's left for us
Are vestiges of a feast table,
Levitating champagne glasses
In the hands of the erased millions.

Mr. So and So, the bridegroom
Of absent looks, lost looks,
The pale reporter from the awful doors
Before identity was leased

At night's delicious close,
A few denizens of insignificance about,
The spider at his trade,
The print of his vermilion foot.

A faded boy in sallow clothes
Badly smudged, his shadow on the wall
Still visible, a wintry shadow
Quieter than sleep.

Soul, take thy risk,
There where your words and thoughts
Come to a stop,
Abbreviate me thus, in marriage.

from *Field*

MARK STRAND

The View

◇　◇　◇

For Derek Walcott

This is the place. The chairs are white. The table shines.
The person sitting there stares at the waxen glow.
The wind moves the air around, repeatedly,
As if to clear a space. "A space for me," he thinks.
He's always been drawn to the weather of leavetaking,
Arranging itself so that grief—even the most intimate—
Might be read from a distance. A long shelf of cloud
Hangs above the open sea with the sun, the sun
Of no distinction, sinking behind it—a mild version
Of the story that is told just once if true, and always too late.
The waitress brings his drink, which he holds
Against the waning light, but just for a moment.
Its red reflection tints his shirt. Slowly the sky becomes darker,
The wind relents, the view sublimes. The violet sweep of it
Seems, in this effortless nightfall, more than a reason
For being there, for seeing it, seems itself a kind
Of happiness, as if that plain fact were enough and would last.

from *The London Review of Books*

Dream On

◇   ◇   ◇

Some people go their whole lives
without ever writing a single poem.
Extraordinary people who don't hesitate
to cut somebody's heart or skull open.
They go to baseball games with the greatest of ease
and play a few rounds of golf as if it were nothing.
These same people stroll into a church
as if that were a natural part of life.
Investing money is second nature to them.
They contribute to political campaigns
that have absolutely no poetry in them
and promise none for the future.
They sit around the dinner table at night
and pretend as though nothing is missing.
Their children get caught shoplifting at the mall
and no one admits that it is poetry they are missing.
The family dog howls all night,
lonely and starving for more poetry in his life.
Why is it so difficult for them to see
that, without poetry, their lives are effluvial.
Sure, they have their banquets, their celebrations,
croquet, fox hunts, their seashores and sunsets,
their cocktails on the balcony, dog races,
and all that kissing and hugging, and don't
forget the good deeds, the charity work,
nursing the baby squirrels all through the night,
filling the birdfeeders all winter,
helping the stranger change her tire.
Still, there's that disagreeable exhalation

from decaying matter, subtle but ever present.
They walk around erect like champions.
They are smooth-spoken, urbane and witty.
When alone, rare occasion, they stare
into the mirror for hours, bewildered.
There was something they meant to say, but didn't:
"And if we put the statue of the rhinoceros
next to the tweezers, and walk around the room three
times,
learn to yodel, shave our heads, call
our ancestors back from the dead—"
poetrywise it's still a bust, bankrupt.
You haven't scribbled a syllable of it.
You're a nowhere man misfiring
the very essence of your life, flustering
nothing from nothing and back again.
The hereafter may not last all that long.
Radiant childhood sweetheart,
secret code of everlasting joy and sorrow,
fanciful pen strokes beneath the eyelids:
all day, all night meditation, knot of hope,
kernel of desire, pure ordinariness of life,
seeking, through poetry, a benediction
or a bed to lie down on, to connect, reveal,
explore, to imbue meaning on the day's extravagant labor.
And yet it's cruel to expect too much.
It's a rare species of bird
that refuses to be categorized.
Its song is barely audible.
It is like a dragonfly in a dream—
here, then there, then here again,
low-flying amber-wing darting upward
and then out of sight.
And the dream has a pain in its heart
the wonders of which are manifold,
or so the story is told.

from *American Poetry Review*

A Calm November.
Sunday in the Fields.

◇   ◇   ◇

The throats of the field are flushed with fall.
Doves and thrushes croon and blush

with pleasure in the diminishing light.
A woman, half-hidden in the wanton leaves

of a book that has strayed from the narrow
margins of its kind, grazes in the reedy marshes

of its sunlit text. An enormous number of canaries
arises, blooming from the radiant script

and quavers on twigs and windowsills.
This flocculent conflagration soon disappears,

the last of the day tucked under its wings.
The moon tapers up in a brilliant column

to illuminate the woman as she rises
from the recently darkened passages. She hums

a low tone and recalls some lines from the Book of Descent:
Rejoice in the form of the pendant head.

The substance of one's autumnal romances
flares in the shadow of large, distant hands.

from *Denver Quarterly*

DEREK WALCOTT

Signs

◇   ◇   ◇

—for Adam Zagajewski

I.

Europe completed its silhouette in the nineteenth century
with steaming train-stations, gas-lamps, encyclopedias,
the expanding waists of empires, the grocer's inventory
of the novel, its structure as a beehive with ideas,
fiction that echoed city-blocks of long paragraphs
with parenthetical doorways, with crowds on the margin
waiting to cross, and slate doves on ledges gurgled epigraphs
for the next chapter where mediaeval cobbles begin
the labyrinth of a contorted plot; leisurely heresies
over coffee in steamed cafes, too chilly outdoors,
opposite the gilt doors of the opera, two green bronze horses
guarding a locked square like bookends, the odours
of a decaying century drift from autumnal gardens
with the smell of old books chained in the National Library.
Cross a small bridge into our time, and the past hardens
into statues of gesturing generals, a magnified cemetery
devoted to the great dead, the linden perspective hazes
into a mist that goes with the clopping horses
of carriages, of a range that was Dickens's and Balzac's
until the grand vision narrows back into ghostly houses
where a plume of smoke rises from distant chimney stacks.

II.

Far from streets seething like novels with their century's sorrow
of charcoal sketches by Kollwitz, the emigre's pain
in feeling his language translated, the synthetic aura
of an alien syntax, an altered construction that will drain
the specific of detail, of damp: creaks of sunlight
on a window-ledge, under a barn door in the hay country
of boyhood, the linen of cafes in an academic light,
in short the fiction of Europe that turns into theatre
over this dry place where there are no ruins only an echo
of what you have read. It is only much later
they will become real: canals, churches, willows, filthy snow.
This is the envy we finally commit, this happens
to us readers, distant devourers, that its pages whiten
our minds like pavements, or fields where a pen's
tracks mark the snow. We become one of those, then,
who convert the scarves of cirrus at dusk to a diva's
adieu from an opera balcony, ceilings of cherubs, cornucopias
disgorging stone bounty, the setting for a believer's
conviction in healing music; then huge clouds pass,
enormous cumuli rumble in trucks like barrels of news-
print and the faith of redemptive art begins to leave us
as we turn back the old engravings, the etched views
that are smudged with terror in dark cobbles and eaves.

III.

The cobbled streets keep to themselves, their gables leaning
to whisper to one another, the walls are scraped of signs
condemning the star of David; there are no grey faces screening
themselves (like the moon drawing a cloud's thin curtains
at the tramp of jackboots, or the shattered store-glass that rains
diamonds on the pavement). Now there is a punishing silence
since they took the old tenants away. There are sins
whose truth no streets dare pronounce, much less the meaning
of why they occurred, then they are various repetitions
of the same sins, blood washed from cobbles, "the cleaning."
And now there is the romance, the movie-setting

for History's enormous soap-opera, the old houses,
the cobbles, the shattered shops, the deliberate forgetting
that changes into drama, even Buchenwald and Auschwitz.
The braille of wet cobbled alleys, the street lamps punctuating
some boulevard's interminable sentence, autumn leaves
blown past the closed opera-house, the soot-eyed crowd waiting
in a bread-line, or near a train line, the camera grieves
for us all now, it moves with the habit of conscience
around the theatrical corners of the old town,
replastering the right paraphernalia, swastikas, signs
of the coming cleansing, until the ancient tongue
that forbade graven images, seems, at last, to make sense.

IV.

That cloud was Europe, dissolving past the thorn branches
of the lignum vitae, the tree of life, but a thunderhead remains
over these islands in crests of arrested avalanches
like a blizzard on a screen in the snow-speckled campaigns,
the same old news just changing its borders and policies,
beyond which wolves founder with red berries for eyes,
and their unheard howling trails off in wisps of smoke
like the frozen smoke over bridges. The barge of Poland
is an agony floating downstream with remote, magisterial
scansion, St. Petersburg's minarets a cloud. Then clouds
are forgotten like battles. Like snow in spring. Also evil.
All that seems so marmoreal is only a veil;
play Timon then, and curse all endeavour as vile,
and the combers will continue to crest, to no avail.
Your shadow stays with you startling the quick crabs
that stiffen until you pass. That cloud means spring
to the Babylonian willows of Amsterdam budding again
like crowds in Pissarro along a wet boulevard's branches,
and the drizzle that sweeps its small wires enshrouds
Notre Dame. In the distance the word Cracow
sounds like artillery; then Serbia. Then snow that clouds
walls riddled with bullet-holes, that like cotton-wool, close.

from *Conjuctions*

ROSANNA WARREN

"Departure"

◇   ◇   ◇

Variations on Max Beckmann and Guido Guinizelli

"I can only speak to people who—"

Unspeaking, unspoken, the full-breasted woman
tied to a dead man upside down

stands center stage with a lamp in her hand,
sheds kerosene glow on the marching band.

That's Cupid, the dark dwarf who tightens her rope;
this is art, this is love, that's the classical shape

of proscenium arch. This is Germany, May '32.
"—can only speak to people who

already carry, consciously or unconsciously, within them—"

You want to buy that center panel, Lilly, but
you can't have that alone

There will always be, on one side, a man bound to a column
with both hands chopped off; there will always be
a still life with hand grenade grapes and a woman kneeling
before an executioner who swings a bag of iron fish

Love always shelters in the gentle heart

And you will always—won't you?—find yourself groping
in a dark stairwell ill-lit by that feeble, dangerous lamp
while you drag along, strapped to you, the corpse of all your errors,
and the drum throbs and shudders like a titanic heart

Love's fire is kindled in the gentle heart
as light kindles in a precious gem

And there's another romance, in which the woman
and man are strapped to each other alive, but head to feet, on a giant fish
and each holds in hand the ritual mask of the other
as they hurtle downwards towards a brilliant, engulfing ocean

as the star beam strikes the water
but the sky keeps the star and all its fire

which is generally known as love. No, you can't
buy the central panel alone, with the king and queen
joyous and powerful in their open boat, the baby bespeaking freedom
and the net full of fish flashing in blessed abundance

"—who already carry, consciously or unconsciously, within them
a similar metaphysical code."

because the oarsman is blindfolded
because the crowned fisherman has his back to us
because that open boat
has not set sail
in our space or in our time
nor will it, while we are alive.

from *The New Republic*

From *Home and Away*

◇   ◇   ◇

I

How different any house looks from outside
and from within. I used to circle mansions
finding out, through guessing and good luck,
what acts of kindness kept the home fires warm
and what was done in dens. Now all unpacked
I feel the leaping flame below the floor,
my dreams consist of madly smoking chimneys
turning into smoking guns. All you
who covet life behind closed doors, look out
for changing views: safe homes can be deceiving
and dusty corners, formerly the mark
of depths unsounded, or of time well spent,
become the cold, gray, fuzzy, woolly monsters
that fill the head before an idea forms.

II

I walked among the gorgeous unturned stones
with rising hopes, a pickax and a plan:
the answers I scraped free would be the bricks
I'd use to build a green and spacious home,
and in this place of knowledge I would glue
wild eyes to lush walls, grateful for the gleams
my mystery, my spur had sent my way.
What I could not predict was that there comes
a time when there are no more stones to scrape

the mossy truth from, that a house composed
of all the answers that I schemed so hard
to get could get so gray. My cellmate and
my stone, who could have known that there was such
a thing as knowing someone else too well?

III

Acting in accordance with your wishes,
let us try a quick experiment:
buy a house and set it down on firm soil
and, completing all the steps required,
fill it to the brim with embryo yous.
When little creatures hang from chandeliers
and steal your treasured hours, ask yourself
the reason for the choice: was it to fill
the wanting world with more endangered lives
like yours? Was it to cauterize old wounds?
Was it to see yourself forever blended
with a beloved other? If the first,
sheer hubris; if the second, lots of luck;
if the third, when water blends with oil.

IV

The oldest story in the book has just
revealed another chapter. There are no
competitors with bedroom eyes who send
encoded notes; no juvenile excuses;
no trio of bored, beautiful delinquents
who flutter past on bicycles, intent
on cigarettes and scandal. In their place
there is a pyramid without a base
on either side of which, the rival lives
of rugged climber, deity of parks
and doomed, descending homeowner, are stationed.
Sometimes they meet in a productive summit
but even then, they cannot miss the sight
of skating eros, red-faced at the bottom.

V

Something, love, is singing in the shower
but it is not me; all the spouts are on
but rather than warm water, I suspect
a flood of doubts comes crashing on my brain.
Wise fools have always said that when you woo,
a breathing world surrounds you; what they save
for later revelations on the stairwell
is how you stand there, listening for clues
leading to the arrest of household objects.
Accessories I use to tame my hair
remind me of the hairpin turns we used
to skirt; cigar butts, fuming in an ashtray,
form just a tiny portion of the troops
gathering daily in this screaming house.

VI

Provocateurs and spies have been among us,
sensitive eyes who knew what we were up to
when we exhaled tornadoes; and when they were
dead to the world or elsewhere, there were portents:
great gusts of rain approved our resolutions,
sunshine meant watch and wait. But in this big house
nobody seems to notice; I could drop hints,
swallow a capsule or a morning toad,
or I could claw the walls until the day came
and there would still be no one there to see it,
no way of telling my heart was not in it
except the banner of decisive action,
the calling of the sharp, impatient helper
that rattles in the cupboard, set on escape.

VII

Before I stab, a moment of polemic:
little fish, aspiring to be big ones,
cannot observe a couple without smirking,
avidly drain the color from our lives
until there is no unrest in our room
except the paper flame that they would put there
to fuel their furnace: we become an excuse.
Great unveilers, chroniclers of the war zone,
certainly talk of the eternal struggle
over the reins, but for our sake remember
there is no background as explosive as its
passionate foreground: get it through your head that
we are not cloth dolls with holes and bulges
but flesh in houses, killing with our own hands.

VIII

We may have our problems, rash explainer,
but at least we are not walking automata,
holding hands to keep a toiler busy,
getting mad to help a tirade along.
The forces of production knock on our door;
I scare them away by the timbre of my voice.
Ghosts barge in and reshuffle the blood on the wall
until it resembles a toolbit or a mother,
but the blood keeps pumping out; I stab and stab
because of a cruel word said the other day,
a gray hair found in the soap scum, a desire
to stop a head from cracking, and most of all
because of the face that flashes past your lashes
and is not mine. I stab at that flinty tempter.

IX

By this I knew I'd never leave my room
to look at cities, parks or art again:
the carnage was a comfort, not a care,
the thing that lay beside me on the bed
improved my mood because it matched the red
around the house, the red that ruled the world.
But even killers singing odes to gore
have lucid intervals. I thought of all
the faces that I never saw because
I was so busy welding them to views:
the bright eyes raised in ecstasy, the head
hung low in grief—for them I carry a torch
that lights the corners of my chamber as
I wait for sirens, as I wait for sleep.

X

Sometimes the flames remind me of your good points;
other times, when I become too bold
and start believing that you might come visit
they leap as if to say, Thus I refute you.
Who knows whether the things I do without you—
making shadow puppets on the walls,
giving private screenings of my crimes—
will cure me of the urge to do it over?
I only know that sometimes when the flames
are cool enough to walk through, I will risk
the shame of being found out by my keeper,
and the worse shame of never being noticed,
by standing at the red-rimmed, steamy window
through which, sometimes, a park bench will appear.

from *The Paris Review*

SUSAN WHEELER

Shanked on
the Red Bed

◊ ◊ ◊

The perch was on the roof, and the puck was in the air.
The diffident were driving, and the daunted didn't care.
When I came out to search for you the lauded hit the breeze
On detonated packages the bard had built to please.

The century was breaking and the blame was on default,
The smallest mammal redolent of what was in the vault,
The screeches shrill, the ink lines full of interbred regret—
When I walked out to look for you the toad had left his net.

The discourse flamed, the jurors sang, the lapdog strained its leash—
When I went forth to have you found the tenured took the beach
With dolloped hair and jangled nerves, without a jacking clue,
While all around the clacking sound of polished woodblocks blew.

When I went out to look for you the reductions had begun.
A demento took a shopgirl to a raisin dance for fun,
And f'r you, for me, for our quests ridiculous and chaste
The lead sky leered in every cloud its consummate distaste.

The mayors queued for mug shots while the banner rolled in the wind
That beat at bolted windows and bore down upon the thin,
And everywhere warped deliverers got bellicose and brave,
When I walked out to find you in the reconstructed rave.

The envelopes were in the slots and paperweights were flung.
When I came down to seek you out the torrents had begun
To rip the pan from handle and horizons from their shore,
To rip around your heady heart looking there for more.

from *The New Yorker*

For C.

◇　◇　◇

After the clash of elevator gates
And the long sinking, she emerges where,
A slight thing in the morning's crosstown glare,
She looks up toward the window where he waits,
Then in a fleeting taxi joins the rest
Of the huge traffic bound forever west.

On such grand scale do lovers say goodbye—
Even this other pair whose high romance
Had only the duration of a dance,
And who, now taking leave with stricken eye,
See each in each a whole new life forgone.
For them, above the darkling clubhouse lawn,

Bright Perseids flash and crumble; while for these
Who part now on the dock, weighed down by grief
And baggage, yet with something like relief,
It takes three thousand miles of knitting seas
To cancel out their crossing, and unmake
The amorous rough and tumble of their wake.

We are denied, my love, their fine tristesse
And bittersweet regrets, and cannot share
The frequent vistas of their large despair,
Where love and all are swept to nothingness;
Still, there's a certain scope in that long love
Which constant spirits are the keepers of,

And which, though taken to be tame and staid,
Is a wild sostenuto of the heart,
A passion joined to courtesy and art
Which has the quality of something made,
Like a good fiddle, like the rose's scent,
Like a rose window or the firmament.

from *The New Yorker*

The Bed

◇　◇　◇

Beds squalling, squealing, muffled in hush; beds pitching, leap-
　　ing, immobile as mountains;
beds wide as a prairie, strait as a gate, as narrow as the plank of
　　a ship to be walked.

I squalled, I squealed, I swooped and pitched; I covered my eyes and
　　leapt from the plank.

Beds proud, beds preening, beds timid and tense; vanquished
　　beds wishing only to vanquish;
neat little beds barely scented and dented, beds so disused you
　　cranked them to start them.

I admired, sang praises, flattered, adored; I sighed and submitted,
　　solaced, comforted, cranked.

Procrustean beds with consciences sharpened like razors slicing
　　the darkness above you;
beds like the labors of Hercules, stables and serpents; Samson
　　blinded, Noah in horror.

Blind with desire, I wakened in horror, in toil, in bondage, my con-
　　science in tatters.

Beds sobbing, beds sorry, beds pleading, beds mournful with
　　histories that amplified yours,
so you knelled through their dolorous echoes as through the
　　depths of your own dementias.

I echoed, I knelled, I sobbed and repented, I bandaged the wrists, sighed
for the embryo lost.

A nation of beds, a cosmos, then, how could it happen still, the
bed at the end of the world,
as welcoming as the world, ark, fortress, light and delight, the
other beds forgiven, forgiving.

A bed that sang through the darkness and woke in song as though
world itself had just wakened;
two beds fitted together as one, bed of arrival, acceptance, patience, bed
of unwaning ardor.

from *Ontario Review*

The Dark Days

◊   ◊   ◊

I. THE COLD WAR

We should have seen it coming back
In June: seeds of unrest, the troubled fiefdoms,
The snipers cloaked in blackjack oaks or sweetgums
    To launch an unprovoked attack

    On us with mace or Minie ball,
The ministers who joked about the sage,
The sage that withered up. In our bronze age
    We missed the heralds of a fall—

    The mounting shades, the Lilliputian
Insurrections waged by night—until
It dawned on us one morning with a chill,
    My God, another revolution.

    The trees ran up new banners, then
In bursts of color on a bombing run
Dropped propaganda leaflets. They had won.
    "Give up," we read, "You'll never win."

    In hindsight there's no mystery:
Too many palace coos, august parades,
Those slow mimosa Sundays, marmelades.
    Plus, we were young. That's history.

We should have seen it coming. Now
The slow smoke coils around the weathercocks,
All pointing north. We have set back our clocks,
    As if we could revive somehow

    Our flagging, fagged esprit de corps.
The parties are over. In personal retreats
The citizens observe the empty streets
    And the dark days of the cold war.

II. S.A.D.

    We should have seen it coming? Back
In June, we're told, while sweets came to the suite,
The green, spring-loaded days were packing heat,
    And, even then, insomniac

    Dark forces lurked in ambuscades;
Shadows were hatching cemetery plots;
And rebel sympathizers took potshots
    With cherry bombs and rusty blades,

    Till one late dawn the songbirds peeled
Away. We woke to catapulting worry:
Hannibal ad portas! With a flurry
    The world turned. Winter swept the field.

    Well, that's poetic elocution,
The civil war of words, that martial art
Ascribing nature with our purple heart.
    For me, another institution.

    The light died like a summer fad.
I should have seen it coming? Naturally.
The season turned, in simple terms, on me.
    I'm sated, saturated, sad.

Sometimes I change the rheostat,
But still the slow smoke coils around the clocks,
All caged in wire. We walk around in socks
    And hear dust falling in the flat

White walls we turn our faces toward.
The poems are over. In partitioned rooms
The residents observe the long, slow brooms
    And the dark daze of the cold ward.

III. Conspectus Against Anthropocentric Assumptions in Polemical Rhetoric

We should have seen it. Coming back
In June, the sun achieved its northernmost
Ecliptic point, the solstice, which we post
    Beforehand in the almanac

And on which day our region sees
The maximum of solar lumination.
Because the planet's axis of rotation
    By 23.5°

Inclines from perpendicular
To the Earth's plane of orbit, seasons change
With variations in the photic range
    Of our G2, main-sequence star.

Cork-celled abscission layers grow
On petioles of leaves. As chlorophyll
Dehydrates, pigments such as xanthophyll
    And carotene begin to show.

Climatic shifts that coincide
With mass migrations can contribute to,
In humans, elevated rates of flu,
    Fatigue, despair, and suicide.

Still, these are biological,
Not indications of occult intent.
We are a protoplasmic accident.
    That is the simple truth. Let all

Of nature's signal flags be furled.
The mysteries are over. God's dead. Nor
Should one detect some latent metaphor
    In the dark days of the cold world.

IV. REVISED WEATHER BULLETIN

We should have seen it coming back.
In "June" we should have heard the vestiges
Of "Juno," goddess of both marriages
    And war, and seen today's snowpack

Foreshadowed in the virgin plain
of someone's bridal gown, blizzards of rice,
The glazed and frosted wedding cake, and ice-
    Bound, listing bottles of champagne,

Portending future dissolution.
We should have seen it coming back because,
While seasons change with scientific laws,
    cf., another attribution:

"All things are metaphors," the Sage
Of Weimar said. And I have evidence,
The inside dope, counterintelligence:
    Flybys of geese, the heavy-gauge

Entanglements of trees, the charge
Of winter storm troops, and the clicking Morse
Of sleet detail the occupation force
    Of nature, standing by and large

For warfare, silencings, and fear.
Now long shades muster in the empty streets,
All choked in ice. The light brigade retreats
    To foothills of the last frontier,

And gray coats move in undeterred.
The year is over. In the studio
I see the long-range forecast calls for snow
    And the dark days of the cold word.

from *The Yale Review*

Returned to the Yaak Cabin, I Overhear an Old Greek Song

◊   ◊   ◊

Back at the west window, Basin Creek
Stumbling its mantra out in a slurred, mid-summer
    monotone,
Sunshine in planes and clean sheets
Over the yarrow and lodgepole pine—
We spend our whole lives in the same place and
    never leave,
Pine squirrels and butterflies at work in a deep dither,
Bumblebee likewise, wind with a slight hitch in its
    get-along.

Dead heads on the lilac bush, daisies
Long-legged forest of stalks in a white throw across
    the field
Above the ford and deer path,
Candor of marble, candor of bone—
We spend our whole lives in the same place and
    never leave,
The head of Orpheus bobbing in the slatch, his song
Still beckoning from his still-bloody lips, bright as a
    bee's heart.

from *Poetry*

CONTRIBUTORS' NOTES AND COMMENTS

JONATHAN AARON was born in Northampton, Massachusetts, in 1941. He is the author of two books of poems, *Second Sight* (Harper & Row, 1982) and *Corridor* (Wesleyan–New England, 1992), and teaches writing and literature at Emerson College in Boston.

Of "Mr. Moto's Confession," Aaron writes: "The poem amounts to a little ode on the actor Peter Lorre. Perhaps best known for his performance as the child-murderer in Fritz Lang's *M,* he was wonderful as Joel Cairo in *The Maltese Falcon,* or as Leyden, the mystery writer whose curiosity gets him into big trouble, in *The Mask of Dimitrios.* And he was terrific as Mr. Moto, the brilliant Japanese detective-philosopher, connoisseur of rare antiques, jujitsu expert, master of disguise.

"Lorre played Mr. Moto in eight films in the late thirties when he himself was in his mid-thirties, thin and wiry, and able to move like a cat. In one of these films (I saw only part of it on TV and have never found it since), Mr. Moto writes something down on a piece of paper—a message for the police, which he cleverly disguises as a haiku. He eventually saves the entire British far eastern fleet from being blown up by gold thieves.

"The poem uses the fact that when Lorre speaks as Mr. Moto, in a delicately clipped English which is meant to sound 'Oriental,' you hear his German accent (or maybe 'middle European' is more exact). It's the accent you hear when he speaks in his other films, and which he seemed to exaggerate (self-parody?) as he got older and rounder, turning from a kind of ballet dancer into a sort of human bowling ball. The poem includes some facts from Lorre's life—his real name was Löwenstein, for example, and late in his life he did act in three Roger Corman 'versions' of Poe. But the poem tries to get beyond biography in seeing Lorre and Mr. Moto as one and the same. It ends up in mystery, which is where I end up whenever I think about Lorre, or watch him on the screen."

AGHA SHAHID ALI directs the M.F.A. program in creative writing at the University of Massachusetts, Amherst. He writes: "I must hold back any information that reminds me of mortality, particularly my own. Any reference to the place and date of my birth is forbidden (though I may acknowledge that I am the final reincarnation of Dionysus). Oh yes, that explains the title of my latest volume of poems, *The Country Without a Post Office,* which includes 'The Floating Post Office.'"

Of "The Floating Post Office," he adds: "Tantalized for years by the sestina, I nevertheless resisted writing one because it always seemed to be doing a bit too well in the convenient realm. Why a poem acquires a certain form is a mystery to me, but when decades of simmering tensions erupted in 1990 into a full-scale uprising in Kashmir, my original home, and those events began to obsess me emotionally and imaginatively, I felt my work 'feeling' radically for departures. I found myself led to various *named* forms to house my obsession—sonnets, canzones, pantoums, ghazals (to name some). And the sestina. Mine somehow resisted the pentameter and settled into, most of the time, a tetrameter line (maybe because a friend once insisted that one can't be emotional in tetrameter). I also enjoyed varying the end words with homonyms."

DICK ALLEN was born in Troy, New York, in 1939. He is the director of creative writing, Charles A. Dana Endowed Chair Professor of English, and president of the Faculty Council at the University of Bridgeport, where he has taught since 1968. The most recent of his five poetry collections is *Ode to the Cold War: Poems New and Selected* (Sarabande Books, 1997). His other books include *Flight and Pursuit* (Louisiana State University, 1987), *Overnight in the Guest House of the Mystic* (Louisiana State University, 1984), *Regions with No Proper Names* (St. Martin's, 1975), *Anon and Various Time Machine Poems* (Dell, 1971), and three teaching text anthologies from Harcourt Brace. Allen has received poetry writing fellowships from the Ingram Merrill Foundation and the National Endowment for the Arts.

Of "The Cove," Allen writes: "The form of the poem, with its sometimes slant and sometimes exact ABCB rhymes and its irregular line length, reflects Stevie Smith's influence. The poem's semi-loose shape seemed appropriate for keeping as much as possible suspended between solid and insubstantial.

"That is, whatever is out there on the lake should be what the reader, kneeling in the narrator's stead, imagines—Death, another task or duty, a wisp of God, sickness, a floating body or tree or tree stump. . . ."

The reader's own fears, sanity firm or slipping, and the particular twilight in which the reader kneels may provide different answers at different times. I do know whatever's out there scares the hell out of me.

"I believe we all live in coves of sorts (I'm perhaps more hermetic than many), that we are continually being called forth from them or having them threatened. But especially at fifty, the tiring is well under way. How much more will be asked from us? How many more demands before we can turn our backs? Or can we, should we, ever?

"It will always be out there.

"There are slight elliptical allusions to Plato and Melville. The poem's nightmare aspect probably came from my memory of seeing the movie version of Dreiser's *An American Tragedy* when I was too young—that dreadful lake. When my even younger brother started screaming, my mother took us from the Saratoga, New York, theater and to this day I've not seen how the movie ends.

"The *sequence* of the images in the poem may be telling; the narrator's attempts at triangulation come from Boy Scout training. I live beside a small lake where there's a diving board and a willow, yet I'm not sure it's this one."

A. R. AMMONS was born on a farm outside Whiteville, North Carolina, in 1926. He started writing poetry aboard a U.S. Navy destroyer escort in the South Pacific. He worked briefly as the principal of an elementary school in Cape Hatteras and later managed a biological glass factory in southern New Jersey. Since 1964 he has taught at Cornell University, where he is the Goldwin Smith Professor of Poetry. He was awarded a MacArthur Fellowship in 1981, the year the "genius awards" were introduced. He has also received the Bollingen Prize (for *Sphere,* in 1975), the National Book Critics Circle Award (for *A Coast of Trees,* in 1981), and the National Book Award, twice—for *Collected Poems: 1951–1971* in 1973 and for the book-length poem *Garbage* in 1993. All these titles were published by Norton. Ammons's other books include *Ommateum* (1955), *Tape for the Turn of the Year* (1965), *The Snow Poems* (1977), *Worldly Hopes* (1982), *The Really Short Poems of A. R. Ammons* (1990), *Brink Road* (1996), and *Glare* (1997). He was the guest editor of *The Best American Poetry 1994.* He and his wife live in Ithaca, New York.

Ammons writes: "I wrote 'Now Then' immediately before driving to Michigan for a reading. I type my poems on a roll of paper, and the poem had not been transcribed from the tape, so I unwound it like a scroll lengthwise and orated it. I read it last, and it was best liked. Not because it is my best poem but because it is a talking poem that flits about, not a literary poem that bears rereading, but a poem easy to be with in flight, I suppose."

DANIEL ANDERSON was born in Cincinnati, Ohio, in 1964. He attended the University of Cincinnati, where he received his B.A., and Johns Hopkins University, where he received an M.A. in the Writing Seminars. His first book of poems, *January Rain,* was the co-recipient of the Nicholas Roerich Poetry Prize and was published in 1997 by Story Line Press. He lives in Morristown, New Jersey, where he teaches English and creative writing at Delbarton School.

Of "A Possum's Tale," Anderson writes: "A couple of years ago, in the middle of an unusually long winter, a possum would come out at dusk each night and walk across the front yard on the icy crust of the snow. It was pretty slow going for him, but he seemed to know where he was headed. This got me started on the poem, and while I was writing it, I remembered the first time I saw one of these fellows when I was a kid. The poem then became a confluence of these two experiences. In the end, it came out as the possum's story, which, when placed in the hands of a sentimentalist like me, is one of isolation and estrangement."

JAMES APPLEWHITE was born in Wilson County, North Carolina, in 1935. His recent books include *Daytime and Starlight: Poems* (1997), *A History of the River: Poems* (1993), and *Lessons in Soaring* (1989), all published by Louisiana State University Press. His avocations include hiking, camping, amateur astronomy, and foreign travel, and his professional pursuits involve postmodern American poetry and poetics and arts administration. He is a professor of English at Duke University and the founding director of the Duke University Institute of the Arts.

Of "Botanical Garden: The Coastal Plains," Applewhite writes: "With its Victorian and Colonial houses behind stone walls and ivy, Chapel Hill has for years served my wife and me as an emblem for the possible completion of our earlier lives. Though it retains much of the village simplicity and southern charm of that past we remember, Chapel Hill is also a university town, with planetarium, art museum, massive library, and modest botanical garden. It has seemed to offer a kind of past-with-understanding—as if, there, we could relive those primal days farther east, with their vitality and intensity, but without the damning ignorance and confusion.

"Since the botanical garden is divided in accordance with the three geographical regions of North Carolina, it lends itself as a paradigm of the progression we've been struggling through. Chapel Hill holds also the address of my analyst (to whom the poem is dedicated). After a particularly illuminating session one summer day a couple of years ago, I stopped by the garden. I felt a pleasure, thinking that I was in the more knowledgeable Piedmont—that the mountains and the coastal plains were only replicas, areas I could revisit briefly and safely.

"But as I stepped into the sand barrens and looked across the swamp pond to the marsh-like pocosin, I felt myself vividly returned to the coastal plain of memory. The very names of the vine-like bushes threatened to choke my throat with consonants. The heat felt suddenly oppressive, as the fierce sun and humidity replicated earlier atmospheres. I watched a snapping turtle slip underwater, then spot the reflection of a cumulus with his sliding shadow. I experienced an archaic, doom-like foreboding.

"I crossed a bridge beside the pond and found myself on a raised boardwalk that gave perspective over wetland. Bushes and vines wore labels, their common and Latin names on the metal tags like protective talismans. Birds and insects native to the actual landscape had been attracted even to this miniature. I felt a narrow space open up between my present on the boardwalk and that earlier self and life still brooding down among the poison oak and fever bark. What looked like a water moccasin unknotting itself in a crotch of ditch bank, in deepest shadow, probably wasn't. If a moccasin, he no longer scared me. It was as if a new terminology had erased the *sin* I'd heard hissing in his name. Sitting in some shade, I wrote, across a map of the garden, this poem."

CRAIG ARNOLD was born on an air force base in 1967. He spent most of his childhood overseas. He received his B.A. from Yale and is currently pursuing a doctorate at the University of Utah. He was the Amy Lowell Poetry Traveling Scholar in 1996–97, a year he spent mostly in the south of Spain, trying to make the perfect gazpacho. He sings, writes, and plays guitar for the band Iris.

For "Hot," Arnold offers the following recipe for Som Tum (Green Papaya Salad): "Peel the skin from a smallish, green (unripe) papaya— the flesh should be firm, dry, and almost white. Split, scoop out the seeds, and shred, with a cleaver or grater, into long thin strips. You should have between two and three cups.

"Peel and remove the shoots from two large cloves of garlic. Pound them thoroughly in a large mortar with a teaspoon of sugar, one or two tablespoons of fish sauce, and as many Thai bird chilies as you feel are safe—one will be enough for most palates. Add the papaya and bruise gently, mixing thoroughly with the spices. You might also add a cup of long beans, julienned. When the strips are limp but not yet pulpy, squeeze in the juice of one lime and toss together. Adjust the seasoning.

"Serve over a lettuce leaf, garnished with coarsely chopped tomatoes, shrimp—either cooked and peeled, or the small dried variety—and a generous portion of ground peanuts. Beer is the preferred accompaniment."

SARAH ARVIO was born in 1954 and grew up near New York City. Educated at schools abroad and at Columbia University, she now lives sometimes in New York, sometimes in Paris, and works as a conference translator for the United Nations. She has translated novels, stories, poems, and essays from the Spanish and the French, and in 1992 won a translators' fellowship from the National Endowment for the Arts. This set of eleven poems, which won *The Paris Review*'s Bernard F. Connors Prize for the long poem, is one third of a book-length sequence.

About *Visits from the Seventh,* Arvio writes: "Years ago, my twin sister, who cultivated occult connections, taught me how to receive voices. At first they were often sinister, not sweet; and they made promises they couldn't keep. After a while I learned to distinguish between the nice ones and the not-so-nice ones, and I made friends with some of them. At a certain point they began to speak to me in rhythmic patterns, and sometimes they blurted out a whole meditation at once. Now and then they signed their names. When they understood that they would be heard, they worked very fast, in a splurge or spree. They like a flat syllabic ten-count, and they prefer triplets. They also like the number and the sense of *seven.* Sometimes the life is such that the inner life is forced to find unusual remedies."

JOHN ASHBERY was born in Rochester, New York, in 1927. He is the author of seventeen books of poetry, including *Wakefulness* (Farrar, Straus & Giroux, 1998), and a volume of art criticism, *Reported Sightings.* His *Self-Portrait in a Convex Mirror* received the Pulitzer Prize, the National Book Critics Circle Award, and the National Book Award. He is currently Charles P. Stevenson, Jr., Professor of Languages and Literature at Bard College. He has been named a Guggenheim Fellow and a MacArthur Fellow, and he is a chancellor of the Academy of American Poets. In 1995 he received the Poetry Society of America's

Robert Frost Medal, the highest honor awarded by that institution. He was the guest editor of *The Best American Poetry 1988*.

FRANK BIDART was born in Bakersfield, California, in 1939. He was educated at the University of California, Riverside, and Harvard University. *Desire,* his most recent book of poems, was published in 1997 by Farrar, Straus & Giroux and was short-listed for both the National Book Award and the National Book Critics Circle prize in poetry. "The Second Hour of the Night" extends a sequence of long poems begun with "The First Hour of the Night," the culminating work in Bidart's *In the Western Night: Collected Poems, 1965–90* (1990). He has received awards from the Lila Wallace–Reader's Digest Fund and from the American Academy of Arts and Letters. He teaches at Wellesley College and lives in Cambridge, Massachusetts.

Of "The Second Hour of the Night," Bidart writes: "In the Egyptian *Book of Gates,* each night the boat of the sun must travel through twelve divisions, or hours, within the underworld, before it can rise again. That's the large myth behind the two 'hours of the night' I've written. Each poem is a journey (only one journey, not the only journey) through a psychic landscape, a territory or set of issues that is part of our psyche. In 'The Second Hour of the Night,' the territory is Eros, the erotic. The poem is a series of linked erotic narratives. In both hours I've written, near the beginning of the journey there is a more or less 'realistic' narrative, then the poem enters a 'mythic' landscape, followed by a dream narrative that partly refigures what has gone before. I hope that I can write more 'hours,' and ideally they will not all have this same shape. But each 'hour' should have within it the seeds of the materials of the others. How we live out each great issue that grips us is connected to how we live out all the others. The series of poems I'm imagining is not meant to be read as one long poem, printed together. The relation I'm imagining is more like that between the numbered sonatas or quartets or symphonies of a composer: the sequence has meaning, though they are not intended to be listened to at one sitting, or in the order of composition. I don't, of course, know if I can write even one more 'hour'; I can see a territory, but am looking from a satellite circling about two hundred and fifty miles up, and its physiognomy isn't visible."

ROBERT BLY was born in Madison, Minnesota, in 1926. His most recent book, *Morning Poems,* is out in paperback from HarperCollins. He recently edited for Ecco Press an anthology of spiritual poetry called

The Soul Is Here for Its Own Joy: Sacred Poems from Many Cultures. His newest work of prose, *The Sibling Society* (Vintage), comments on American consumer culture.

Of "A Week of Poems at Bennington," Bly writes: "I wrote all of these poems, except the first, during a week I spent at Bennington College in January 1996, having been invited to give several lectures on the art of poetry at the semi-annual gathering of Liam Rector's low-residency writing program.

"Several years ago I adopted—following the lead of William Stafford—the delight of writing a poem each morning before getting out of bed. It's a way of staying in bed longer. But it does help to keep in touch with daily moods as well, since the poem starts with whatever phrase or sentence is floating in the mind on waking up.

"Sunday morning I had spent on an airplane flying to Vermont, so I pulled in a ringer for that day, a poem written several weeks before, on a subject suggested by a friend's poetry: 'It's time to prepare myself not to be here.' The friend was Stafford.

"I arrived on Sunday and that night gave a poetry reading from some recent poems. It went well. About four A.M. a voice penetrated my ear asking, 'Why did you say *that*?' Many poetry readers experience that voice. It's a kind of demon of four A.M. When I woke again at dawn, the words floating in my mind were: 'Well, there it is. There's nothing to do.' The cat came in, I think, because there is something in a poetry reading about stealing milk. Perhaps I am the cat stealing my own poems, or perhaps the audience is the cat.

"The next night as I slept and woke, my body itself felt happy. I remembered meeting animals in my dream, and we laughed together. In the middle of the poem, relatives in Norway turned up dancing and kicking their hard heels on the floor. Perhaps my happiness came from reading so many good books. Sven Birkerts was staying at the same guest house as I, and I dedicated the poem to him because in *The Gutenberg Elegies* he wrote so beautifully about an experience he calls 'deep reading.'

"Donald Hall and I are endlessly old friends. We've sent poems back and forth to each other regularly for forty-five years. At Bennington, Don's room was across the hall from mine, and so I'd hear his cough in the morning when he woke. On this day he was driving down to Boston to see a basketball game with his son, Andrew. Jane Kenyon had died only a few months before in April of 1995, and we were all aware how hard it was for him to get used to living alone. There's some suggestion of that in the poem. He has always revised extensively, and it's not unusual for him to make forty drafts of a poem or an essay. He often scolds me about improvisation, but I did do twelve drafts of the poem for him.

"On Thursday morning the new snow was beautiful, as were the sunlight and the icicles. I did say to a woman friend, 'Let's all make fun of other people. That would bring us closer.' When talking about poetry with friends, it's easy to feel that mood.

"In the talk I gave on Thursday I brought up the idea of not making assertions too early in the poem. If one says, as Wallace Stevens does, 'In my room, the world is beyond my understanding,' we can accept that. He next says, 'The house was quiet and the world was calm.' The more disturbing assertions, harder for the reader to accept, one can bring up later. The day before, some of the students, at my request, had given me a poem each, simply because I was curious about what they were writing. I quoted lines of several student poems as examples of violent assertions spoken so early in the poem that it wasn't likely the reader would hang around to read more. Several students complained that even though I had not mentioned names, I had not asked their permission to read their poems aloud. They were right. So the next morning the poem turned out to be a kind of apology, beginning: 'Well I do it, and it's done. And it can't be taken back.'

"On Saturday morning I began with the sentence, 'Don't tell me there's nothing that can be done.' I remembered Rumi in one of his poems mentioning the different ways his hands and his legs would respond to a given question, so I adopted that mode. I mentioned the tongue's idea, and the toe and the heart and eventually got to the buttocks. They want us to see everything upside down, so I followed that.

"The poems probably have too much improvisation and too little thought, but there's something playful about just watching what happens six days in a row."

GEORGE BRADLEY was born in Roslyn, New York, in 1953. He is the author of three books of poetry (*Terms to Be Met,* Yale University Press, 1986; *Of the Knowledge of Good and Evil,* Knopf, 1991; and *The Fire Fetched Down,* Knopf, 1996) and the editor of *The Yale Younger Poets Anthology* (Yale University Press, 1998). Though never a cabby, Bradley has nonetheless had a checkered career, employed variously as a construction worker, a hospital orderly, a sommelier, a copywriter, an editor, and a teacher. At the moment, he is participating in a venture to import and distribute Italian olive oil.

Of "In an Old Garden," Bradley writes: "In what is no doubt a knee-jerk reaction to taking up residence in small-town Connecticut, over the past few years I have been writing sonnets about the New England landscape. One of the problems/pleasures of this one was to cast it in couplets, a form that, simple as it is, would get my vote for the most satisfying rhyme scheme in English. English, of course, is notorious as a rhyme-poor language, but I wonder if it hasn't gotten a bad rap in that regard. It is poor in all those *-ado* and *-ini* words that make for musical but unsurprising verse, but with its vast vocabulary, it is not lacking in the unpredictable *trouvailles* that are the delight of rhyme."

JOHN BRICUTH was born in Houston, Texas, in 1940. After serving in the U.S. Navy, he worked at the NASA Manned Spacecraft Center in Houston, received his doctorate from Rice University in 1970, and taught school; he now lives in seclusion. His poetry has appeared in numerous magazines, including *Shenandoah, The Southern Review, Southwest Review, Virginia Quarterly Review,* and *The Yale Review.* He won an Emily Clark Balch Prize in 1970 for his long poem "The Musical Emblem." And he published his first volume of poems, *The Heisenberg Variations,* in 1976, presently available from the Johns Hopkins University Press.

Bricuth writes: "This poem is the fourth section of a longer work entitled *Just Let Me Say This About That,* a work that runs to 2,076 lines. It was written over a period of fifteen years. The author tried to combine as many vocabularies as possible to convey his sense of the diversity of the contemporary world, and he cast the overall poem in that omnipresent modern form—the question-and-answer format of the press conference. The book-length version of the poem will be published in the fall of 1998 by Overlook Press as the first volume in the Sewanee Writers' Series."

ANNE CARSON was born in Toronto, Canada, in 1950. She is a professor of classics who has taught at the universities of Calgary, Toronto, Emory, Princeton, McGill, and Berkeley, as well as at the 92nd Street Y in New York City, where she was Rockefeller Scholar in Residence for 1986–87. She is the author of *Eros the Bittersweet* (rep. Dalkey Archive, 1998), *Glass, Irony and God* (New Directions, 1995), *Plainwater* (Knopf, 1995), and a novel in verse, *Autobiography of Red* (Knopf, 1998).

Of "TV Men: Antigone (Scripts 1 and 2)," Carson writes: "The poem was occasioned on a cold winter day when I was walking behind someone (into the wind) and noticed it was warmer."

TURNER CASSITY was born in Jackson, Mississippi, in 1929, and was educated at Millsaps College, Stanford University, and Columbia University. He retired in 1991 from Emory University Library, where he had worked from 1962. He has been publishing for forty years. *The Destructive Element: New and Selected Poems* will appear from Ohio University Press in 1998.

Cassity writes: "If you disallow *Paradise Lost,* there are very few science fiction poems in English. Thom Gunn's *Misanthropos* comes to mind. 'Symbol of the Faith' is my contribution to a neglected genre. The Hofmannsthal quotation that heads the poem was made in regard to the decision to costume the ballet *Josephslegende* in Renaissance rather than biblical fashion."

HENRI COLE was born in Fukuoka, Japan, in 1956. He grew up in Virginia and graduated from the College of William and Mary. In 1989 he received the Amy Lowell Poetry Traveling Scholarship and in 1995 he was the recipient of the Rome Prize in Literature from the American Academy of Arts and Letters. He has published three collections of poetry: *The Marble Queen* (Atheneum, 1986), *The Zoo Wheel of Knowledge* (Knopf, 1989), and *The Look of Things* (Knopf, 1995). A new book entitled *The Visible Man* is forthcoming from Knopf. He has worked as a soda jerk, flower delivery boy, cake decorator, gardener, bank teller, busboy, waiter, bartender, editorial assistant, arts administrator, and teacher. At present, he is Briggs-Copeland Lecturer in Poetry at Harvard University.

Cole writes: "I wrote 'Self-Portrait as Four Styles of Pompeian Wall Painting' over a period of a year while living in Rome. I saw many paintings during this time, most of them religious and violent. My goal was not so much to put pictures into words, but to take something of their naked realism and project it into the realm of the abstract, where the lyric poem exists. Yet it was in the secular Pompeian wall paintings (200 B.C.–A.D. 100) that I found the simplest trope for autobiography. At first I saw the four styles as chronological representations of four stages in my life. But as I began to write and scrutinize myself, the four styles became mixed up and seemed to coexist metaphorically in me.

"In the first style there are vivid stucco reliefs made to look like Greek mortar and drafted blocks; it is more a plastic than a painted style; there is rarely a presence of figures. The second style substituted stucco work with illusionistic representations of architectural elements, colonnades, podia, views of gardens and landscapes. The third style abandoned perspective and flattened out into unified fields with inserted figurative scenes and portraits, often erotic. Ornamentation is clean and subtly calligraphic. And the fourth style is eclectic and fantastic. It continued after the eruption of Mt. Vesuvius (A.D. 79). Unexpectedly, by writing in the imaginary voice of Pompeian wall paintings, I came closer than ever before to the truths of my life. I am indebted to the classical scholar Malcolm Bell for guiding me aesthetically through the Pompeian ruins."

BILLY COLLINS was born in New York City. His recent books include *Picnic, Lightning* (University of Pittsburgh Press, 1998), *The Art of Drowning* (University of Pittsburgh Press, 1995), and *Questions About Angels* (William Morrow, 1991), selected by Edward Hirsch for the National Poetry Series. He has won the Bess Hokin Prize, the Frederick Bock Prize, the Oscar Blumenthal Prize, and the Levinson Prize awarded by *Poetry* magazine. A recipient of a Guggenheim Fellowship and a grant from the National Endowment for the Arts, he is a professor of English at Lehman College (City University of New York).

Of "Lines Composed Over Three Thousand Miles from Tintern Abbey," Collins writes: "As the title suggests, this poem is a flagrant example of the notion that what poems are really about is other poems, in this case Wordsworth's 'Tintern Abbey.' My poem begins with a dry look at the familiar Romantic habit of falling into sudden bouts of depression, especially in the midst of outrageously pleasant landscapes. For a while there, it seemed that no literate person in England could go for a walk without succumbing to some form of Anglo-melancholia in which neurotic longings for childhood were lovingly combined with the dread of mortality.

"Moving on from there, the poem uses the presumptuous 'we' in an attempt to draw the reader into this dim view of Romantic *Angst* before making its move, simultaneously stepping into the present and shifting indoors, specifically into my study where I invite the reader to join me for a nap. Here, the problem of time is collapsed into an uneventful afternoon, landscape is reduced to domestic trappings, and the yearning for vanished splendors in the grass is disparaged. Also, the poem's true indebtedness to the shorter 'daffodil poem' is revealed, for that poem also moves indoors—reversing the usual Romantic direction—from 'vales and hills' to a Wordsworthian couch.

"But, believe me, it took getting in touch with my Inner Professor to put all these afterthoughts together."

ALFRED CORN was born in Bainbridge, Georgia, in 1943. His most recent collection of poems, *Present* (Counterpoint), was published in

1997, along with a novel titled *Part of His Story* (Mid-List Press) and a study of prosody, *The Poem's Heartbeat* (Story Line Press). He is the author of six earlier volumes of poetry and a collection of critical essays titled *The Metamorphosis of Metaphor* (Viking). He has received a Guggenheim Fellowship and an Award in Literature from the Academy and Institute of Arts and Letters. He currently teaches at Columbia University. A frequent contributor to *The New York Times Book Review* and *The Nation,* he also writes art criticism for *Art in America* and *ARTnews* magazines. He lives in New York City.

Corn writes: "In November 1987, J. D. McClatchy and I traveled in Israel. (The *intifada* began less than a month after our departure.) I'd wanted to make that trip since childhood, and 'Jaffa' is one in a sequence of poems concerning several sites visited. Because it's my way, I read quite a lot about each stop on the itinerary. None of that preparation prevented me from being overwhelmed by what I felt— the weight of historical tragedy, the immensity of the religions that had been fostered in this small corner of Asia Minor. Left speechless, I still knew I would have to try to write about what I'd seen. Even so, the sequence was nearly ten years in the making. It appears in my most recent book, *Present,* although two of the poems were not included, one about the death of Moses on Mount Nebo, and one about Jerusalem. I'm still making revisions, hoping to complete them someday.

"Modern Jaffa is built on the site of the biblical Joppa. In classical mythology it was the chief city of Cepheus's Ethiopian kingdom, where the story of Andromeda and Perseus took place. To return to modern history, the period of the British Mandate (or temporary colonial administration) began six years after the 1917 Balfour Declaration in which Britain undertook to establish a national homeland for the Jews in Palestine—though the terms of the proclamation weren't fulfilled until 1948. The population of Jaffa is largely Palestinian and 'Tel Jaffa' is Arabic for 'the hill of Jaffa.'"

JAMES CUMMINS was born in Columbus, Ohio, in 1948, and grew up in Indianapolis and Cleveland. He is curator of the Elliston Poetry Collection at the University of Cincinnati, where he teaches literature and writing. His first book, *The Whole Truth,* was published by North Point Press in 1986; his second, *Portrait in a Spoon,* came out in 1997 from the University of South Carolina Press. He has received grants from the National Endowment for the Arts, the Ingram Merrill Foundation, and the Ohio Arts Council.

Of "Echo," Cummins writes: "Given my track record, I'm a little embarrassed to say that this poem was destined for a long sestina sequence; I'm going to have to join a twelve-step program for poets who admit to be 'enabled' by the mad energy and design of works like *The Dream Songs, Mirabell: Books of Number,* or John Hollander's 'Cupcake' poems. ('Hi. My name's Jim. It's been two years since I last read *Ko, or a Season on Earth.*') Though it's hard to believe, I conceived of a work in which the role of the teleutons in a sestina would be filled by individual sestinas, so that six individual 'narratives' or themes would develop through smaller cycles of six poems each. I didn't even want to think about what I was going to do with the envoi. The project seemed to have a certain ambition, but not really; it was merely insane. I ended up with eight poems, four of which survive.

"I wanted to write a 'Narcissus' poem, so naturally it ended titled 'Echo.' I wanted to write about the inability to love back, taking the last, most important step; and the loss that's perceived, even within that self-absorption."

TOM DISCH was born in Des Moines, Iowa, in 1940. He grew up in Minnesota and moved to New York City in 1957. His latest collection of poems, *A Child's Garden of Grammar,* from the University Press of New England, can be found either in the gardening or reference sections of many bookstores. His collection of poetry criticism, *The Castle of Indolence* (Picador, 1995), was a finalist for the National Book Critics Circle award in criticism. *The Dreams Our Stuff Is Made Of: How Science Fiction Conquered the World* was published this year by the Free Press, and his novel *The Sub: A Study in Witchcraft* is forthcoming from Knopf. He lives in New York City and out of it.

Disch writes: " 'What Else Is There' is one of a set of eleven uniformly imperfect rondeaus, each of which is missing a line in the third stanza, the result of cloning from defective RNA. It is the poet's hope that others will realize that this seeming mistake actually represents an improvement of the rondeau, a poetic form that has undergone little change for many centuries, and that they will want to follow the poet's innovative example."

DENISE DUHAMEL was born in Providence, Rhode Island, in 1961, and was educated at Sarah Lawrence College and Emerson College. "The Difference Between Pepsi and Pope" is forthcoming in 1999 in *The Star-Spangled Banner* (Southern Illinois University Press; winner of the Crab

Orchard Poetry Prize). Her other poetry books include *Exquisite Politics* (a collaborative volume with Maureen Seaton; Tia Chucha Press, 1997), *Kinky* (Orchises Press, 1997), *How the Sky Fell* (Pearl Editions, 1996), *Girl Soldier* (Garden Street Press, 1995), and *The Woman with Two Vaginas* (Salmon Run Press, 1995). She has been awarded grants from the Ludwig Vogelstein Foundation, the Puffin Foundation, and the New York Foundation for the Arts. She lives with her husband, the poet Nick Carbo, in New York City.

Of "The Difference Between Pepsi and Pope," Duhamel writes: "A combination of astigmatism and nearsightedness makes me a rather creative reader when I don't wear my glasses."

LYNN EMANUEL was born in Mt. Kisco, New York, in 1949. She directs the writing program at the University of Pittsburgh. Her two books, *Hotel Fiesta* and *The Dig,* have been collected in a double volume by the University of Illinois Press. Her work previously appeared in *The Best American Poetry 1995,* guest-edited by Richard Howard.

Emanuel writes: " 'Like God,' is my homage to Italo Calvino's novel, *If on a winter's night a traveler.* I intend both to imitate and to honor the affect of this book in which the reader is simultaneously absorbed in a narrative and aware of his or her role as a reader absorbed in a narrative. Writing 'Like God,' I thought about an observation in John Berger's book *Ways of Seeing.* Berger describes the convention established in Renaissance painting whereby 'Perspective . . . centers everything on the eye of the beholder. . . . The visible world is arranged for the spectator as the universe was once thought to be arranged for God. According to the convention of perspective there is no visual reciprocity. There is no need for God to situate himself in relation to others: he is himself the situation.' In my poem, I have extended Berger's observation to include the activity of reading. In place of the spectator viewing the painting, I inserted the reader reading a book."

IRVING FELDMAN was born in Brooklyn, New York, in 1928. He is the author of *New and Selected Poems* (Viking Penguin, 1979), *Teach Me, Dear Sister* (Viking Penguin, 1983), *All of Us Here* (Viking Penguin, 1986), and *The Life and Letters* (University of Chicago Press, 1994). In 1986 he received a grant from the National Endowment for the Arts, and in 1992 he was made a MacArthur Fellow. He is Distinguished Professor of English at the State University of New York at Buffalo.

Of "Movietime," Feldman writes: "Sometimes my writing develops a momentum that, in turn, runs away with it, as their momentum does with this poem's lovers. So, to slow the locomotive and make its passage more interesting, less devastating: more switches and cars and a richer freight—the long lines here, and 'tiny textures of being/and time.'"

EMILY FRAGOS was born in Mt. Vernon, New York, in 1949. She currently teaches poetry and fiction workshops at Fordham University, Lincoln Center, New York. She was educated at Syracuse University, the Sorbonne, and Columbia University. Her first book, *Little Savage,* won the David Craig Austin Poetry Prize (1996), judged by Ann Lauterbach. She is an amateur pianist and cellist and has worked as an English tutor for the young dancers at the School of American Ballet.

Of "Apollo's Kiss," Fragos writes: "When I first read the myth of Apollo and Cassandra, it stunned and hurt me. The elusive nature of obsession, the god-given gift that is altered to nightmare and turns in upon the bearer, the terrible vulnerabilities, the ancient punishments. I could not find a way to inhabit the conundrums until I came to the poem's first two words: 'Devise Cassandra.' Then I wrote the poem."

DEBORA GREGER was born in Walsenburg, Colorado, in 1949. She teaches in the creative writing program at the University of Florida. Her books of poetry include *Movable Islands* (Princeton, 1980), *And* (Princeton, 1986), *The 1002nd Night* (Princeton, 1990), *Off-Season at the Edge of the World* (Illinois, 1994), and *Desert Fathers, Uranium Daughters* (Penguin, 1996).

ALLEN GROSSMAN was born in Minneapolis, Minnesota, in 1932. His most recent publications are *The Ether Dome* (1991) and *The Philosopher's Window* (1995), both from New Directions, and *The Long Schoolroom: Lessons in the Bitter Logic of the Poetic Principle* (1997) from the University of Michigan Press. He is the Mellon Professor in the Humanities at the Johns Hopkins University. "Weird River" is part of a volume not yet completed called *New Poems;* further poems toward this collection can be found, as they are written, on the Web at <http://jhuvms.hcf.jhu.edu/~gross_a/index.html>.

Grossman writes: "The 'weird river' in this poem is the swift dark flood of the always already *unwritten*—fatal—and the star Asper is the knowledge of it, poetic consciousness—*'per astra ad aspera.'* The three crows ('corbies' of tradition) flap up out of the simile and perform their tiny drama, the name of which is 'We Do Our Best,' subject to the one Commandment or Law of all human discourse which the poet knows: 'Will what is. Just let it be known.'"

THOM GUNN was born in England in 1929. He came to California in 1954 and has lived in San Francisco for many years. His first book was published in 1954, and he recently published *The Man with Night Sweats* (1992) and *Collected Poems* (Farrar, Straus & Giroux, 1994). He teaches English at Berkeley.

Of "To Cupid," Gunn writes: "I labored so long over writing this poem that I can still see only the labor. Thus I'm reassured that it has been chosen for the anthology, because I do like *what* the poem says, very much.

"Fabrice is the hero of Stendhal's *Charterhouse of Parma,* and if you don't know that novel, you've missed one of the most enjoyable stories ever written. It's all about spontaneities and calculation, too."

MARILYN HACKER was born in the Bronx, New York, in 1942. She is the author of eight books, including *Winter Numbers* (Norton, 1994), which received the Lenore Marshall Prize of the Academy of American Poets and *The Nation,* and the verse novel *Love, Death and the Changing of the Seasons,* reissued by Norton in 1995. *Edge,* her translations of the French poet Claire Malroux, was published by Wake Forest University Press in 1996. A former editor of *The Kenyon Review,* she now teaches at Hofstra University and divides her time between New York and Paris.

Hacker writes: " 'Again, the River' is a tribute to a friend, herself a poet, novelist, and classical scholar (so why not Sapphics?) and a meditation on the mutability of life and language."

RACHEL HADAS was born in New York City in 1948. She is the author of twelve books of poetry, essays, and translations, most recently *Halfway Down the Hall: New and Selected Poems* (Wesleyan University Press, 1998), *The Empty Bed* (poems; Wesleyan University Press, 1995), and *The Double Legacy* (essays; Faber & Faber, 1995). She has received a Guggenheim Fellowship, an Ingram Merrill Foundation grant, and an award in literature from the American Academy of Arts and Letters. She teaches English at the Newark campus of Rutgers University and has also taught at Columbia and Princeton universities.

Of "Pomegranate Variations," Hadas writes: "This sequence is a kind of poetic record of a writing course I taught at Rutgers Newark in the fall of 1994; it was completed at the Atlantic Center for the Arts early in 1995. Most of my courses at Rutgers, where I've taught since 1981, are large-ish literature classes; when I have taught poetry writing, it's often been elsewhere, for example Gay Men's Health Crisis of the Sewanee Writers' Conference. Thus this poetry course was relatively unusual in the Newark setting. It felt intense and intimate; there were maybe ten students, from very diverse backgrounds, and they worked beautifully together. Including some of their names or images from their poems in my own poem was something I'd never done before, but it felt right this time.

"The erotics of teaching is a phenomenon that has long been evident to me (and, I should think, to anyone who sets foot in a classroom). That fall the emotional cast of the workshop felt like a renewal; the deaths of my mother and a dear friend a couple of years before were beginning to recede, and I sometimes felt joyful, possessive, fierce about teaching, poetry, truth-telling. All semester, I looked forward to the classes. The door would close and the process would begin again, over and over—a cyclical miracle.

"As I recall the writing of 'Pomegranate Variations,' I kept rough records of various things that were said and done in class, or simply remembered them—notably the day I actually brought a pomegranate into Hill Hall, Room 216. The beautiful and poetically rich story of Demeter and Persephone certainly entered into my imagination, and I am indebted, as the epigraphs note, both to Christina Rossetti's immortalizing of fruit in 'Goblin Market' and to Eavan Boland's poem 'Pomegranate.'

"I can't claim any settled symbolic or mythological meaning in my 'Variations,' which range over remembered parts of my own youth, the process of teaching, the atmosphere of a particular class, and attitudes toward language. I do see a similar kind of aggregation in the writing, a year or so later, of my 'Helen Variations,' a linked series of poems all connected to the fact that I was in the process of translating Euripides' romance *Helen*. Do the two sets of variations mean I'm embarked on a venture in mythology? Not necessarily. What interests me is the fact that both sets work through triangulation: the poet/speaker/teacher/translator (and her own past) in constellation with a text, or a set of texts, on the one hand, and with the class, or the world out there, on the other."

DONALD HALL was born in Connecticut in 1928. Since 1975 he has lived in New Hampshire and supported himself as a freelance writer.

His most recent book of poems, *Without* (Houghton Mifflin, 1998), is about the illness and death of his late wife, the poet Jane Kenyon.

Hall writes: "Jane's leukemia was diagnosed in January 1994, and she died in April 1995. Shortly after her death I began 'Letter with No Address.' I wasn't sure that I was writing a poem, nor did I think about writing further letter-poems. After someone dies, all survivors have the same experience. You hear good news, and your first thought is: 'Oh, Jane will be happy too. . . .' You correct yourself with a wrench. I needed to tell Jane what was happening: Maggie Fisher was pregnant; Joyce and I met at the Mall of New Hampshire, where Jane and Joyce used to meet. When I had drafted my letter, I began to revise it, trying out of long habit to *make a poem*. I worked on 'Letter with No Address' for a couple of years, with help from my friends—but the poem was mostly there after a month. Then I wrote other letters, ending with 'Letter After a Year.' Writing these pieces, trying to make them poems, gave me a reason to get out of bed in the morning. Although I did not undertake the form with literary forethought, the epistolary device turned out to be right. I could look out the window and tell Jane about the weather; I could tell her what flowers were blooming. I could tell Jane about a grandchild's birthday party; I could reminisce about our old life together. The wandering paragraphs of a letter suited my wandering, albeit obsessed, mind. I could zip back and forth from subject to subject, from my uncle and aunt Dick and Nan in Tilton to the drive back from Tilton. These letters provided a place where I could work out the feelings of that first year of grief."

JOSEPH HARRISON was born in Richmond, Virginia, in 1957, grew up in Virginia and Alabama, and took degrees at Yale University and Johns Hopkins. He lives in Baltimore, and teaches at Goucher College, the Johns Hopkins part-time graduate writing program in Washington, and privately. His poetry has appeared in *The Kenyon Review, The Paris Review, Western Humanities Review,* and elsewhere; a group of poems, introduced by Rachel Hadas, was featured in *Boston Review.* His manuscript is entitled *Someone Else's Name.*

Of "The Cretonnes of Penelope," Harrison writes: "As many readers will recognize, the title comes from a line in Wallace Stevens's beautiful lyric, 'The World as Meditation': 'A form of fire approaches the cretonnes of Penelope.' The form is a variation on the sestina (the editor who published it suggested we call it a 'quintina'), which I made up as I went along: I had no formal intentions, beyond the pentameter, until I rhymed the sixth line. Penelope's situation (in Homer, of course, it's a death shroud she's weaving) seems to me an interesting figure for the predicament of the writer or artist: making something, ripping it up, making something, ripping it up, all the while vaguely hoping for one's ship to come in, whatever that would mean, with nobody in the immediate vicinity paying much attention."

ANTHONY HECHT was born in New York City in 1923. His B.A. from Bard College was granted in absentia (1944) while he was overseas with the army; he later earned his M.A. from Columbia University. After forty years of teaching at Bard College, Kenyon College, Smith College, the University of Rochester, Iowa State University, and Georgetown University, he retired in 1993. Most of his poetry has been assembled in *The Collected, Earlier Poetry, of Anthony Hecht* and *The Transparent Man,* both published by Knopf. His other works include *Obligatti: Essays in Criticism* (Atheneum); a critical study of W. H. Auden's poetry, *The Hidden Law* (Harvard University Press); *On the Laws of the Poetic Art: The Andrew Mellon Lectures, 1992* (Princeton, 1995); and *The Presumptions of Death* (Gehenna Press, 1995). His latest publications include a collection of poems, *Flight Among the Tombs* (1996), and the Introduction to the New Cambridge Shakespeare edition of the sonnets (1996). Hecht has received the Pulitzer Prize, the Bollingen Prize, and the Eugenio Montale Award. He and his wife live in Washington, D.C. He has three sons.

Of "Rara Avis in Terris," Hecht writes: "While this is a love poem for my wife, and was part of a Christmas present (it accompanied a small brooch described in the poem—just as Emily Dickinson composed poems to accompany gifts), it was partly prompted by a sense that the truculence of national and international politics, a hankering for definitive solutions imposed by coercion, had finally entered the formerly thoughtful and civil corridors of higher education, where I had been happy among students and colleagues for most of my career. But then, as it seemed, quite suddenly, the literature that I loved and taught came to be regarded as nothing more than a symptom of social ills, gender and sexual orientation, unacknowledged racial agendas, and other base motives that could be exposed only by employing techniques that not only had little to do with literature but were actively hostile to it. Having long since pronounced the death of God, *philosophes* now rejoiced to proclaim the death of the author, leaving themselves and their kind in sole possession of departments of English. I was very content to retire."

DARYL HINE was born in British Columbia in 1936. His books include translations of Homer, Theocritus, and Ovid, as well as numerous volumes of his own verse, the most recent of which is entitled *Postscripts: Poems* (Knopf, 1991). Formerly the editor of *Poetry* magazine and a MacArthur Fellow, he is now working on a metrical translation of Hesiod and a memoir of the philosopher Samuel J. Todes.

About "The World Is Everything That Is the Case," Hine writes, "This sonnet is a cento of quotations, direct and indirect, from the writings of Ludwig Wittgenstein."

EDWARD HIRSCH was born in Chicago, in 1950, and currently teaches in the creative writing program at the University of Houston. He has published five books of poems, all with Knopf: *For the Sleepwalkers* (1981; reprinted Carnegie Mellon Press, 1998), *Wild Gratitude* (1986), *The Night Parade* (1989), *Earthly Measures* (1994), and *On Love* (1998).

Of "The Lectures on Love," Hirsch writes: "I decided to call a symposium on love. I would invite only those writers I was most deeply interested in hearing from; I wouldn't be deterred by the fact that we lived at different times. Each of the voices would be intimate and formally charged, unsparing, ruthlessly authentic. It would be a gathering of household gods, a group of litanies and treatments, a festival of reliefs and inscriptions, a set of fever papers, a fever jubilee, a paradise of instruction. . . .

"Desire before knowledge. I began by developing a shocking squib from Baudelaire's *Intimate Journals.* When I moved on to Heine speaking from his mattress-grave, I realized that some of the 'lectures' would be turning into love poems. The forms would be a form of praise, a fever psalm. Suddenly, I was setting sail for happiness. . . ."

RICHARD HOWARD was born in Cleveland, Ohio, in 1929. He was educated at Columbia University and the Sorbonne. The most recent of his eleven books of poems is *Trappings* (Counterpoint, 1998); for his third, *Untitled Subjects,* he was awarded the Pulitzer Prize in 1970. He has translated more than 150 works from the French and received the American Book Award for his translation of Baudelaire's *Les Fleurs du mal.* He is a member of the American Academy of Arts and Letters and a chancellor of the Academy of American Poets, and in 1994–1995 he served as the Poet Laureate of New York State. In 1996 he was named a fellow of the MacArthur Foundation. He is poetry editor of both *The Paris Review* and *Western Humanities Review,* and he teaches in the writing division of the School of the Arts at Columbia University. He was guest editor of *The Best American Poetry 1995*.

Of "The Job Interview," Howard writes that it was "originally written for a Festschrift in honor of André Breton" but was "rejected by the editor (Anna Balakian) as insufficiently laudatory (of A. B.—André Breton, not Anna Balakian, who has since died)."

ANDREW HUDGINS was born in Killeen, Texas, in 1951, while his father was stationed at nearby Fort Hood. He teaches at the University of Cincinnati, where he is a professor of English. He has published five books of poetry, all with Houghton Mifflin, including *After the Lost War* (1988) and *The Glass Hammer* (1994). In 1997 a collection of his essays was published by the University of Michigan under the title *The Glass Anvil*. His fifth book of poems, *Babylon in a Jar* (1998), includes the poem "The Hanging Gardens."

Of "The Hanging Gardens," Hudgins writes: "This poem let me revel in two of my fixations: history and gardens. When I was a child, I got out of the library a children's book about the seven wonders of the ancient world, and I was fascinated by the description of the Hanging Gardens of Babylon, because I could almost but not quite imagine them. But I felt like I should be able to imagine them. I knew what gardens were and, from the Bible, what Babylon was. Because the Bible was read to me as absolute spiritual and historical truth from the time I was very young, I have always felt a strong connection, even kinship, with the world of the ancient Middle East. The chapters in the Book of Wonders about, say, the Temple of Artemis at Ephesus or Phidias's Statue of Zeus at Olympia meant little to me. Statues were simply statues and other children's books I read made me think of the ancient gods as comic and trivial.

"My book about the wonders of the world was vague on just what the Hanging Gardens were or how they worked, and I realize now that that's because the historians disagree about whether the gardens even existed or were myth. Because the book paraphrased Philo's statement that the gardens grew in the air, I saw the garden as something like Jonathan Swift's Flying Island of Laputa, but with lush vines draped over its sides. An image I loved, though I knew it made no sense—a habit of mind that seems to drive much of the thinking about the Hanging Gardens of Babylon.

"Several years ago a friend offered to give me her art history notes about the Hanging Gardens and those confusing notes, along with

John Dixon Hunt's very interesting *Oxford Book of Garden Verse,* sent me back to the library to find out what I could about those fabulous gardens. And this poem is the result."

MARK JARMAN was born in Mount Sterling, Kentucky, in 1952. He is a professor of English at Vanderbilt University in Nashville, Tennessee. He is the author of six books of poetry: *North Sea* (Cleveland State University Poetry Center, 1978), *The Rote Walker* (Carnegie-Mellon University Press, 1981), *Far and Away* (Carnegie-Mellon University Press, 1985), *The Black Riviera* (Wesleyan University Press, 1990), *Iris* (Story Line Press, 1992), and *Questions for Ecclesiastes* (Story Line Press, 1997), which was nominated for the National Book Critics Circle Award in poetry. With Robert McDowell, he is the co-author of *The Reaper Essays* (Story Line Press, 1996), and with David Mason, he has edited *Rebel Angels: 25 Poets of the New Formalism* (Story Line Press, 1996). Story Line Press will publish his book of essays, *The Secret of Poetry,* in 1999. *The Black Riviera* won the Poets' Prize for 1991.

Of "The Word 'Answer,'" Jarman writes: "I was reading Karl Barth's essay on 'The Lord's Prayer,' when I came to the passage I have used as an epigraph for my poem. Barth's essay, like his theology generally, is very down-to-earth. When he speaks of asking God for our daily bread, he believes we should mean just that. But I was also struck by his suggestion that prayer is a catalyst or stimulus to God or as he says 'an influence' that can affect not only God's behavior but his very being. He seemed to suggest that a prayer's answer might be inherent in the act of praying itself. What else he suggested, at least to me, I have tried to represent in the poem."

DONALD JUSTICE was born in Miami, Florida, in 1925. He currently resides in Iowa. For his poetry he has received the Pulitzer Prize, the Bollingen Prize, and, in 1996, the Lannan Literary Award. His recent books include *A Donald Justice Reader* (University Press of New England, 1992), *New and Selected Poems* (Knopf, 1995), and *Oblivion* (Story Line Press, 1998), a book of critical prose.

Of "Stanzas on a Hidden Theme," Justice writes: "The first stanza was written in 1984, the third and last in 1997. In that stanza I seem to have been thinking of Chekhov. On the advice of Alice Quinn, the poetry editor of *The New Yorker,* two other stanzas were cut; I was grateful for the good advice. Whether the three remaining stanzas connect I am not at all sure; they do share something, I would like to believe, besides the verse form. The poem's original title was from the first line: 'There is a gold light in certain old paintings.'"

BRIGIT PEGEEN KELLY was born in Palo Alto, California, in 1951. She teaches in the creative writing program at the University of Illinois at Urbana-Champaign. Her first book, *To the Place of Trumpets,* was published by Yale University Press in 1988 as part of the Yale Series of Younger Poets. Her second book, *Song,* was published in 1995 by BOA Editions, Ltd., and was awarded the Lamont Poetry Prize from the Academy of American Poets.

KARL KIRCHWEY was born in Boston in 1956, and educated at Yale College and Columbia University. He is the author of three collections of poetry: *A Wandering Island* (Princeton University Press, 1990), *Those I Guard* (Harcourt Brace, 1993), and *The Engrafted Word* (Henry Holt, 1998). His work-in-progress, based on the *Alcestis* of Euripides, received *The Paris Review*'s Prize for Poetic Drama in 1997. He has been director of the Unterberg Poetry Center of the 92nd Street YM-YWHA in New York since 1987, and has taught at Smith College, Yale, and Columbia. He lives in Manhattan with his wife and two children.

Kirchwey writes: "The three parts of 'Roman Hours' were composed during a fellowship year I spent with my family at the American Academy in Rome, and had their origins in sources dynastic, scientific, and domestic, respectively. Nowhere is the past more simultaneously present than in modern Rome; the investigation of timekeeping devices which forms the ostensible organizing principle of the poem came naturally.

"Octavian Caesar (Augustus) erected an obelisk pillaged from Egypt on the Campus Martius in Rome to celebrate his victory over Cleopatra. The obelisk was in fact the pointer on a gigantic sundial (*horologium*), traces of which survive below modern Rome's streets. This sundial was so constructed that the sun appeared to complete an annual 'walk' between Augustus's own Mausoleum and his Altar of Peace (an ironically named monument, if ever there was one): thus Augustus had effectively co-opted the heavens themselves, involving the sun in his own waltz of power, as the Italian scholar Salvatore Settis has interestingly discussed. "The Horologium of Augustus" is in stanzas which, by the increasing numerical squares of their syllable count, pun on another sense—the mathematical one—of the word 'gnomon,' or pointer.

"An historian of science at the University of Wisconsin (Madison) named James Lattis most patiently explained to me the relation between the movement of the heavenly bodies and timekeeping methods, and part two of 'Roman Hours' arose from these conversations. Another kind of 'clock,' called a meridian, focuses light through a hole in a building wall: the sun's light, for an austral meridian, and the light of the North Star, for a polar meridian. The beam of light, or its point, once again travels along a 'track'—in this case, on the floor of the Baths of Diocletian, long ago converted to a church (Santa Maria degli Angeli e Martiri) by the same Christians whose slave labor supposedly built the edifice in the first place. The italicized passages in this second poem are from Edward Gibbon's *Decline and Fall of the Roman Empire.*

"One popular Sunday afternoon destination for Romans and tourists alike is the park atop the Janiculum, Rome's highest hill, where a cannon is still fired out over the city to mark the hour of noon and where Punch and Judy puppet shows take place, near the row of herms bearing busts of Garibaldi's officers in the doomed battle against the French in 1849. There is also a merry-go-round, and in our first days in Rome, these diversions provided us with a dependable recourse in an unfamiliar environment, giving rise eventually to 'The Janiculum Cannon.'"

CAROLYN KIZER was born in Spokane, Washington, in 1925, and educated in Spokane public schools. Her father was a noted civil liberties lawyer and urban planner. She has three children and is married to John Woodbridge, FAIA, also a city planner. She graduated from Sarah Lawrence College in 1945, and then was a fellow of the Chinese government at Columbia University; she subsequently went to China, where her father directed Chinese relief. She founded the poetry quarterly *Poetry Northwest* and was the first director of literature for the National Endowment for the Arts. Her most recent collection is *Harping On: Poems 1985–1995* (Copper Canyon, 1996). She received the Pulitzer Prize in 1985 for *Yin: New Poems* (BOA Editions, 1984).

Of "Second Time Around," Kizer writes: "Nearly every male poet of my generation has been married more than once, their first wives often women of considerable attainments on their own. A certain English poet comes to mind as well! I don't mean to be invidious. I have been married twice myself (my second being a vast improvement on the first. As I often say, 'I don't mind egotism as long as the man has something to be egotistical about.') Unlike most of my work, which I revise extensively, this poem wrote itself. Perhaps for that reason, I don't consider it of any importance."

KENNETH KOCH was born in Cincinnati, Ohio, in 1925. He teaches at Columbia University and lives in New York City. His most recent books of poetry are *Straits* (Knopf, 1998), *On the Great Atlantic Rainway: Selected Poems 1950–1988* (1994), and *One Train* (1994), for which he was awarded the Bollingen Prize for Poetry (1995) and the Bobbitt National Poetry Prize (1996). Other recently published books are *Making Your Own Days: The Pleasures of Reading and Writing Poetry* (Scribner, 1998), *The Gold Standard: A Book of Plays* (Knopf, 1996), and *Hotel Lambosa and Other Stories* (Coffee House Press, 1993). *The Banquet,* an opera for which he wrote the libretto, with music by Marcello Panni, was presented in Bremen in June 1998.

Of "Ballade," Koch writes: "Villon's line *'En l'an trentiesme de mon age'* (which begins his 'Testament') inspired me, just before reaching my thirtieth year, to write a poem with that line as its title. It began: 'O red-hot cupboards and burning pavements, alas it's summer; my cheeks fall into somewhere and alas for the Rainbow Club. / Flowery pins bluejay introspection anagrams. On this day I complete my twenty-ninth year! . . .' This new poem, 'Ballade,' with its seventeen stanzas written from the viewpoints of seventeen different years, was partly suggested by the work I did revising the earlier poem when I decided to include it in my selected poems, *On the Great Atlantic Rainway.*"

JOHN KOETHE was born on Christmas Day 1945 in San Diego, and was educated at Princeton and Harvard. He is a professor of philosophy at the University of Wisconsin, Milwaukee. "The Secret Amplitude" is included in his most recent book of poems, *Falling Water* (Harper-Collins, 1997). His other books of poetry include *The Late Wisconsin Spring* (Princeton University Press, 1984), *Domes* (Columbia University Press, 1973), for which he received the Frank O'Hara Award, and *Blue Vents* (Audit/Poetry, 1968). He is the author of *The Continuity of Wittgenstein's Thought* (Cornell University Press, 1996). *Falling Water* won the Kingsley Tufts Award for poetry in 1998.

Koethe writes: "I'd intended for a long time to write a poem in the form of Wallace Stevens's 'The Auroras of Autumn,' but after I'd written several sections of 'The Secret Amplitude' I remembered that Stevens's sections were twenty-four lines each, whereas I'd been writing sections of thirty lines. So I said farewell to that idea. The poem is written in tercets with lines of ten syllables, with a rhyme scheme that varies from section to section in a sort of concentric pattern: the first, fifth, and ninth sections have the same rhyme scheme, as do the second and eighth, the third and seventh, and the fourth and sixth. The title refers to a powerful kind of inner experience that may or may not be illusory, but the poem also incorporates ruminations about two friends of mine who killed themselves, and about trips to Paris and other places."

RIKA LESSER was born in Brooklyn, New York, in 1953. She is the author of three collections of poetry: *Etruscan Things* (Braziller, 1983), *All We Need of Hell* (North Texas, 1995), and *Growing Back: Poems 1972–1992* (University of South Carolina Press, 1997). Educated at Yale and Columbia, she is a translator of Swedish and German literature and has won the Landon Poetry Translation Prize from the Academy of American Poets. *What Became Words* (Sun & Moon, 1996) is her selection of poems by jazz pianist, politician, and psychiatrist Claes Andersson, Finland's minister of culture. In 1996 she was awarded the Poetry Translation Prize of the Swedish Academy.

Lesser writes: "I began to write 'About Her' in April 1996, nearly two and a half years after 'that day that time' described in the poem's first section, described in greater detail in the first section of 'Epilogue: Dödsdansen,' the poem that concludes *All We Need of Hell*. (Perhaps in some future reprinting of that book, 'About Her' will serve as an epilogue to the epilogue.)

"It is now (January 1998) more than four years since 'then,' and still I recall nothing of that day. Was writing the poem a continuing attempt to recover it, as writing the poems in *All We Need of Hell* was an attempt to recover my pre-sick, pre-manic-depressive identity?

"Lonely children who read converse with their playthings, create playmates, invent 'twins.' In doing so, in glancing in the mirror, they may discover not themselves but others: cultures, languages, poets. Civilization."

PHILLIS LEVIN was born in Paterson, New Jersey, in 1954, and was educated at Sarah Lawrence College, and the Johns Hopkins University. She teaches at the Unterberg Poetry Center of the 92nd Street Y in New York City, and is an associate professor of English at the University of Maryland, College Park. Her second collection, *The Afterimage,* was published by Copper Beech Press in 1995; her earlier books, *Temples and Fields* (University of Georgia Press, 1988), received the Norma Farber First Book Award from the Poetry Society of America. A Fulbright Fellowship has taken her to Slovenia.

PHILIP LEVINE was born in Detroit, Michigan, in 1928. For his writing he has won two Pulitzer Prizes, two National Book Awards, two National Book Critics Circle Awards, the Lenore Marshall Award, and the Ruth Lilly Award. His most recent books of poetry are *What Work Is* (1991) and *The Simple Truth* (1994), both from Knopf, and *Unselected Poems* (Greenhouse Review Press, 1997). In 1994 Knopf also published *The Bread of Time: Toward an Autobiography*. After having recently taught at the University of California at Wilmington, he returns this fall to New York University.

Of "Drum," Levine writes: "My favorite Michigan poet is Theodore Roethke, and my favorite poems by him are the so-called greenhouse poems. I too was a gardener on a small scale in my teens, but I was not drawn to using his marvelous attention to detail to capture that world, for he'd already done that far better than I could ever. No, I wanted to focus the same intensity and precision that he gave to his weed-pulling, bulb-planting days to a time and place out of my urban, industrial years. I went back in memory to a particular 'shop' I'd never written about before, one that for me had a powerful taste and texture, and tried as best I could to get my first 'greenhouse poem.'"

REBECCA McCLANAHAN was born in Indiana in 1950. She is the author of four books, most recently *The Intersection of X and Y* (Copper Beech Press, 1996). Having taught writing for more than twenty-five years, she is currently a freelance writer and teacher in Charlotte, North Carolina. Her newest project, a book focusing on the craft of writing, is due from Story Press in January 1999.

McClanahan writes: "The experience of writing 'Making Love' was similar to the process alluded to in the poem. Like the first stirrings of love or lust, the affair began effortlessly. The poem shrugged its bare shoulder and I followed, delirious with possibility. But the faster I ran and the more I tried to capture it, the more the poem eluded me, taking turns that left me breathless. Exhausted, I slowed. The poem slowed, as if waiting for me to catch up. We walked for months, hand in hand, a slow and steady pace—one day this line; another day, that one. I nudged, the poem whispered. Reluctantly, it gave up its secrets, one by one, until one rainy morning it allowed its last line."

J. D. McCLATCHY was born in Bryn Mawr, Pennsylvania, in 1945. He is the author of four books of poems, *Scenes from Another Life* (1981), *Stars Principal* (1986), *The Rest of the Way* (1990), and *Ten Commandments*

(Knopf, 1998), and two collections of essays, *White Paper* (1990) and *Twenty Questions* (1998). He has edited many other books, including *The Vintage Book of Contemporary World Poetry* (1996), and written opera libretti for several composers. He is a chancellor of the Academy of American Poetry, and since 1991 has been editor of *The Yale Review*. He lives in New York City and in Stonington, Connecticut.

Of "Descartes's Dream," McClatchy writes: "The genius of René Descartes (1596–1650) was recognized and cultivated while he was still a child. When he was a student at the Jesuit school at La Flèche, allowances were made for his poor health and he did most of his work in bed. But brilliant work it was, and when Henri IV was assassinated, Descartes was one of the pupils assigned to receive the monarch's heart for burial in the church at La Flèche. Following his education, he traveled, and in 1619 was staying in Ulm, a city renowned for its mathematicians (Einstein was born there 260 years later). He was suddenly wracked by terrifying doubts and despair, and prayed for light. His prayers seem to have been heard, for he was soon seized by an extraordinary series of dreams and illuminations. During one of these—on November 10, 1619—it flashed on him that the method of analytical geometry could be extended to other studies as well. Three famous dreams followed this revelation. My poem is an amalgam of the first two of these dreams. In the third, he chanced upon a poem by Ausonius and happened to see the line *Quid vitae secatabor iter?* (What way of life shall I follow?). The rest of the story belongs to the history of philosophy."

HEATHER McHUGH was born to Canadian parents in San Diego in 1948. She teaches at the University of Washington in Seattle and in Warren Wilson College's low-residency M.F.A. Program for Writers in Asheville, North Carolina. Her most recent collection, *Hinge & Sign: Poems, 1968–1993* (Wesleyan University Press), was short-listed for the National Book Award in poetry. For the past three years she has been using a Lila Wallace–Reader's Digest grant to work with rural elementary school students who make their own paper and books and also post their poems on the Internet. Her URL is <http://weber.u.washington.edu/~amanuen>.

Of "Past All Understanding," which first appeared under the title "Flap Copy," McHugh writes: "Dog driven by fear and love. Man driven by fear and love. Earth driven by God. (The rest is singing.)"

SANDRA McPHERSON was born in San Jose, California, in 1943, and is currently a professor of English at the University of California, Davis.

Her most recent collections of poetry are *The Spaces Between Birds: Mother/Daughter Poems 1967–1995* (Wesleyan University Press, 1996), *Edge Effect: Trails and Portrayals* (Wesleyan University Press, 1996), *The God of Indeterminacy* (University of Illinois Press, 1993), and a fine-press construction, *Beauty in Use,* from Janus Press, West Burke, Vermont, 1997.

McPherson writes: " 'Chalk-Circle Compass' was one of the first of my 'extinct object' poems to be accepted for publication. I am exploring this century's history through objects that are no longer made, diaries of lives now ended, militaria, scrapbooks, telegrams, schooling materials, children's games, and so forth. 'The Hectograph,' for instance, about a classroom printing set from 1932, was published in *Field,* fall 1997, but sounds and looks very different from this compass poem; 'With Respect to the Palmer Method,' about a 1920s penmanship course, will appear in *The Missouri Review.* 'Chalk-Circle Compass' is pleased to think about irregularity vs. 'perfection' of form and how our child bodies ingest these alternatives as part of ourselves."

W. S. MERWIN was born in New York City in 1927. *A Mask for Janus,* his first book of poems, was chosen by W. H. Auden as the 1952 volume in the Yale Series of Younger Poets, and *The Carrier of Ladders* (1970) won the Pulitzer Prize. He has translated *The Poem of Cid* and *The Song of Roland,* and his *Selected Translations 1948–1968* won the PEN Translation Prize for 1968. In 1987 he received the Governor's Award for Literature of the State of Hawaii. In 1994 he received both the Dorothy Tanning Prize from the Academy of American Poets and a three-year writer's award from the Lila Wallace–Reader's Digest Fund. His most recent books include *The Vixen* (Knopf, 1996) and *The Folding Cliffs,* a narrative poem set in Hawaii (Knopf, 1998). *Flower and Hand* (Copper Canyon, 1997) restores to print three earlier books: *The Compass Flower, Feathers from the Hill,* and *Opening the Hand.* He lives in Hawaii—in a place called Haiku, on the island of Maui.

Of "The Chinese Mountain Fox," Merwin writes: "Foxes and wolves, representatives of the great canine presence among our elders, have appeared from time to time in what I have written, and I am not able to say altogether what they are doing there though they are certainly welcome. Something of that relation I hope is apparent in the poem. I knew of no zoological predecessor of the fox in this poem, but since it was written Peter Matthiessen has told me that there was, or is, such a creature in the world that we claim to know. I have no idea what the relation of the two might be."

ROBERT MEZEY was born in Philadelphia, Pennsylvania, in 1935. He attended Kenyon College and received his B.A. from the University of Iowa in 1959. He was a fellow at Stanford University and has taught at several schools, including Fresno State, the University of Utah, and Franklin and Marshall. Since 1976 he has been a professor and poet in residence at Pomona College. His first book, *The Lovemaker* (Cummington Press), won the Lamont Poetry Prize in 1960; other books include *White Blossoms, The Door Standing Open,* and *Evening Wind.* He has translated (with Richard Barnes) the more than four hundred collected poems of Borges; his own *Collected Poems* will be published by the University of Arkansas Press in 1999.

Mezey writes: "I've written many sonnets over the years but only three that I think are any good, 'Joe Simpson' being the most recent of the three. I wrote it in response to a request, the hardest kind of poem for me. Joe Simpson was a former brother-in-law, and I was told that he had asked on his deathbed if I would write something about him. (He had always liked an elegy I had written for his father many years before.) As the poem says, I didn't really know him very well, but one can hardly refuse a deathbed request. I read the poem at the memorial service, and my dear friend Harry Duncan (whose Cummington Press published my first two books) printed it as a handsome bereavement card, the last work he ever did; he finished setting the type the day he went into the hospital for the last time, and two of his young assistants printed it the day after his death. What I like best about the poem is that the first four and a half lines comprise four short sentences and the rest of the poem one long one."

A. F. MORITZ was born in Niles, Ohio, in 1947, and was educated at Marquette University. Since 1974 he has lived in Toronto. His books of poems include *The Tradition* (Princeton, 1986) and several published in Canada, including *Mahoning* (Brick Books, 1994). He is co-author with Theresa Moritz of *The Oxford Literary Guide to Canada* (1987) and *Stephen Leacock: A Biography* (Stoddart, 1985), and has translated books of poems by Ludwig Zeller, Benjamin Péret, and Gilberto Meza. He and Theresa Moritz have just finished a translation of Zeller's *conte philosophique, Rio Loa, Station of Dreams,* and a biography of Emma Goldman emphasizing her years in Canada, both to be published in 1998. His poetry has received Guggenheim, Ingram Merrill, and Canada Council fellowships and the Award in Literature of the American Academy of Arts and Letters. He works as a writer and an occasional teacher of literature and creative writing at the University of Toronto.

Moritz writes: " 'Artisan and Clerk' came after my book *Mahoning,* which takes its name from the main river of my native region in northeastern Ohio, and which is about the social, historical, natural, and spiritual character of that place. It is thus a book of origin and 'roots' partly in the American tradition of Williams, Olson, Faulkner, etc.; its manner, however, descends not at all from such writers but from Trakl, Bobrowski, Bonnefoy, Seferis, Ritsos, Quasimodo, and others. Afterward, the impulse of the subject matter went on to dictate some poems, like 'Artisan and Clerk,' in a form less purely symbolic, gestural, and 'mute.' One thing I'm concerned with is to end analysis and begin transformation, always remembering that satire and vision are two faces of the same coin. This poem ends not just with an indomitable outcast; there is the assertion that what casts him or her out is finally nothing but a small gargoyle in a 'divine' scene, which this gargoyle has nevertheless prevented from being realized on the physical plane. Still, human life requires accomplishment outwardly, on the social, political, and architectural levels, as well as inwardly. Preserving the revolutionary possibility is something, but I'm not satisfied."

THYLIAS MOSS was born in Cleveland, Ohio, in 1954. A 1996 Fellow of the MacArthur Foundation, she teaches in the M.F.A. program at the University of Michigan. This year she celebrates the twenty-fifth anniversary of her marriage and the publication of two books: her sixth volume of poetry, *Last Chance for the Tarzan Holler,* from Persea Books, and *Tale of a Sky-Blue Dress,* a memoir from Avon. Previous publications include appearances in *The Best American Poetry* in 1989, 1990, 1991, and 1992; *The Best of the Best American Poetry 1988–1997, Pyramid of Bone* (*Callaloo*/University of Virginia Press, 1989), which was shortlisted for the National Book Critics Circle Award, *Rainbow Remnants in Rock Bottom Ghetto Sky* (Persea, 1991), winner of the National Poetry Series Open Competition, and *Small Congregations* (Ecco, 1993), a volume of new and selected poems. The recipient of numerous grants and awards, including a Guggenheim Fellowship, a Whiting Writer's Award, and the Witter Bynner prize, she lives in Ann Arbor with her husband and sons, who sometimes still enjoy, without her coercion, reading *I Want to Be* (Dial Books for Young Readers, 1993), her first book for children.

Of "The Right Empowerment of Light," Moss writes: "Naturally, it was an accident. I certainly did not intend to find something. Indeed, I would prefer at least a day of no discovery at all, but I erred in how I set about trying to exercise that preference, turning to a book of photography by Linda Butler. There on the cover and repeated on plate forty-five to which the book opened (practically of its own accord since I that day was no intentional seeker) were these slender illuminated objects. These were not lamps, not generators of any sort, yet they were privy to luminosity. They appeared to be the source of the radiance and not some mere reflective surface no more a seeker than I. How long before metaphor, my usual adored captor, claimed me? It was instantaneous, as absolutes must be, instantaneous and never-ending, true love of the luminous, but the luminous what (oh, don't yet surrender to the caption despite its purpose; seek first metaphors!)? Were these not the glowing tubes of old televisions? Were they not cylindrical oracles and wasn't that my white gas of a future filling all the glassy space? Were these not, say, even condoms holding radioactive deposit—ah, metaphor; keep on evoking such interactions and mergers, so intense is your hold, so intense is my delight in the holding—ah, this corrupt science, these crooked, out-of-line, wayward, crippled (bad word) test tubes of a milkiness that dared to glow, *dared* to glow. They're brilliant.

"It was daring that I found and finding it could not let it go until it was released to a poem. And I found myself again with preference, this time for the audacity of these radishes (despite caption, boundary), for their vanity possible only through their crookedness, their bent ways that led them to light, for their delicious (wouldn't it be?) arrogance to shine, shine, not with the little light (hymn and gospel) considered so proper—no, no; these radishes held back not so much as a photon, bright for just a minute, but that was the minute in which they were found, in which they are held so that the burnout, inevitable or not, did (or) does not happen, held off by that fine little arrogance. And then I realized that were this (and I certainly wanted it to be dished up) served me on some surely inadequate plate (even if gold-plated along the rim), I would be so thoroughly unprepared to eat the glowing (arrogance had not appeared on any menu given me) that I would sit, stare, until the glowing penetrated my eyes, taught me to shine down the house with just a glance until only that shine was there, only arrogance, even though, as bright as it is, some could think it so, so clean; absolutely, astonishingly clean."

WILLIAM MULLEN was born in 1946, and grew up in Little Rock, Arkansas. In 1968 he graduated from Harvard College, where he took poetry seminars with Robert Fitzgerald and Robert Lowell. He is the author of *Choreia: Pindar and Dance* (Princeton, 1982). More recent publications include *Jefferson and Rome: Foundation and Fabric* (de Gruyter, 1998) and *The Agenda of the Milesian School* (Archaeo Press, Oxford, 1998), an exploration of pre-Socratic thinkers in the light of catastrophism.

Mullen writes: " 'Enchanted Rock' is an homage to Tu Fu's 'Autumn Meditations,' often called, in Chinese literary tradition, China's greatest poem. It imitates it formally by adopting its structure of eight eight-line stanzas, each with no rhyme on the four odd-numbered lines and a single rhyme throughout on each of the four even-numbered lines (here varied by off-rhyme). It also imitates 'Autumn Meditations' thematically: the speakers in both poems are in later life remembering with sadness the happiness of their younger days in a remote place.

"The ghats at Banaras are the famous steps down which thousands crowd daily to immerse themselves in the sacred waters of the Ganges. It may interest readers to know that because of recent cleanups the Hudson River, even in New York harbor itself, is now considerably less polluted than the Ganges.

"The capitalized 'Spirit' of the fourth and sixth stanzas may be conceptualized by the reader as an incoherent amalgam of the *Brahman* of the Upanishads and Hegel's *Geist*.

"The phrase 'Epicurus' gods' at the end of the seventh stanza refers to the gods of Epicurean philosophy, who were completely different from traditional Homeric gods in that they were beings who existed in the space between worlds, had no interest in humans (neither in our prayers nor in our ethical behavior), and who were of interest to us only insofar as they could be imagined as models of that state of *ataraxia,* serenity or imperturbability, which was the goal Epicureans strove to achieve in their own lives."

ERIC ORMSBY was born in Atlanta, Georgia, in 1941, and grew up in Miami. In 1986 he moved to Montreal, where he is currently a professor of Islamic Studies and classical Arabic at McGill University. His poems have been anthologized in the fourth edition of *The Norton Anthology of Poetry.* His most recent book is *For a Modest God: New and Selected Poems* (Grove, 1997).

Of "Flamingos," Ormsby writes: "Somewhat to my own surprise I often find myself writing about birds, even though (or maybe because) birds impress me as supremely strange and rather alarming creatures. Flamingos (which I observed as a child in Florida, in the wild and in zoos) have always fascinated me, perhaps because their gait and demeanor appear to combine the rankly sexual and the demurely ecclesiastical; they display a prim flamboyance all their own. In my poem I wanted to evoke both the oddity of their form and coloration as well as to mimic in the poem's cadences their singular stride, which suggests a spookily sinuous Carmen Miranda decked out in cardinal's vestments to participate in some festive procession. In the final section, I also wanted to pay an oblique tribute, again through the cadences as well as the hues of the lines, to Wallace Stevens, a poet I admire very much."

JACQUELINE OSHEROW was born in Philadelphia in 1956. She is the author of *With a Moon in Transit* (Grove, 1996), *Conversations with Survivors* (1994), and *Looking for Angels in New York* (1988) (both from the University of Georgia Press). She has been awarded a Guggenheim Fellowship, the Witter Bynner Prize from the American Academy of Arts and Letters, an Ingram Merrill Foundation grant, and a number of prizes from the Poetry Society of America. "Views of *La Leggenda della Vera Croce*" will appear in her forthcoming collection *Dead Men's Praise* (Grove).

Of "Views of *La Leggenda della Vera Croce*," Osherow writes: "This poem is the result of a grant from the University of Utah research committee, which enabled me to travel to Italy to visit (or, in most cases, revisit) the places out of which the poem was written. I brought my then twenty-month-old youngest daughter with me (a born traveler who still asks when we're going back) and so the poem is also, at least in part, the product of pushing a stroller through the high grass beyond Ostia Antica in the purported direction of the remains of the ancient synagogue, as well as barging with the same stroller into the office of the assistant to the superintendent of fine arts in Arezzo, to beg to be permitted to see the half of *The Legend of the True Cross* fresco cycle (including *The Torture of the Jew*) which was then being restored. I'm convinced that it was my daughter who charmed the exceedingly friendly and helpful woman into talking her boss into letting me climb the scaffolding with the head restorer. I then had the unforgettable experience of seeing from close up what I had only ever looked at, with my head tilted far back, from what now seemed like the enormous distance of the floor. Perhaps this is what gave me the nerve to try, finally, to write something about these frescoes, which I really have visited (I don't exaggerate in the poem) dozens and dozens of times."

ROBERT PINSKY was born in Long Branch, New Jersey, in 1940. His most recent collection, *The Figured Wheel: New and Collected Poems 1968–1996,* was awarded the Lenore Marshall Prize and the Ambassador Prize of the English Speaking Union. His translation of Dante's *Inferno* was published to wide acclaim by Farrar, Straus & Giroux in 1994. A professor of creative writing at Boston University, he is currently Poet Laureate of the United States.

Pinsky writes: "The summer before I turned eleven, my mother fell through an unfinished floor and received a head injury. For years afterward, she had various symptoms that made the household somewhat chaotic. Meaning became a prized rarity. 'Ode to Meaning' grows out of that experience more directly than do many of my other poems. The opposite meaning is not necessarily meaninglessness: it might be the arbitrary. Thus, in the third stanza, the words appear in alphabetical order."

REYNOLDS PRICE was born in Macon, North Carolina, in 1933. Educated in the public schools of his native state, he earned an A.B. summa cum laude from Duke University, graduating first in his class. In 1955 he traveled as a Rhodes Scholar to Merton College, Oxford University, to study English literature. After three years and the B.Litt. degree, he returned to Duke, where he continues in his fourth decade of teaching. He is James B. Duke Professor of English. In 1962 his novel *A Long and Happy Life* received the William Faulkner Award for a notable first novel. Since then, he has published nearly thirty books. His novel *Kate Vaiden* received the National Book Critics Circle Award in 1986. His *Collected Stories* appeared in 1993, his *Collected Poems* in 1997. His tenth novel, *The Promise of Rest,* appeared in 1995 and completed—with *The Surface of Earth* and *The Source of Light*—a trilogy of novels, entitled *A Great Circle,* concerned with nine decades in a family's life.

Price writes: " 'The Closing, the Ecstasy' is several kinds of poem. My two most apparent intentions were to write in convincing detail about a specific instance of sexual longing and, beyond that immediate occasion, to write a fresh and valid contemporary example of an old kind of poem that has always interested me—the frank reflection of sexual intent that only half disguises itself as a metaphysical but nonetheless physically overwhelming snowstorm composed of nothing more coercive than words and images. John Donne's 'The Ecstasy' is the most famous such poem in English; and while my structure differs radically from his, my hopes in the act of writing were similar."

WYATT PRUNTY was born in Humbolt, Tennessee, in 1947. He is currently the director of the Sewanee Writers' Conference and teaches in the English Department at Sewanee. His books include *Since the Noon Mail Stopped* (1977), *The Run of the House* (1993), *Balance as Belief* (1989), *What Women Know, What Men Believe* (1986), and *The Time Between* (1982), all from Johns Hopkins University Press, as well as *Fallen from the Symboled World: Precedents for the New Formalism* (Oxford University Press, 1990) and *Domestic of the Outer Banks* (Inland Boat Press, 1980).

STEPHEN SANDY was born in Minneapolis, Minnesota, in 1938. His first collection of poetry, *Stresses in the Peaceable Kingdom,* was published by Houghton Mifflin in 1967 and was followed by *Roofs,* in 1971. Knopf published *Riding to Greylock* in 1983, *Man in the Open Air* in 1988, and *Thanksgiving Over the Water* in 1992. His most recent volume is *The Thread, New and Selected Poems* (Louisiana State University Press, 1998). He has received fellowships from the National Endowment for the Arts and the Ingram Merrill Foundation and has held a Fulbright Lectureship in Japan at the University of Tokyo. He has been McGee Professor of Writing at Davidson College in North Carolina and is on the faculty of Bennington College in Vermont.

Of "Four Corners, Vermont," Sandy writes: "This poem is not new, having been sketched out some years ago; the title is intended to make the poem more vivid, but it is not 'about' Vermont or any particular place. It might be any listless little town, and 'Four Corners,' a generic intersection. Thus, the poem does not allude to any specific governor."

ALAN SHAPIRO was born in Boston in 1952. He received his B.A. from Brandeis University in 1974. He has published five books of poetry: *After the Digging* (Elpenor Books, 1981), *The Courtesy* (University of Chicago Press, 1983), *Happy Hour* (University of Chicago Press, 1987), *Covenant* (University of Chicago Press, 1991), and *Mixed Company* (University of Chicago Press, 1996), which won the 1996 *Los Angeles Times* Book Award for poetry. He has also published three books of prose: *In Praise of the Impure: Poetry and the Ethical Imagination* (TriQuarterly Books, 1993), *The Last Happy Occasion* (University of Chicago Press, 1996), and *Vigil* (University of Chicago Press, 1997). He has received awards and fellowships from the National Endowment for the Arts, the Guggenheim Foundation, and the Lila Wallace–Reader's Digest Fund. He teaches English and creative writing at the University of North Carolina, Chapel Hill, where he lives with his wife and two children.

Shapiro writes: " 'The Coat' is less about depression than about the comfort one can find in being depressed. The comfort is genuine, and all the more insidious for being so."

ROBERT B. SHAW was born in Philadelphia in 1947. He was educated at Harvard, where he studied with Robert Fitzgerald and Robert Lowell, and at Yale, where he received a Ph.D. He is currently a professor of English at Mount Holyoke College. His three books of poems are *Comforting the Wilderness* (Wesleyan, 1977), *The Wonder of Seeing Double* (Massachusetts, 1988), and *The Post Office Murals Restored* (Copper Beech, 1994). He has also published a critical study, *The Call of God: The Theme of Vocation in the Poetry of Donne and Herbert* (Cowley, 1981).

Of "A Geode," Shaw writes: "The geode, brown and pleasantly hefty, is very much as described in the poem. It was a gift from my father-in-law, and sat on one bookcase or another for several years before making its way into verse. Its blend of familiarity and strangeness must have caught my attention at last: to all appearances an unassuming rock, it gives out that remarkable sloshing sound when shaken. It traveled a long way, both in time and distance, to get to where it is now. Conveniently for a poet, it seemed to exude its own natural symbolism.

"If the lines on 'the worth of hiddenness' toward the end of the poem have a religious tinge, that is because I persist in an old-fashioned conviction that natural objects can serve a sacramental function if patiently contemplated. I would say the same of works of art when they aim to make transcendental realities palpable—if only for a moment, for the time it takes to read a poem or to listen to the water harbored in the rock."

CHARLES SIMIC was born in Belgrade, Yugoslavia, in 1939, and emigrated to the United States in 1953. Since 1967 he has published about sixty books in this country and abroad. His latest poetry collections include *Walking the Black Cat, A Wedding in Hell,* and *Hotel Insomnia,* all from Harcourt Brace. He won the Pulitzer Prize in 1990 for his book of prose poems *The World Doesn't End.* Four volumes of his prose have appeared in the University of Michigan Press's Poets on Poetry Series, most recently *The Unemployed Fortune-Teller* (1994) and *Orphan Factory* (1998). Awarded a MacArthur Fellowship in 1984, he was the guest editor of *The Best American Poetry 1992.* Since 1973 he has lived in New Hampshire.

Of "Ambiguity's Wedding," Simic writes: "One day I was thinking about Emily Dickinson's poetry when I realized that I knew many of her lines, though not a whole poem by heart. I started writing them down, and the poem—a kind of homage to her—began to emerge."

MARK STRAND was born in Canada of American parents in 1934. After many years of teaching at the University of Utah, he moved to Baltimore in 1992 to teach at Johns Hopkins. He is now on the University of Chicago's Committee on Social Thought. He has held a MacArthur Foundation Fellowship and has served as the nation's Poet Laureate. His recent books include *Dark Harbor* (1993) and *The Continuous Life* (1990), both from Knopf, and a monograph on Edward Hopper (Ecco). *A Blizzard of One,* his latest collection, appeared in 1998. He has published short stories and translations from the Spanish and the Portuguese. He was the guest editor of *The Best American Poetry 1991.*

Strand writes: "I dedicated 'The View' to Derek Walcott, because (1) years ago he dedicated a poem to me, and (2) something about 'The View' reminded me of a poem of his, in which a movie scene was taking place on a balcony. Also, I was thinking of a Caribbean island while writing the poem. Something in the back of my mind kept urging a tropical view forward."

JAMES TATE was born in Kansas City, Missouri, in 1943. For his *Selected Poems* (1991) he received the Pulitzer Prize and the William Carlos Williams Award. *Worshipful Company of Fletchers,* published in 1994, was awarded the National Book Award. In 1995 the Academy of American Poets presented him with the Tanning Prize. His latest book of poems, *Shroud of the Gnome,* was published in 1997 by the Ecco Press. Since 1971 Tate has taught at the University of Massachusetts. He was guest editor of *The Best American Poetry 1997.*

Of "Dream On," Tate writes: "The poem is having a lot of fun as it goes along, but it turns humble at the end, realizing that poetry is a fleeting thing and that anyone is lucky who can touch it."

SIDNEY WADE was born in Englewood Cliffs, New Jersey, in 1951. She is currently on sabbatical leave from the University of Florida, where she is an associate professor of English. Her books of poetry are *Empty Sleeves* (University of Georgia Press, 1991) and *Green* (University of South Carolina Press, 1998).

Of "A Calm November. Sunday in the Fields," Wade writes: "My title is a line lifted from Wallace Stevens's 'Like Decorations in a Nigger Cemetery.' One is rarely encouraged to read eroticism into Stevens, but I find it can be done, if one plays seriously enough with him."

DEREK WALCOTT was born in Saint Lucia, the West Indies, in 1930. His books of poems include *Another Life* (1973), *The Star-Apple Kingdom* (1979), *The Fortunate Traveller* (1982), *Midsummer* (1984), and *The Arkansas Testament* (1987), all from Farrar, Straus & Giroux. Walcott won a MacArthur Fellowship in 1981 and the Nobel Prize for literature in 1992. His recent works include *Omeros* (1990) and *The Bounty* (1997), both from Farrar, Straus & Giroux. He is the founder of the Trinidad Theater Workshop, and his plays have been produced by the New York Shakespeare Festival, the Mark Taper Forum in Los Angeles, and the Negro Ensemble Company. He has published four books of plays with Farrar, Straus & Giroux, and he wrote the libretto for Paul Simon's Broadway musical, *The Capeman*. He divides his time between Boston, where he teaches at Boston University, and Trinidad.

ROSANNA WARREN was born in Connecticut in 1953. She teaches comparative literature at Boston University. Her books include a verse translation of Euripides' *Suppliant Women,* with Stephen Scully (Oxford University Press, 1995); collections of poems, *Stained Glass* (Norton, 1994) and *Each Leaf Shines Separate* (Norton, 1984). She has also edited an anthology, *The Art of Translation: Voices from the Field* (Northeastern University Press, 1989), and two chapbooks of poems by prison inmates: *In Time* and *From this Distance* (Boston University Publications, 1995 and 1996).

Warren writes: " 'Departure' is a poem of its age, the fin de siècle in which the personal voice has been fractured and scattered. Not wildly scattered, however. There is a controlled and ritual element to the scattering, and to the lyric unities the poem recalls. And there is a logic, I hope, in the juxtaposition of the apparently incongruous visions of love from Guido Guinizelli, the Italian poet of the 'dolce stil nuovo' (sweet new style) of metaphysical love poetry that inspired Dante, and from the German painter Max Beckmann. The lines I have translated from Guinizelli (c. 1240–1276) come from his poem 'Al cor gentil rempara sempre Amore'; the lines from Beckmann (1884–1950) are adapted from remarks made by the painter and recorded in *Max Beckmann's Triptychs* by Charles S. Kessler (Harvard University Press, 1970). *Departure* is the title of one of Beckmann's great triptychs, begun in 1932 and now in the collection of the Museum of Modern Art in New York City."

RACHEL WETZSTEON was born in New York City in 1967, and currently lives there. She has received a B.A. from Yale, an M.A. from Johns Hopkins, and an M.Phil. from Columbia, where she is completing a dissertation on W. H. Auden. Her first book of poems, *The Other Stars*, was chosen for the 1993 National Poetry Series and published by Viking Penguin in 1994; her second collection, *Home and Away*—which includes the poems in this book—will be published by Viking Penguin in the fall of 1998. She has received a grant from the Ingram Merrill Foundation. She teaches at Columbia and the Unterberg Poetry Center of the 92nd Street Y in New York City.

Wetzsteon writes: "These are the final ten poems in a sequence of fifty unrhymed sonnets called *Home and Away*, which tells the story of a love affair from its earliest, thrilling moments to its terrible, violent conclusion. Although I hope all fifty of these dark poems can be read straight through without too much difficulty—and maybe even some pleasure—I also hope that each group of ten poems can stand on its own. I've tried to make this happen by setting each ten poems in a different place. The anthologized poems take place inside a house. The 'park bench' I mention in the last poem is a reference to the setting of the first ten poems; it's meant as a small gleam of hope in an otherwise quite bleak ending, as it is the place where the lovers first met. One final note about point of view: if it is unclear whether the husband or the wife is speaking in a particular poem, it is supposed to be; I don't want readers to be able to tell who is narrating *any* of the poems. This isn't to say that I set out to write a confusing poem—only that I needed ways to represent the confusion inherent in the story itself. Simply designating either the husband or the wife as the narrator—or, more equitably, alternating between his point of view and hers—didn't feel right; hence the deliberately slippery perspective in these ten poems, and throughout the entire sequence."

SUSAN WHEELER was born in Pittsburgh, Pennsylvania, in 1955. Her books include *Bag 'o' Diamonds* (University of Georgia Press, 1993) and *Smokes* (Four Way Books, 1998), and her poems have appeared in *The New Yorker, Mirage, The Paris Review, Lingo,* and *The Colorado Review,* as well as in four previous editions of *The Best American Poetry.* Having worked as an automobile mechanic in Vermont, a promotions manager at *Interview* magazine, and a public affairs director for the Art Institute of Chicago, she now teaches on the core faculty of the M.F.A. program in creative writing at the New School for Social Research in New York, and in the department of English at New York University.

Of "Shanked on the Red Bed," Wheeler writes: "It is my valentine to Auden."

RICHARD WILBUR was born in New York City in 1921. After teaching at Harvard, Wellesley, Wesleyan, and Smith, he has now retired to write. Published in 1988, when he was serving as Poet Laureate, his *New and Collected* won him a second Pulitzer Prize. Recently, he has finished his eighth translation from Molière—the prose play *Don Juan*. Harcourt Brace will soon publish his children's book *The Disappearing Alphabet*, and he is putting together a new book of his poems.

Wilbur writes: " 'For C.' was written for my wife of fifty-five years, and was suitably published in *The New Yorker*'s Valentine's Day issue (February 17, 1997). What I wanted to say was that a lasting love may have as much enchantment, wildness, and dimension as do brief, poignant affairs and broken-off romances. The challenge I felt in writing the poem was to get the tone right—to say my say with an entire sympathy for lovers of all kinds and fortunes, and without a shadow of smugness."

C. K. WILLIAMS was born in Newark, New Jersey, in 1936. He currently teaches at Princeton University one semester a year, and lives the rest of the time in Paris. His latest books include *The Vigil* (1997) and *Selected Poems* (1994), both from Farrar, Straus & Giroux, and a collection of essays, *Poetry and Consciousness* (University of Michigan Press, 1998).

Of "The Bed," Williams writes: "Sometimes one wishes to acknowledge experience while at the same time for whatever aesthetic or moral reasons deliteralize it. In this poem I wanted to account for a series of desperately repetitive though often exuberant and vividly singular sexual adventures (I almost said undertakings). Luckily for me, the poem has a happy ending."

GREG WILLIAMSON was born in 1964, and grew up in Nashville, Tennessee. He teaches in the Writing Seminars at Johns Hopkins University in Baltimore. His first book, *The Silent Partner*, received the Nicholas Roerich Poetry Prize and was published by Story Line Press in 1995.

Of "The Dark Days," Williamson writes: "I started the poem in October 1995, as leaves fell and the days grew short. At first, it was just going to be, more or less, the first section. Not long into it, however, I began to sketch out other responses to nature, metaphor, the pathetic fallacy, and so forth. By the time I got around to 'Revised Weather Bulletin,' it was January, and we were getting round-the-clock coverage of the 'Mitsubishi Blizzard of the Century Extravaganza VII,' or whatever it was called. Anyhow, it was snowy, and winter malingered for a long time."

CHARLES WRIGHT was born in Pickwick Dam, Tennessee, in 1935. Educated at Davidson College, he served in the army for four years, then attended the Writers' Workshop at the University of Iowa. He lectured at the universities of Rome and Padua under the Fulbright program. He has received fellowships from the National Endowment for the Arts and the Guggenheim Foundation and won a PEN award for his translation of Eugenio Montale's *The Storm and Other Things*. He is a professor of English at the University of Virginia at Charlottesville, where he lives with his family. In 1996 he was awarded the Lenore Marshall poetry prize for his book *Chikamauga* (Farrar, Straus & Giroux, 1995). His most recent collection, *Black Zodiac* (Farrar, Straus & Giroux, 1997), won the *Los Angeles Times* Book Prize, the National Book Critics Circle award in poetry, and the Pulitzer Prize.

MAGAZINES WHERE THE POEMS
WERE FIRST PUBLISHED

Agni, ed. Askold Melnyczuk. Boston University, 236 Bay State Road, Boston, Massachusetts 02215.

American Poetry Review, eds. Stephen Berg, David Bonanno and Arthur Vogelsang. 1721 Walnut Street, Philadelphia, Pennsylvania 19103.

The Antioch Review, poetry ed. Judith Hall. P.O. Box 148, Yellow Springs, Ohio 45387.

Boston Review, poetry eds. Mary Jo Bang and Timothy Donnelly. E53-407, MIT, 30 Wadsworth Street, Cambridge, Massachusetts 02139-4307.

Chelsea, ed. Richard Foerster. P.O. Box 773, Cooper Station, New York, New York 10276-0773.

Conjunctions, ed. Bradford Morrow. Bard College, Annandale-on-Hudson, New York 12504.

Connecticut Review, ed. Vivian Shipley. Southern Connecticut State University, 501 Crescent Street, New Haven, Connecticut 06473.

Denver Quarterly, poetry ed. Bin Ramke. Department of English, University of Denver, Denver, Colorado 80208.

Field, poetry eds. Stuart Friebert, David Young, Alberta Turner, and David Walker. Rice Hall, Oberlin College, Oberlin, Ohio 44074.

The Gettysburg Review, ed. Peter Stitt. Gettysburg College, Gettysburg, Pennsylvania 17325.

The Hudson Review, eds. Paula Deitz and Frederick Morgan. 684 Park Avenue, New York, New York 10021.

The Kenyon Review, ed. David Lynn. Kenyon College, Gambier, Ohio 43022.

The London Review of Books, 28–30 Little Russell Street, London WC1A 2HN, England.

Michigan Quarterly Review, ed. Laurence Goldstein. 3032 Rackham Building, University of Michigan, Ann Arbor, Michigan 48109.

The New Criterion, poetry ed. Robert Richman. 850 Seventh Avenue, New York, New York 10019.

New England Review, ed. Stephen Donadio. Middlebury College, Middlebury, Vermont 05753.

The New Republic, poetry ed. Mark Strand. 1220 19th Street NW, Washington, D.C. 20036.

The New Yorker, poetry ed. Alice Quinn. 20 West 43rd Street, New York, New York 10036.

Ontario Review, ed. Raymond J. Smith. 9 Honey Brook Drive, Princeton, New Jersey 08540.

The Paris Review, poetry ed. Richard Howard. 541 East 72nd Street, New York, New York 10021.

Partisan Review, poetry ed. Rosanna Warren. 236 Bay State Road, Boston, Massachusetts 02215.

Ploughshares, eds. Don Lee and David Daniel. Emerson College, 100 Beacon Street, Boston, Massachusetts 02116-1596.

Poetry, ed. Joseph Parisi. 60 West Walton Street, Chicago, Illinois 60610-3380.

Raritan, ed. Richard Poirier. 31 Mine Street, New Brunswick, New Jersey 08903.

River Styx, ed. Richard Newman. 3207 Washington Avenue, St. Louis, Missouri 63103-1218.

Salt Hill, ed. Peter S. Fendrick. English Department, Syracuse University, Syracuse, New York 13244-1170.

The Southern Review, poetry eds. James Olney and Dave Smith. 43 Allen Hall, Louisiana State University, Baton Rouge, Louisiana 70803.

Southwest Review, ed. Willard Spiegelman. 307 Fondren Library West, Box 374, Southern Methodist University, Dallas, Texas 75275.

The Threepenny Review, ed. Wendy Lesser. P.O. Box 9131, Berkeley, California 94709.

Western Humanities Review, poetry ed. Richard Howard. Department of English, University of Utah, Salt Lake City, Utah 84112.

The Yale Review, ed. J. D. McClatchy. P.O. Box 208243, New Haven, Connecticut 06520-8243.

ACKNOWLEDGMENTS

The series editor thanks his assistant, Mark Bibbins, for his invaluable work on this book. Warm thanks also go to Glen Hartley and Lynn Chu of Writers' Representatives, and to Gillian Blake, Erich Hobbing, and Giulia Melucci of Scribner.

Grateful acknowledgment is made to the publications from which the poems in this volume were chosen. Unless specifically noted otherwise, copyright to the poems is held by the individual poets.

Jonathan Aaron: "Mr. Moto's Confession" appeared in *The New Republic*. Reprinted by permission of the poet.

Agha Shahid Ali: "The Floating Post Office" from *The Country Without a Post Office*. Originally published in *The Kenyon Review*. Copyright © 1997 by Agha Shahid Ali. Reprinted with the permission of the author and W. W. Norton & Company, Inc.

Dick Allen: "The Cove" appeared in *The Hudson Review*. Reprinted by permission of the poet.

A. R. Ammons: "Now Then" appeared in *Michigan Quarterly Review*. Reprinted by permission of the poet.

Daniel Anderson: "A Possum's Tale" appeared in *Raritan*. Reprinted by permission of the poet.

James Applewhite: "Botanical Garden: The Coastal Plains" from *Daytime and Starlight: Poems* (Louisiana State University Press, 1998). Copyright © 1998 by James Applewhite. Originally appeared in *The Southern Review*. Reprinted by permission.

Craig Arnold: "Hot" first appeared in *Poetry,* copyright © 1997 by Craig Arnold. Reprinted by permission of the poet and the Editor of *Poetry*.

Sarah Arvio: from *Visits from the Seventh* appeared in *The Paris Review*. Reprinted by permission of the poet.

John Ashbery: "Wakefulness" from *Wakefulness*. Copyright © 1998 by John Ashbery. Reprinted by permission of Farrar, Straus & Giroux, Inc. Originally appeared in *The New Yorker*.

Frank Bidart: "The Second Hour of the Night" from *Desire*. Copyright © 1997 by Frank Bidart. Reprinted by permission of Farrar, Straus & Giroux, Inc. Originally appeared in *The Threepenny Review*.

Robert Bly: "A Week of Poems at Bennington" appeared in *Agni*. Reprinted by permission of the poet.

George Bradley: "In an Old Garden" originally appeared in *The New Yorker*. Reprinted by permission; copyright © 1997 by George Bradley.

John Bricuth: from *Just Let Me Say This About That* appeared in *Southwest Review*. Reprinted by permission of the poet.